MODERN TOURISM IN 21ST CENTURY

MODERN TOURISM IN 21ST CENTURY

Mahesh Chandra Singh

CENTRUM PRESS
NEW DELHI-110002 (INDIA)

CENTRUM PRESS
H.O.: 4360/4, Ansari Road, Daryaganj,
New Delhi-110002 (India)
Tel: 23278000, 23261597, 23255577, 23286875
B.O.: No. 1015, Ist Main Road, BSK IIIrd Stage,
IIIrd Phase, IIIrd Block, Bangalore-560085 (INDIA)
Tel: 080-41723429
Email: centrumpress@gmail.com
Visit us at: www.centrumpress.com

Modern Tourism in 21st Century

First Edition, 2010

ISBN 978-93-80540-68-9

PRINTED IN INDIA

Printed at Balaji Offset, Delhi.

Contents

Preface

The main difference between modern tourism and tourism in the past, is that modern tourism involves the mass availability and mass participation in holidays by what can be regarded as the entire population. This is distinct from tourism before the railway age when there were only two classes of people those who were on a holiday all the time and the masses whom never took a holiday.

Modern tourism involves a universal access to travel for individuals in the western world with destinations on an international scale competing for these tourists. Speed, comfort and value for money are the bases for gaining and maintaining market share in the highly competitive tourist market.

The principle task of this essay is to demonstrate how each transport mode contributed to the growth of this highly competitive market for tourism. Modern tourism involves many different types each that in turn have had an impact on the transport means. The different types of tourism can be divided based on the tourist's main interest of their trip. Tourism can involve one of the following; adventure, pleasure, sports, cultural, sports, study, incentive, research, professional and country.

We need to consider how certain technological changes have made mass tourism possible. This question is so crucial to understanding mass tourism because modern tourism and transport are inseparably linked. Tourism has always depended on the transport modes available and transport is also a component of the tourist product itself. Tourism is vital for many countries due to the income generated by the consumption of goods and services by tourists, the taxes levied on businesses in the tourism industry and the opportunity for employment and economic advancement by working in the industry.

The book focuses on the theme that in the truer sense tourism is predominantly for recreational or leisure purpose.

—Mahesh Chandra Sharma

1

The Organisation of Tourism

World Tourism Organization

The World Tourism Organization (UNWTO), based in Madrid, Spain, is a United Nations agency dealing with questions relating to tourism. It compiles the World Tourism rankings. The World Tourism Organization is a significant global body, concerned with the collection and collation of statistical information on international tourism. This organization represents public sector tourism bodies, from most countries in the world and the publication of its data makes possible comparisons of the flow and growth of tourism on a global scale. The official languages of UNWTO are Arabic, English, French, Russian and Spanish.

Organizational Aims

The World Tourism Organization plays a role in promoting the development of responsible, sustainable and universally accessible tourism, paying particular attention to the interests of developing countries. The Organization encourages the implementation of the Global Code of Ethics for Tourism, with a view to ensuring that member countries, tourist destinations and businesses maximize the positive economic, social and cultural effects of tourism and fully reap its benefits, while minimizing its negative social and environmental impacts. UNWTO is committed to the United Nations Millennium Development Goals, geared toward reducing poverty and fostering sustainable development.

History

The origin of the World Tourism Organization stems back to 1925 when the International Congress of Official Tourist Traffic

Associations ICOTT) was formed at The Hague. Some articles from early volumes of the Annals of Tourism Research, claim that the UNWTO originated from the International Union of Official Tourist Publicity Organizations (IUOTPO), although the UNWTO states that the ICOTT became the International Union of Official Tourist Propaganda Organizations first in 1934.

Following the end of the Second World War and with international travel numbers increasing, the IUOTPO restructured itself into the International Union of Official Travel Organizations (IUOTO). A technical, non-governmental organization, the IUOTO was made up of a combination of national tourist organizations, industry and consumer groups.

The goals and objectives of the IUOTO were to not only promote tourism in general but also to extract the best out of tourism as an international trade component and as an economic development strategy for developing nations.

Towards the end of the 1960's, the IUOTO realized the need for further transformation to enhance its role on an international level. The 20th IUOTO general assembly in Tokyo, 1967, declared the need for the creation of an intergovernmental body with the necessary abilities to function on an international level in cooperation with other international agencies, in particular the United Nations.

Throughout the existence of the IUOTO, close ties had been established between the organization and the United Nations (UN) and initial suggestions had the IUOTO becoming part of the UN. However, following the circulation of a draft convention, consensus held that any resultant intergovernmental organization should be closely linked to the UN but preserve its "complete administrative and financial autonomy".

It was on the recommendations of the UN that the formation of the new intergovernmental tourism organization was based. Resolution 2529 of the XXIVth UN general assembly stated:

"[The general assembly] believes that a formula that would allow agreement to be reached more readily among governments for the establishment of an international tourism organization of an intergovernmental, particularly to assist the developing countries would be:

(a) The conversion of the International Union of Official Travel Organizations into an intergovernmental organization through a revision of its statutes:

(b) The establishment of operational links between the United Nations and the transformed Union by means of a formal agreement."

In 1970, the IUOTO general assembly voted in favour of forming the World Tourism Organization (WTO), based on statutes of the IUOTO, and after ratification by the prescribed 51 states, the WTO came into operation on November 1, 1974.

Most recently, at the fifteenth general assembly in 2003, the WTO general council and the UN agreed to establish the WTO as a specialized agency of the UN. The significance of this collaboration, WTO Secretary-General Mr. Frangialli claimed, would lie in "the increased visibility it gives the WTO, and the recognition that will be accorded to [it]. Tourism will be considered on an equal footing with other major activities of human society".

As of 2007, its membership included 150 countries, seven territories and some 350 affiliate members, representing the private sector, educational institutions, tourism associations and local tourism authorities.

The frequent confusion between the two WTOs – World Tourism Organization and the Geneva-based World Trade Organization – officially ended on 1 December 2005, when the General Assembly approved to add the letters UN (for United Nations) to the start of abbreviation of the leading international tourism body in English and in Russian. UNWTO abbreviation remains OMT in French and Spanish. UNWTO General Assembly concluded its work at its 16th session in Dakar, Senegal, on 2 December 2005.

Secretaries-General of UNWTO

General Assembly

The General Assembly is the supreme organ of the Organization. Its ordinary sessions, held every two years, are attended by delegates of the Full and Associate members, as well as representatives from the Business Council. It is the most important meeting of senior tourism officials and high-level representatives of the private sector from all over the world.

Regional Commissions

Established in 1975 as subsidiary organs of the General Assembly, the six Regional Commissions normally meet once a year. They enable member States to maintain contact with one another and with the Secretariat between sessions of the General assembly, to which they submit their proposals and convey their concerns. Each commission elects one Chairman and its Vice-Chairmen from among its Members for a term of two years commencing from one session to the next session of the Assembly.

Executive Council

The Executive Council's task is to take all necessary measures, in consultation with the Secretary-General, for the implementation of its own decisions and recommendations of the Assembly and report thereon to the Assembly.

The Council meets at least twice a yearly the Council consists of Full Members elected by the Assembly in the proportion of one Member for every five Full Members, in accordance with the Rules of Procedure laid down by the Assembly with a view to achieving fair and equitable geographical distributional The term of office of Members elected to the Council is four years and elections for one-half of the Council membership are held every two years. Spain is a Permanent member of the Executive Council.

Committees

World Committee on Tourism Ethics Programme Committee on Budget and Finance committee on Market and Competitiveness Committee on Statistics and the Tourism Satellite account Sustainable Development of Tourism Committee on Poverty Reduction Committee for the Review of Applications for Affiliate Membership

Secretariat

The Secretariat is led by Secretary-General ad interim Taleb Rifai of Jordan, who supervises about 110 full-time staff at UNWTO's Madrid Headquarters. He is assisted by the Deputy Secretary-General. These officials are responsible for implementing UNWTO's programme of work and serving the needs of Members. The Affiliate Members are supported by a full-time Executive Director at the Madrid Headquarters. The Secretariat also includes a regional support office for Asia-Pacific in Osaka, Japan, financed by the Japanese Government.

Transport and Tourism

Managing Crises: UK Civil Aviation, BAA Airports and the August 2006 Terrorist Threat

The travel and tourism industry is expanding rapidly, but it has proved itself susceptible to crises which have both internal and external causes. Outside threats originate in the economic, environmental, socio-cultural and political domains and there is increasing concern about terrorism. This paper examines the dynamics and outcomes of a terrorist-related travel and tourism crisis with particular reference to the UK civil aviation industry in the summer of 2006. Reports of a planned terrorist strike against air travellers led to the imposition of unprecedented security measures which brought London's Heathrow Airport, one of the busiest in the world, to a standstill. Disruption was greatest on the day the news became public and continued for a period of ten days with lingering impacts which were felt nationally and globally.

After a brief introduction to the relevant literature, the circumstances are reviewed within the context of a model of the evolution of crises and their management. Phases cover the situation prior to the crisis, the alleged plot and the responses of the principal actors of government, airports and airlines. The focus is on airports run by BAA, formerly the British Airports Authority which was privatised after the 1986 Airports Act and acquired by the Spanish Ferrovial Group in June 2006. Consequences of the events recounted are considered and the paper ends with an overall assessment and some general conclusions derived from the case. Similar incidents seem likely to recur in the future and it is hoped that examination of the particular experiences will improve knowledge of the characteristics of this distinctive type of crisis and afford insights into effective preparation and management. A case study methodology was selected as the most appropriate and the analysis is based on secondary data drawn from a range of electronic and print media sources. The limitations of the absence of an insider perspective and reliance on news reporting are acknowledged, but direct access to decision making by public and private agencies and their documentation was not available to the researcher.

Travel and Tourism Crisis and Crisis Management

Crisis management as a whole has its own literature, but the principles are applicable to the travel and tourism industry and there is a growing volume of specific research. Travel and tourism crises are found to share features common to all crises, but also to possess certain distinctive qualities due to the nature of the product and industry. They often evolve with speed and can have far reaching commercial reverberations (Evans and Elphick, 2005). There is a possibility of personal injury and high fatalities and transport safety failures and accidents are a theme of several studies. Transport crises can also be the result of economic pressures separate from or linked to terrorism, the latter exemplified by the aftermath of what happened in the USA on 11 September 2001 (Nolan *et al.*, 2004; WTO, 2002). The relationship between terrorism and tourism is a topic of mounting interest (Pizam and Smith, 2000; Sonmez, 1998), indicative of the spate of terrorist outrages in the past decade.

There are great variations in scale and crises can be confined to an individual business or embrace a destination (Aktas and Gunlu, 2005). The latter may be engendered by political instability, one manifestation of which is terrorism, but natural disasters are a common catalyst. Management becomes more complex as the geographical area extends and more stakeholders have to be taken into account. Dilemmas were apparent in some of Thailand's coastal resorts after the devastating Indian Ocean tsunami of 2004. Handling of the subsequent tourism crisis was directed by officials and larger tourism businesses and the formal industry was deemed to be nearing recovery while the informal sector of hawkers and small enterprises still faced disruption (Rice, 2005). Inclusiveness and allocation of responsibilities for managing crises are thus important considerations and mechanisms for stakeholder dialogue and participation should be built into any models, although strong leadership is also essential.

Both generic and industry theories of crises and their management suggest that crises unfold in a sequence of steps which can be broadly labelled precrisis, crisis and post-crisis (Fink, 1986; Nankervis, 2000). Management tasks encompass signal detection, preparation, prevention, containment, recovery and learning. The ultimate aim is the return to normality and restoration of the status quo, although it is appreciated that this may be unrealistic due to fundamental changes engendered by the crisis. Faulkner's (2001) work is frequently cited and his model for managing disasters at destinations.

The model commences with a period when there is no evidence of a looming crisis and, while some can be predicted by means such as environmental scanning, others may be inconceivable in their particularities. Warnings of the imminence of a crisis then ensue, materialising in a situation demanding action. Recovery commences, divided into shorter and longer term, and resolution concludes the process. Responses comprise activity suitable to each phase with a movement from preparation and adoption of a position of readiness to first reactions and then measures directed at recovery, leading to a final review. These activities both inform and are informed by strategies of risk assessment and crisis management planning through a network of communication loops which also connect to future crises, allowing use to be made of understanding gained in order to prevent recurrence or limit damage when this is impossible. The model seeks to capture the cycle of crisis and is a useful analytical tool. It is employed as a framework for this paper in which the following sections are devoted to the seven phases, questions of the model's shortcomings being returned to in the conclusion.

Phase One: Pre-event and Phase Two: Warning

The parameters of the pre-event phase are not easily delineated in the August 2006 case due to the relatively longstanding hazard in the modern era of terrorists targeting airports and aircraft, illustrated by the history of plane hijackings and occasions like the Pan Am Lockerbie bomb in 1988 (Ray, 1999). A turning point might be 11th of September 2001 that demonstrated the potential for devastation by employing civilian aircraft to further terrorist ends. It signified the enhanced capabilities of terrorists and the sophistication of their methods as well as an intensification of fanaticism, underlining the need for constant vigilance and tighter security (Gunaratna, 2007). The bombings in London in July 2005 were another pivotal incident, confirming the vulnerability of the UK and its capital to terrorist attack (The Economist, 2005).

The onset of the warning phase, however, may predate 2001 and be determined by the political forces which were creating more extreme manifestations of terrorism and a new generation of terrorists, members of which are willing to sacrifice themselves as suicide bombers (Thackrah, 2004). International affairs, especially the circumstances in Iraq, have also engendered hostilities among nations whereby certain countries, their citizens and business interests have become attractive targets. General warnings were thus perhaps implicit in wider developments. Whatever the timetable, the climate in 2006 was one in which government, the air transport industry and passengers had been made keenly aware of the capacity of terrorism to wreak havoc among air travellers. The manner in which this occurred in the UK in August of that year is outlined in the next sections where accounts are founded on information published by two news media during the period under examination and BAA.

Phase Three: Event

Given the prevailing circumstances, the alleged plot was perceived to be highly credible by the UK authorities and deserving of urgent attention. The conspiracy reportedly involved the detonation of liquid explosives, carried onto planes in sports drinks bottles, in as many as ten passenger aircraft flying from the UK to the USA. It had been uncovered after an international surveillance exercise lasting over a year and was linked to the al-Qaeda organisation. British police and intelligence services were told of the threatened strike, expected to take place within 48 h, at 9pm on 9 August and a total of 21 suspects had been arrested by 11.50pm. The British Home Secretary claimed that the country was facing the gravest risk to security since the Second War and senior officials were quoted as saying, had the plan succeeded, it would have meant 'mass murder' on an 'unprecedented' and 'unimaginable' scale.

Whether such language was fitting and the dangers were inflated (Parkes, 2007) are outside the remit of this study. Nevertheless, it must be acknowledged that there had been criticisms of the record of the British security services over their investigations into terrorist suspects. Resultant scepticism in some quarters about the competence of the government and its agencies and underlying agendas constituted an element of the crisis, as did foreign policy decisions, and domestic and international political considerations cannot be entirely overlooked in any evaluation of its root causes and progression.

The discovery of the plan can be seen as the event which precipitated the crisis, although this demarcation is again debatable. Some observers might argue that it was the stances taken by the government and airport authorities that acted as a catalyst and aggravated the scale of the crisis, an interpretation adhered to by a number of airlines. Any such dispute highlights the complexity of the crisis which reverberated across the industry with different implications for government, airports and airlines. The government had responsibility for national security and the safety of citizens as well as obligations to the international community while airports and airlines had to deal with the practicalities of urgently executing radical security measures. Perspectives and priorities varied and there was room for tension and conflict as each party had to contend with its own crisis. However, these were interconnected and all were embroiled in the same drama and united by certain concerns pertaining to averting any further plots and appeasing public anxieties. Decisions made by one had ramifications for others and shaped advances towards individual and collective resolution.

Phase Four: Immediate Emergency

A meeting at 10pm on 9 August of the civil service Civil Contingencies Committee which was led by the Home Secretary, the Prime Minister being overseas, decreed that action must be taken to avert an attack. The UK was put on the maximum state of alert at 2am on 10 August and the Department of Transport announced details of enhanced security at airports. All the baggage of air travellers beginning their journey in the UK or transiting at UK airports was to be conveyed in the hold and they could take only specified essentials into the cabin in a single (ideally transparent) plastic carrier bag. The list covered travel documents, pocket-size wallets and purses, keys, spectacles (without cases), contact lens holders (without solution), tissues and feminine hygiene products (unboxed), prescription medical items (except in liquid form unless verified as authentic) and baby foods and sanitary items for those travelling with an infant. The contents of any bottles of baby milk had to be tasted by their owners. Every passenger would be hand searched and nothing was to be carried in pockets.

Any other liquids and gels, including most types of cosmetics and toiletries and foodstuffs, were not permitted. Prams and walking aids would be screened and only airport wheelchairs could enter the departure area. Those flying to the USA and their belongings would be screened again at the boarding gate. Passengers were advised to postpone travel if possible, to arrive early at the airport and to anticipate lengthy delays. The regime was in force for four days and prolonged completion of airport check-in and security clearance and boarding.

A key agency in the implementation of the scheme was BAA which is in charge of Heathrow, Gatwick, Stansted, Southampton, Aberdeen, Edinburgh and Glasgow airports. Emphasis is given to its role hereafter, but it should not be forgotten that the many other UK airport owners and operators (Humphreys *et al.*, 2007) were also compelled to act. Passengers at Heathrow heard that they could carry only essential hand luggage on board at 5am on 10 August when the first aircraft were scheduled to leave. Stansted airport asked passengers to travel only if it was essential at 7.30am, extra security personnel were installed at Scottish airports at 8.10am and all incoming services to Heathrow, not already in the air, were suspended at 8.50am.

The American government stated at 1.30pm that the terrorists were focusing on United, American and Continental airlines with the intention of bombing flights to New York, Washington and California.

Most of the approximately 400,000 passengers around the UK directly caught up in the turmoil of 10 August were BAA customers and those journeying to, from and through Heathrow were the worst hit. The airport was so congested that marquees were erected outside the terminals to house the crowds and some, among them travellers with young children and elderly relatives, faced at least a 58 h wait. Individuals interviewed talked of their discontent about the treatment received and paucity of information and being unable to join allocated flights because of overcrowded check-in desks and security screening points.

With regard to airlines, British Airways (BA) cancelled all domestic and short haul international flights from Heathrow and some from Gatwick on 10 August. Passengers flying from Stansted with Ryanair and easy Jet were told to leave the airport and rebook their flights. Most foreign airlines also abandoned their services to London even before the formal suspension of flights. BA offered to refund or rebook customers who chose not to travel from affected airports and volunteers from throughout the company were recruited to assist in staffing the crisis. Cancellations continued on 11 August, but BA anticipated operating 70 percent of its flights on that date while easy Jet and Ryanair cancelled 112 and 30, respectively.

Phase Five: Intermediate

Airport Security

Just after midnight on 14 August, the security threat was downgraded from critical to severe by the government which judged a terrorist attack now to be highly likely rather than imminent. Passenger searches were reduced from 100 to 50 percent and the hand baggage ban was lifted to allow one item, measuring no more than 45 cm long, 35 cm wide and 16 cm deep. Laptops and electronic devices which had previously been forbidden could now be carried if they were contained in the single piece of luggage, but had to be unpacked for security scanning.

Liquids and gels were still banned, apart from baby foods and certain prescribed medication. Liquid, cream or gel essential prescription medicines weighing over 50 ml were not permitted in the cabin while those under 50 ml had to be verified by tasting; if the individual was unable to taste the medicine, they were referred back to the airline and a representative would accompany them to an airport pharmacist for approval. All goods purchased in departure lounges, however, could be taken onboard. These arrangements did not apply to travellers to the USA who could not carry toiletries or cosmetics bought in the departure area or any liquid items and were subjected to secondary searches at the boarding gate.

Changes were implemented immediately at some provincial airports, but BAA said that they would not come into force at Heathrow and Gatwick until Tuesday 15 August at 4.30am in order for time for a full briefing of security staff. Passengers using these airports and Stansted, also serving London, were therefore requested to abide by the original restrictions. The authorities stressed that the rules would persist for as long as it was deemed necessary, despite protests from the airlines. Updated details of regulations were made available on the BAA website and explanatory leaflets were distributed at airports where signage was erected.

The government and BAA expressed their commitment to passenger safety as the further relaxation of restrictions was discussed between the authorities and airlines. More changes were eventually announced on 21 September, effective from 22 September, whereby the internationally agreed standard hand baggage size (56 cm by 45 cm by 25 cm) was restored and musical instruments were again permissable, as were solid cosmetics. Laptops and other electronic equipment were approved, but had to be separately screened and the embargo on nonessential liquids remained. Stricter security was, however, retained for American flights.

There was an opportunity for reflection as well as recrimination in the aftermath of the immediate emergency and speaking at the end of August, the Director General of IATA was quoted as saying that BAA had 'failed miserably in business continuity' by 'stopping the travellers' and that the police and military should have been deployed. While the foiling of the alleged plot was reassuring, deficiencies in airport management had been exposed in what was a 'wake-up call for the industry'. He urged improvements in contingency planning, the acceptance by governments of their obligations and the harmonisation of cross-border security (IATA, 2006a).

Airlines

By mid-August, airlines were cancelling fewer services and the backlog of delayed flights and passengers had eased. August 16 saw 35 BA cancellations from Heathrow and 11 from Gatwick, with 19 the following day, and the company was hopeful that it would be back to normal by 18 August. It did run a full timetable from Heathrow and Gatwick for the first time on 19 August, Ryanair and easy Jet having done so from Stansted on 15 August. There was, however, an additional problem of displaced luggage to deal with and over 20,000 bags were calculated to have gone astray. Most of these belonged to BA customers and arrangements had to be made for their delivery to owners.

The UK's airlines had endorsed the airport authorities and government policy at first, but some started to openly query the way in which the crisis was being handled. BA's Chief Executive said that BAA was 'unable to provide a robust security search process and baggage operation', compelling the airline to cancel flights or leave without all passengers on board (Shah and Mesure, 2006). The chaos and ongoing uncertainty was a victory for the terrorists, in the opinion of the Chief Executive of Ryanair, who called for the army and police to help man airport security. Others practitioners denounced draconian security measures which were unsustainable. There were criticisms of BAA's apparent lack of preparedness and planning and the issue of compensation was raised. Ryanair accused BAA of 'paralysing' its London base of Stansted because of inadequate staffing and condemned baggage policies as 'nonsensical', insisting on the reinstatement of normal security systems. It also launched a campaign to 'get Britain flying again' with a million seats on sale on 100 routes at a price of £25, inclusive of taxes and charges, and a further million at 99 pence subsequently. Ryanair then declared that it would be suing the government for 3m after its seven day ultimatum about a return to the status quo was ignored (Ryanair, 2006).

Air Travellers

From the outset, there was a great deal of confusion about security regulations and complaints from the public who were not always well informed and sometimes received contradictory advice. Airline crews also voiced their dissatisfaction at measures, from which they were not excluded, such as the liquids ban which embraced contact lens solution and toothpaste. Any anger and frustration seemed to give way to resignation after a few days, however, as travellers were pictured in the media waiting patiently in the still lengthy queues.

There were no mass cancellations and the International Air Transport Association (IATA) discounted the idea of a worldwide slump of the magnitude seen in 2001 (IATA, 2006b). Annual comparisons can be misleading, but details of BAA terminal passengers for the month of August over a four-year period hint at negative outcomes of a slowdown in rates of growth and reversals at Heathrow and Edinburgh in 2006. Circumstances appear to have depressed air travel as a whole with BAA's domestic market dipping by 7.6 percent, European charter traffic by 6.8 percent and North Atlantic flyers by 3.3 percent (BAA, 2006b). A similar pattern was observed at non-BAA airports such as Manchester where there was a rise of 1.7 percent in scheduled passengers in contrast to one of 13.8 percent the previous year while Birmingham saw a slump of 7.9 percent (CAA, 2007a).

It can be argued that there were also signs of resilience and that more dramatic cuts might have been expected, many commentators believing that the industry and travelling public were less sensitive to and more stoical about terrorism than in the past (The Economist, 2006a; Harrison, 2006). The fact that the alleged plot had been foiled was also of importance, in marked contrast to previous tragedies. Nevertheless, several occurrences still indicated nervousness among air travellers and airlines. Security alerts incited by disruptive passengers, intentional and unintentional possession of banned items and bomb hoaxes led to flights being delayed and diverted. Heightened sensitivity was apparent elsewhere in Europe, Asia and the USA with a succession of false alarms reported.

Phase Six: Longer Term

Stringent cabin baggage rules were partially relaxed in the UK in a series of steps while efforts were made to secure greater inter-governmental cooperation and consistency in approach. The European Commission (EC) started talks about upgraded counter-terrorism programmes and the exchange of data on airline passengers, pledging investment in research into the detection of liquid explosives. Intelligence gathering and sharing was believed to be a vital tool in stopping terrorists and EU and US officials did come to some agreement regarding trans-Atlantic traveller information, although European privacy laws limited the release of personal data and this complicated discussions. EC nations had concurred about a uniform stance by September 2006 and European wide rules took effect from the beginning of November. These meant that passengers must carry duty-free goods in sealed bags and any fluids in containers no larger than 100 ml in a plastic bag. The ICAO (International Civil Aviation Organisation) also announced its intention to introduce a common policy in all member country airports by March 2007 (ICAO, 2006).

The confrontation between BAA and the airlines became a factor in the five-year review of BAA's landing fees being conducted by the Civil Aviation Authority, price control proposals finally announced in late 2007 (CAA, 2007b). Airlines, which had been critical of BAA's performance prior to August 2006, were prepared to cite the handling of affairs in August as symptomatic of mismanagement. BAA was also under scrutiny by the Office of Fair Trading because of its dominant position which it was accused of abusing by critics who denounced the company as uncaring and unresponsive to the needs of its customers. There was a possibility that BAA would be called on to divest itself of one or more airports and a decision was eventually made at the end of 2006 to refer it to the Competition Commission for more detailed investigation (Office of Fair Trading, 2006). The commercial ramifications of the disclosure of the alleged plot were evidenced by the drop in value of airline shares and disturbed financial markets (Financial Times, 2006). City analysts forecast that easy Jet would forfeit 3m (Shah and Mesure, 2006), Ryanair put its losses at 3m (Ryanair, 2006) and BA stated a figure of 10m for August (BA, 2006). Budget carriers were especially vulnerable as the new measures contradicted their endeavours to accelerate the speed of boarding in order to maximise fleet utility. Ryanair had additionally been encouraging passengers to fly only with hand luggage to reduce turnaround time and its baggage handling fees. The decree that the size of permissible cabin bags be substantially reduced clearly undermined this strategy, albeit on a temporary basis. Airport authorities too faced economic damage and spending attributable to security contributed to BAA losses of 13m in August alone (BAA, 2006c).

Phase Seven: Resolution?

Despite the advance of one year, certain elements of the crisis remained outstanding and this suggests a lingering effect whereby consequences of crises can obscure or delay full and final resolution. Compensation matters and legal disputes may be judged an element of a crisis, for example, and settlements are frequently protracted. Perpetrators of criminal deeds underlying a crisis must be brought to justice before the case is fully closed and the trials of those eventually charged with terrorist offences connected to the bomb plot are due to begin in early 2008.

Debate about the quality of security and responsibilities for setting standards and bearing the costs stimulated by the events of August 2006 has led to ongoing reforms. Certain security procedures adopted seem set be in place indefinitely, reinforced by new steps. Passenger profiling founded on ethnicity and religion as well as age and unusual travel histories was mooted, although opponents complained of its tendency to promote racial stereotyping and discrimination. Other potential tools rely on sophisticated technologies of electronic and biometric analyses, but constraints of resources and reliability will have to be overcome (The Economist, 2006b). Progress will be an international affair given that terrorism and civil aviation both function at a global level and establishing consensus may not be easy, but air travellers can expect to undergo continued rigorous security checks with the attendant inconveniences. The degree to which governments will heed the exhortations of IATA and industry representatives to subsidise security, thereby helping to ameliorate the financial burden imposed on airlines, has not been determined and there is a possibility of higher fares due to mounting security expenses.

In addition, there have been reductions in the duty-free revenues of airport authorities because of the evolving rules governing purchase of liquid goods. Tax paid revenues may also be hit as passenger involvement in lengthy security procedures means less time and money spent on all types of landside and airside shopping. Steady rises in amounts charged to airline customers by airports in a bid to recoup some of this loss would be a blow to a civil aviation industry struggling with escalating fuel bills and competitive pressures. Developments could erode profitability, not least for companies in the budget market, with doubts about the survival of some enterprises.

Regular repetition of chaotic scenes at airports might well provoke interest in alternative modes of transport when these are a viable option, illustrated by the surge in bookings for Eurostar trains between London and Paris and Brussels at the peak of the August 2006 emergency. Nearby destinations could be favoured by holiday makers with a growing partiality for domestic tourism, the latter trend perhaps underway. BTMICE (business travel, meetings, incentives and conferences) participants may also switch to virtual communications (Arnfalk and Kogg, 2003) and facilities such as video-conferencing to escape the stresses and uncertainties of air travel.

Looking ahead, a future of intense security and the persistence of terrorist alarms and outrages can be envisaged. Flying may come to be widely viewed as excessively arduous for all but the most unavoidable of journeys. Travellers could be unwilling to arrive at the airport at least three, and maybe four, hours before departure for a relatively short flight when they may be prevented from carrying important personal possessions and have to risk the transportation of valuable items in the hold. Business travellers might again be denied use of laptops and equipment which enables them to work while on the move. Passengers and airlines could be approaching a threshold of acceptability and tolerance regarding official air security regimes which they may be reluctant to cross. The crisis exposed the often competing demands of security, passenger comfort and convenience and commercial realities. Identifying and securing an acceptable balance is an ongoing exercise which is perhaps prolonging total resolution.

Travel Agency and Tour Operation

A travel agency is a retail business, that sells travel related products and services to customers, on behalf of suppliers, such as airlines, car rentals, cruise lines, hotels, railways, sightseeing tours and package holidays that combine several products. In addition to dealing with ordinary tourists, most travel agencies have a separate department devoted to making travel arrangements for business travellers and some travel agencies specialize in commercial and business travel only. There are also travel agencies that serve as general sales agents for foreign travel companies, allowing them to have offices in countries other than where their headquarters are located.

Origins

The British company Cox & Kings is sometimes said to be the oldest travel agency in the world, but this rests upon the services that the original bank, established in 1758, supplied to its wealthy clients. The modern travel agency first appeared in the second half of the 19th century. Thomas Cook, in addition to developing the package tour, established a chain of agencies in the last quarter of the 19th century, in association with the Midland Railway. They not only sold their own tours to the public, but in addition, represented other tour companies. Other British pioneer travel agencies were Dean and Dawson, the Polytechnic Touring Association and the Co-operative Wholesale Society. The oldest travel agency in North America is Brownell Travel; on July 4, 1887, Walter T. Brownell led ten travellers on a European tour, setting sail from New York on the SS Devonia.

Travel agencies became more commonplace with the development of commercial aviation, starting in the 1920s. Originally, travel agencies largely catered to middle and upper class customers, but the postwar boom in mass-market package holidays resulted in travel agencies on the main streets of most British towns, catering to a working class clientèle, looking for a convenient way to book overseas beach holidays.

Operations

As the name implies, a travel agency's main function is to act as an agent, that is to say, selling travel products and services on behalf of a supplier. Consequently, unlike other retail businesses, they do not keep a stock in hand. A package holiday or a ticket is not purchased from a supplier unless a customer requests that purchase. The holiday or ticket is supplied to them at a discount. The profit is therefore the difference between the advertised price which the customer pays and the discounted price at which it is supplied to the agent. This is known as the commission. A British travel agent would consider a 10-12% commission as a good arrangement. In Australia, all individuals or companies that sell tickets are required to be licensed as a travel agent.

In some countries, airlines have stopped giving commission to travel agencies. Therefore, travel agencies are now forced to charge a percentage premium or a standard flat fee, per sale. However, some companies still give them a set percentage for selling their product. Major tour companies can afford to do this, because if they were to sell a thousand trips at a cheaper rate, they still come out better than if they sell a hundred trips at a higher rate. This process benefits both parties. Other commercial operations are undertaken, especially by the larger chains. These can include the sale of in-house insurance, travel guide books and timetables, car rentals, and the services of an on-site Bureau de change, dealing in the most popular holiday currencies.

The majority of travel agents have felt the need to protect themselves and their clients against the possibilities of commercial failure, either their own or a supplier's. They will advertise the fact that they are surety bonded, meaning in the case of a failure, the customers are guaranteed either an equivalent holiday to that which they have lost or if they prefer, a refund. Many British and American agencies and tour operators are bonded with the International Air Transport Association (IATA), for those who issue air tickets, Air Travel Organisers' Licensing (ATOL) for those who order tickets in, the Association of British Travel Agents (ABTA) or the American Society of Travel Agents (ASTA), for those who sell package holidays on behalf of a tour company.

A travel agent is supposed to offer impartial travel advice to the customer. However, this function almost disappeared with the mass-market package holiday and some agency chains seemed to develop a 'holiday supermarket' concept, in which customers choose their holiday from brochures on racks and then book it from a counter. Again, a variety of social and economic changes have now contrived to bring this aspect to the fore once more, particularly with the advent of multiple, no-frills, low-cost airlines.

Commissions

Most travel agencies operate on a commission-basis, meaning that the compensation from the airlines, car rentals, cruise lines, hotels, railways, sightseeing tours and tour operators, etc., is expected in form of a commission from their bookings. Most often, the commission consists of a set percentage of the sale.

In the United States, most airlines pay no commission at all to travel agencies. In this case, an agency usually adds a service fee to the net price.

Types of Agencies

There are three different types of agencies in the UK: Multiples, Miniples and Independent Agencies. The former comprises a number of national chains, often owned by international conglomerates, like Thomson Holidays, now a subsidiary of TUI AG, the German multinational. It is now quite common for the large mass-market tour companies to purchase a controlling interest in a chain of travel agencies, in order to control the distribution of their product. The smaller chains are often based in particular regions or districts.

In the United States, there are four different types of agencies: Mega, Regional, Consortium and Independent Agencies. American Express and the American Automobile Association (AAA) are examples of mega travel agencies.

Independent Agencies usually cater to a special or niche market, such as the needs of residents in an upmarket commuter town or suburb or a particular group interested in a similar activity, such as sporting events, like football, golf or tennis.

There are two approaches of travel agencies. One is the traditional, multi-destination, out-bound travel agency, based in the originating location of the traveller and the other is the destination focused, in-bound travel agency, that is based in the destination and delivers an expertise on that location. At present, the former is usually a larger operator like Thomas Cook, while the latter is often a smaller, independent operator.

Consolidators

Airline consolidators and other types of travel consolidators and wholesalers are high volume sales companies that specialize in selling to niche markets. They may or may not offer various types of services, at a single point of access. These can be hotel reservations, flights or car-rentals, for example. Sometimes the services are combined into vacation packages, that include transfers to the location and lodging. These companies do not usually sell directly to the public, but act as wholesalers to retail travel agencies. Commonly, the sole purpose of consolidators is to sell to ethnic niches in the travel industry. Usually, no consolidator offers everything, they may only have contracted rates to specific destinations. Today, there are no domestic consolidators, with some exceptions for business class contracts.

Criticism and Controversy

"Racking"

Travel agencies have been accused of employing a number of restrictive practices, the chief of which is known as 'racking'. This is the practice of displaying only the brochures of those travel companies whose holidays they wish to sell, the ones that pay them the most commission. Of course, the average customer tends to think that these are the only holidays on offer and is unaware of the possible alternatives.

Conversely, by limiting the number of companies that a travel agency represents, this can bring a better and more profitable, working relationship between the agency and its suppliers. Travel agencies can then obtain special benefits for their customers, from a supplier, by concentrating their bookings with that supplier. Some examples of these special benefits would be room upgrades or the waiver of change and cancellation fees.

("Racking" is a British expression, not used in the United States.)

The Internet Threat

With general public access to the Internet, many airlines and other travel companies began to sell directly to passengers. As a consequence, airlines no longer needed to pay the commissions to travel agents on each ticket sold. Since 1997, travel agencies have gradually been disintermediated, by the reduction in costs caused by removing layers from the package holiday distribution network. However, travel agents remain dominant in some areas such as cruise vacations where they represent 77% of bookings and 73% of packaged travel. In response, travel agencies have developed an internet presence of their own by creating travel websites, with detailed information and online booking capabilities. Several major online travel agencies include: Expedia, Voyages-sncf.com, Travelocity, Orbitz, Cheap Tickets, Priceline, Cheap Oair and Hotwire.com. Travel agencies also use the services of the major computer reservations systems companies, also known as Global Distribution Systems (GDS), including: SABRE, Amadeus CRS, Galileo CRS and Worldspan, which is a subsidiary of Travelport, allowing them to book and sell airline tickets, hotels, car rentals and other travel related services. Some online travel websites allow visitors to compare hotel and flight rates with multiple companies for free. They often allow visitors to sort the travel packages by amenities, price, and proximity to a city or landmark.

Travel agents have applied dynamic packaging tools to provide fully bonded (full financial protection) travel at prices equal to or lower than a member of the public can book online. As such, the agencies' financial assets are protected in addition to professional travel agency advice.

All travel sites that sell hotels online work together with GDS, suppliers and hotels directly to search for room inventory. Once the travel site sells a hotel, the site will try to get a confirmation for this hotel. Once confirmed or not, the customer is contacted with the result. This means that booking a hotel on a travel website will not necessarily result in an instant answer. Only some hotels on a travel website can be confirmed instantly (which is normally marked as such on each site). As different travel websites work with different suppliers together, each site has different hotels that it can confirm instantly. Some examples of such online travel websites that sell hotel rooms are Expedia, Orbitz and World Hotel-Link.

The comparison sites, such as Kayak.com, Trip Advisor and Side Step search the resellers site all at once to save time searching. None of these sites actually sell hotel rooms.

Often tour operators have hotel contracts, allotments and free sell agreements which allow for the immediate confirmation of hotel rooms for vacation bookings.

Mainline service providers are those that actually produce the direct service, like various hotels chains or airlines that have a website for online bookings. Portals will serve a consolidator of various airlines and hotels on the internet. They work on a commission from these hotels and airlines. Often, they provide cheaper rates than the mainline service providers as these sites get bulk deals from the service providers. A meta search engine on the other hand, simply culls data from the internet on real time rates for various search queries and diverts traffic to the mainline service providers for an online booking. These websites usually do not have their own booking engine.

Careers

With the many people switching to self-service internet websites, the number of available jobs as travel agents is decreasing. Most jobs that become available are from older travel agents retiring. Counteracting the decrease in jobs due to internet services is the increase in the number of people travelling. Since 1995, many travel agents have exited the industry, and relatively few young people have entered the field due to less competitive salaries. However, others have abandoned the 'brick and mortar' agency for a home-based business to reduce overheads and those who remain have managed to survive by promoting other travel products such as cruise lines and train excursions or by promoting their ability to aggressively research and assemble complex travel packages on a moment's notice, essentially acting as a very advanced concierge.

Cargo

A small number of companies work with cargo airlines and cargo ships.

Who is a travel agent?

A travel agent is any individual or company that:

- Sells, resells, or offers to sell travel tickets
- Makes or offers to make travel arrangements
- Advertises any of those things.

Many businesses are regarded as travel agents, including retail and corporate agents, tour wholesalers, consolidators, inbound tour operators, general sales agents, some bus or coach operators and some airlines.

Travel Technology

Travel technology is a term used to describe applications of Information Technology (IT), or Information and Communications Technology (ICT), in travel, tourism and hospitality industry. Travel technology may also be referred to as tourism technology or even hospit Definition of Travel Technology

Since travel implies locomotion, travel technology was originally associated with the computer reservations system (CRS) of the airlines industry, but now is used more inclusively, incorporating the broader tourism sector as well as its subset the hospitality industry. While travel technology includes the computer reservations system, it also represents a much broader range of applications, in fact increasingly so. Travel technology includes virtual tourism in the form of virtual tour technologies. Travel technology may also be referred to as *e-travel / etravel* or *e-tourism / etourism* (eTourism), in reference to "electronic travel" or "electronic tourism".

In other contexts, the term "travel technology" can refer to technology intended for use by travellers, such as light-weight laptop computers with universal power supplies or satellite Internet connections. That is not the sense in which it is used here.

Applications of Travel Technology

Travel technology includes many processes such as dynamic packaging which provide useful new options for consumers. Today the tour guide can be a GPS tour guide, and the guidebook could be an audioguide, podguide or I-Tours, such as City audio guides. The biometric passport may also be included as travel technology in the broad sense.

Tour Operator

A tour operator typically combines tour and travel components to create a holiday. The most common example of a tour operator's product would be a flight on a charter airline plus a transfer from the airport to a hotel and the services of a local representative, all for one price. Niche tour operators may specialise in destinations e.g. Italy, activities and experiences e.g. skiing, or a combination thereof. The original raison d'etre of tour operating was the difficulty of making arrangements in far-flung places, with problems of language, currency and communication. The advent of the internet has led to a rapid increase in self-packaging of holidays. However, tour operators still have their competence in arranging tours for those who do not have time to do DIY holidays, and specialize in large group events and meetings such as conferences or seminars. Also, tour operators still exercise contracting power with suppliers (airlines, hotels, other land arrangements, cruises, etc.) and influence over other entities (tourism boards and other government authorities) in order to create packages and special departures for destinations otherwise difficult and expensive to visit.

The two major tour operator associations in the US are the National Tour Association (NTA) and the United States Tour Operator's Association (USTOA), in Europe it is the European Tour Operators Association-ETOA and in the UK it is ABTA and AITO. The primary association for receptive North American inbound tour operators is the Receptive Services Association of America (RSAA).

Tour Operators and Travel Agents

Sometimes there is confusion over the difference in functions of tour operators and travel agents. Tour operators are the organisers and providers of package holidays. They make contracts with hoteliers, airlines and ground transport companies then print brochures advertising the holidays that they have assembled.

Travel agents give advice and sell and administer the bookings for a number of tour operators. It is estimated that there are some 7,000 travel agency shops ranging size from the multiples, with several hundred outlets each, to the individual shop. Some travel agents also undertake tour operating-be it on a small scale, e.g. a local agent packaging a group holiday for a local club, or on a larger scale-most famously by the legendary Thomas Cook, who was the first tour operator, and Sir Henry Lunn (Lunn Poly) who is widely credited with "inventing" skiing as a leisure activity. Agents can also sell the 'components' (flights, ferry bookings, car hire etc.) for those who travel independently.

Although most package holidays are sold through travel agents a significant and growing percentage are sold direct to the consumer through advertising -Teletex, TV Travel Shops and the internet.

Package Holiday

A package holiday or package tour consists of transport and accommodation advertised and sold together by a vendor known as a tour operator. Other services may be provided like a rental car, activities or outings during the holiday. Transport can be via charter airline to a foreign country. Package holidays are a form of product bundling. Package holidays are organised by a tour operator and sold to a consumer by a travel agent. Some travel agents are employees of tour operators, others are independent.

Package Tours

An early form of package holiday was organised by Thomas Cook in 1841, offering customers a return trip between Leicester and Loughborough. The first package tour of Europe was organised by Cook in 1855, and by 1872 he was undertaking world-wide tours, albeit with small groups.

Vladimir Raitz, the co-founder of the Horizon Holiday Group, pioneered the first mass package holidays abroad with charter flights between Gatwick airport and Corsica in 1950, and organised the first package holiday to Palma in 1952, Lourdes in 1953, and the Costa Brava and Sardinia in 1954. In addition, the amendments made in Montreal to the Convention on International Civil Aviation on June 14, 1954 was very liberal to Spain, allowing impetus for mass tourism using charter planes.

By the late 1950s and 1960s, these cheap package holidays — which combined flight, transfers and accommodation — provided the first chance for most people in the United Kingdom to have affordable travel abroad. One of the first charter airlines was Euravia, which commenced flights from Manchester Airport in 1961 and Luton Airport in 1962. Despite opening up mass tourism to Crete and the Algarve in 1970, the package tour industry declined during the 1970s. On 15 August 1974, the industry was shaken when the second-largest tour operator, Court Line which operated under the brand names of Horizon and Clarksons, collapsed. Nearly 50,000 tourists were stranded overseas and a further 100,000 faced the loss of booking deposits.

In 2005 a growing number of consumers were avoiding package holidays and were instead travelling with budget airlines and booking their own accommodation. In the UK, the downturn in the package holiday market led to the consolidation of the tour operator market, which is now dominated by a few large tour operators. The major operators are Thomson Holidays and First Choice part of TUI AG and Thomas Cook AG. Under these umbrella brands there exists a whole range of different holiday operators catering to different markets, such as Club 18-30 or Simply Travel. Budget airlines have also created their own package holiday divisions such as Jet2 Holidays.

The trend for package holiday bookings saw a comeback in 2009, as customers sought greater financial security in the wake of a number of holiday and flight companies going bust, and as the hidden costs of 'no-frills' flights increased. Coupled with the search for late holidays as holidaymakers left booking to the last moment, this led to a rise in consumers booking package holidays.

Dynamic Packaging is a method that is becoming increasingly used in package holiday bookings that enables consumers to build their own package of flights, accommodation, and a hire car instead of a pre-defined package. Dynamic packages differ from traditional package tours in that the pricing is always based on current availability, escorted group tours are rarely included, and trip-specific add-ons such as airport parking and show tickets are often available. Dynamic packages are similar in that often the air, hotel, and car rates are available only as part of a package or only from a specific seller. The term "dynamic packaging" is often used incorrectly to describe the less sophisticated process of interchanging various travel components within a package, however, this practice is more accurately described as "dynamic bundling". True Dynamic Packaging demands the automated recombination of travel components based on the inclusion of rules that not only dictate the content of the package, but conditional pricing rules based on various conditions such as the trip characteristics, suppliers contributing components, the channel of distribution, and terms of sale. Dynamic packages are primarily sold online, but online travel agencies will also sell by phone owing to the strong margins and high sale price of the product.

Free Independent Traveller

Free Independent Traveller (or Tourist) refers to both a way of travelling and, from an industry viewpoint, a sector within the tourism market. FITs practise a form of dynamic packaging but the emphasis is from the end-user point of view and includes the wider economic effects that FITs "spread" in their destination country as opposed to more traditional, consolidated forms of travel.

2

Tourism and Hospitality in Twenty First Century

Promotion of Barrier-free Tourism for People with Disabilities in the Asian and Pacific Region

Tourism is a rapidly growing industry in the Asian and Pacific region. Following the trauma of the recent Asian financial crisis, the region has regained its status as one of the world's fastest growing destinations. As reported by the World Tourism Organization (WTO), the Asian and Pacific region, after two years of decreasing tourist arrivals, registered in 1999 a growth rate of 7.5 percent reaching a new record of more than 94 million international tourists. It is also expected that such a positive trend will continue into the early years of the new millennium.

Tourists, today are not content with staying within the confines of a resort hotel compound, being bussed to individual sites and entertained in places that mainly cater to tourists. Instead, tourists are increasingly interested in experiencing diversity of holiday environment in all aspects, including its people, culture, nature, architecture and way of life. This trend will be even more marked as consumers become better informed about options and entitlements, as well as more sophisticated and less willing to accept poor quality facilities and services that entail discomfort and stress. Tourists want access to everything that a city or a country has to offer. In view of the changing consumer demand, tourism for all is an increasingly important sales argument in a competitive market. At the same time, it can serve as an effective tool in furthering the human rights of people with disabilities in the destination communities.

People with disabilities and older persons are becoming a growing group of consumers of travel, sports, and other leisure-oriented products and services. Furthermore, with regard to physical access, families with young children, who are also becoming part of this increasing tourist market, have similar needs to persons with disabilities and older persons. Thus large numbers of people require tourism to be made barrier-free.

Although the number of tourists who would benefit from accessible facilities and services is on the increase, most tourism services providers in the Asia-Pacific region have still not yet recognized the importance of taking action on this issue. Most hotels, transportation facilities and tourist sites are not physically accessible for many people with disabilities and older persons. Their staff members have not been trained to provide disabled person-friendly services. This is associated with an absence of explicit government policies and strategies for promotion of accessible tourism, lack of training for tourism service personnel on means of meeting the access needs of tourists with disabilities, and shortage of tourism programmes that address such needs.

Disability and Access

Present policies and programmes suffer from a dearth of disability data and inadequacy of existing data. In the majority of the countries and areas of the Asia-Pacific region, it is difficult to estimate the number of people with disabilities. There is a wide variation in the estimated disability rates reported by the developed and developing countries. The variation depends, to a large extent, on the definitions of disability used. The types of disability range from hearing, vision, and mobility impairment to intellectual impairment and psychiatric disorders.

For example, Australia's 1993 survey indicated that persons with a disability comprise 18 percent of its population. New Zealand's first national household survey (1996) yielded a disability rate of 19.1. In 1994, the United States Census Bureau estimated that some 54 million Americans were covered under the Americans with Disability Act (ADA) of 1990, constituting nearly 21 percent of the United States population. In contrast, China's (1987) and Pakistan's (1984-85) sample surveys both indicated a 4.9 percent disability rate. The 1991 National Sample Survey of India, covering four disabilities — visual, hearing, speech and locomotor — yielded a prevalence rate of 1.9 percent.

The share of the older people in the populations of developed countries is already rising dramatically. The same phenomenon is occurring in developing countries. According to United Nations projections, by the year 2025, about 14 percent of the Asia-Pacific region's total population will be 60 years or older, and the region will be home to 56 percent of the world's older persons. Among older persons, a significant percentage presents some type of disability. For example, in Western Australia over 50 percent of people over 60 years of age have a disability 2.

It is now widely recognized from many quarters that people with disabilities, together with carers, friends and relatives, and older persons constitute a large potential consumer market segment for the tourism and hospitality industry. However, to take advantage of this potential niche market will depend on how the tourism sector as a whole and the tourism industry in particular will address the issue of tourism accessibility for people with disabilities. Indeed good access will benefit not only people with disabilities, but also many other members of the community, especially senior citizens.

Access varies depending on disability and goes well beyond the physical type alone.

Darcy (1998) 3 has characterized access from three main dimensions:

(a) Physical access which involves people with physical disabilities requiring the use of wheelchairs or walking aids and requires the provision of, for example, handrails, ramps, lifts and lowered counters.

(b) Sensory access which involves people with hearing or sight impairments requiring the provision of, for example, tactile markings, signs, labels, hearing augmentation-listening systems and audio cues for lifts and lights.

(c) Communication access, which involves those people who have difficulty with the written word, vision, speech, and hearing impairment of persons from other culture.

In one way or another, all travellers who move out of their familiar surroundings are handicapped by new environments, the exciting aspects notwithstanding. Thus, the degree of sensitivity, clarity, safety and convenience required in designing tourism facilities from the perspective of disabled travellers will benefit everyone else.

Main Constraints of Disabled Travellers

People with disabilities have a right to, and do want to enjoy travel and leisure experiences. Tourism is a means of broadening horizons and developing friendships for a social group, which increasingly is less willing to remain segregated from mainstream society. Furthermore, as more people acquire disabilities or survive with disabilities, they too wish to enjoy travel, just like everyone else. However, their travel experiences are still characterized by transportation constraints, inaccessible accommodation and tourism sites, and inadequate customer services.

Transportation

While air travel in general has become easier and airlines increasingly provide friendly services to the average travellers, still some problems arise from time to time, such as misplaced luggage or delays in flight schedules. However, these mishaps might seriously inconvenience travellers with disability. For example, an issue among some travellers with disabilities is the damage to and loss of wheelchairs on airplanes. Indeed, being without one's wheelchair is much more distressing than having the misfortune of lost or delayed luggage for the average travellers. Other constraints facing wheelchair-travellers include the difficulty of boarding and disembarking the aircraft, changing flights and the inaccessibility of airplane restrooms. For blind people, identifying and retrieving luggage becomes another additional obstacle in the course of their already difficult journey. The pain of long-haul travel in air economy class seat for someone with stiff limbs or arthritis, the sheer size of modern airports for those with mobility problems and endless forward planning for all are some of the challenges still facing travellers with disabilities.

Most travellers negotiate structural constraints associated with air travel by using other modes of transportation – car, bus or train. Private automobiles equipped with customized features have the advantage of providing schedule flexibility if used for pleasure travel. However, only a small group of affluent people with disability can afford such cars.

Modern technology greatly facilitates bus travel by people with disabilities. People with physical disabilities can now journey in buses equipped with hydraulic lifts, which help them to board easily. So-called "low-floor" buses are gradually becoming the standard for intra-urban public transportation in a growing number of countries. These buses have the floor some 50 cm above street level. They feature a hydraulic "kneeling" function, which reduces the step to some 25 cm. However, in most developing countries the availability of such specially designed buses remains limited. While trains could better accommodate disabled persons travel needs, often the gap between car doors and the platform are too wide; access to toilets and compartments remains a constraint, especially for people with physical disabilities and wheelchair users.

Accommodations

Reasonable accommodations for people with disabilities constitute still another set of challenges. For example, very few hotels offer accessible disabled person-friendly rooms with wider entrances; low-level switches, hand dryers, towels racks and beds; chair lifts and room information written in simple and concise language for people with cognitive disabilities. Of the rooms available, few have ground floor access. Access throughout hotels is also problematic. Few hotels have lifts to all floors on slow timers, access to reception, pool and bar areas, clear signage, visual alarms and clear access through the entire building. While the majority of hotels provide special parking areas, often these are uncovered and quite distant from the main hotel entrances, requiring that steps be negotiated in order to access the buildings.

Another issue relating to accommodation facilities and amenities concerns the different types of disability to be provided for. Indeed the needs for people with vision or hearing impairment or intellectual disability are quite different from those with physical disability. Most of the hotels provide facilities and amenities responding more to the special needs of people with physical disabilities and specifically those in wheelchairs. For example, among hotels that offer wheelchair access, few provide information available in Braille or in audiovisual format.

Many travellers with disabilities find facilities at eating and drinking establishments within tourist destination areas to be difficult to access. Some others encounter problems when making hotel reservations. It was observed that in some hotels, specific accessible rooms even when available, could not be reserved by an individual. In some other instances, some room accommodations, which were promoted as accessible rooms, actually appeared to be inaccessible to people with disabilities. For example, showers with handrails may well accommodate some people, but for many wheelchair users, bathtubs present a major barrier.

Tourism Sites

Attractions are the elements of a tourism destination that stimulate the purpose of a journey and visit. They may be of a leisure-type, such as visiting theme parks or participating in sport events; nature-based, such as seaside tourism or mountain trekking; historical, such as visiting museums or antique shopping; or socio-cultural, such as festivals or visiting friends or relatives. Most of the constraints encountered by tourists with disabilities in the course of these activities focus on site inaccessibility. For example, beaches are often not equipped to accommodate wheelchair users. Similarly, poor access to museums, historical monuments or shopping areas restricts people with disabilities from enjoying the opportunity of participating in these activities.

Travel Planning

For people with disabilities, planning a vacation can be somewhat more complicated. Depending on the type of disability, the would-be travellers need to ensure that during the envisaged vacation due attention will be given to their special needs such as special lifts for coaches and adapted hotel rooms. Such arrangements cannot be made without the assistance of travel agencies that cater to those special needs. As for several years accessible tourism shows promising sign of expansion, tour operators have started to appreciate the potential of a market that has traditionally been poorly served. However, tailoring packages to people with various disabilities requires labour intensive work, making therefore a low-margin business. Yet specialized agents, especially in Europe, are joining forces through transnational association to exchange information, set up data banks, launch joint marketing campaigns and lobby for better services. At the same time, specialized European travel agents and non-profit organizations have been cooperating by pooling what they have learned about the availability of special facilities in various countries.

Conditions to Promote Barrier-free Tourism for people with Disabilities

People with disabilities are being acknowledged as a consumer group of travel, sports, and other leisure-oriented products and services. If professionals of the tourism industry are to succeed in accessing this potential new market, they must understand the needs involved and learn how to respond to these challenges for the benefit of both parties.

Legislation Framework

One crucial element in meeting this goal is the existence of a legal framework, which ensures that people with disabilities have the right to access to tourism facilities and services and to encourage tourism professionals to adopt related measures. Several governments in the region have passed comprehensive legislation to protect the rights of persons with disabilities. Others are in various stages of adoption, formulation and planning such legislation. Those countries, which have already adopted such legislation, enacted additional laws and regulations or amended existing one to further protect the rights of persons with disabilities in specific areas crucial to the equalization of opportunities.

For example, in Australia the Commonwealth Disability Discrimination Act 1992 (DDA) and the Disability Service Act 1993, plus various other State legislation, require departments, public authorities and the tourism industry to ensure that people with disabilities have the same fundamental rights as the rest of the community. Furthermore, the 1993 Act specifically relates to access to appropriate accommodation and services and allows people with disabilities the opportunity to make decisions, which affect their life. Tourism providers are subject to all requirements of both acts, which means that all premises, good and services used by the public must be accessible to people with disabilities. Failure to provide equal access is illegal, unless it is proved to cause unjustifiable difficulties such as excessive cost.

Legislation on access should also apply to a variety of public areas and services — including information services – such as travel agents, cafes, restaurants, libraries, transport, shops, theatres and other places of entertainment. Accordingly, related information needs to be provided to people with disabilities. Lack of proper physical access to transport, buildings and sites will not only exclude people with disabilities from participating in community life but also affect tourism and leisure providers. In this connection, the appropriate legislation would indeed help to design an air travel transportation system able to remove barriers to travel for people with disabilities. In Australia, the Air Carrier Access Act

(1986) ensures that no air carrier might discriminate against disabled persons in the provision of air transportation. This Act represents a major advance towards a comprehensive adaptive air travel system for people with disabilities.

One great challenge regarding legislation implementation is the provision of information to tourism professionals, such as for instance hospitality providers, of the key relevant legislation relating to people with disabilities and their obligations under the legislation. According to the findings of a recent survey, the majority of the hospitality providers interviewed in Western Australia stated that they were not aware of any specific legislation regarding issues of access for people with disabilities. This was further supported by representatives from disability agencies who said that there was a general lack of awareness on those issues. There is also evidence that most of the laws enacted lack of any credible legislative power, due to low enforcement.

Tourism Services Providers

To fully harness the potential of barrier-free tourism, it is essential that the tourism industry improve its services to people with disabilities. This includes improved access of hotel facilities within all areas of the property to the entire disabled community, including those with physical, sensory and communication disabilities. For example, particular attention should be given to providing people with physical disabilities with a clear accessible route to the main entrance of an establishment and then to the reception desk. Similarly, persons with sight or hearing impairments need to be provided for with adequate facilities to facilitate their free mobility within the premises. Accessible rooms should also be made available and designed with features, which can accommodate wheelchair users as well as people with sight and hearing impairments.

In the area of transportation, efforts need to be pursued to upgrade and improve the level of facilities for people with disabilities. Accessible transportation features, such as toilets in aircrafts, are fundamental requirements for barrier-free travel. Airport authorities should ensure that basic accessible infrastructure adjustments for people with disabilities are included in the design of new and/or renovated airports, such as the introduction of greater areas of level access as well as the provision of easy access to toilets.

Travel operators that specialize in services for, and provide tailoring packages to, people with disabilities are instrumental in assisting them with their vacation planning.

They are able to provide them with the information regarding the availability of accessible facilities suited to their needs. People with disabilities are more likely to rely on tourism professionals, such as specific travel agents and hotels that best serve their needs. It is therefore imperative that specific barrier-free tourism promotional activities be undertaken by travel agents in close cooperation with other professionals of the tourism industry such as hospitality providers.

Disability organizations may also contribute to these promotional efforts by drawing the attention of the tourism industry to the needs and desires of the people with disabilities, especially with regard to flexibility in travel options.

Training and Education

Training and education is one of the major challenges facing the tourism industry in relation to meeting the needs of people with disabilities. Sensitive and willing staff with the right attitude and strong interpersonal skills can overcome many of the barriers that persons with disabilities face and turn what may be perceived as an inaccessible property into a accessible one. It is essential for the tourism industry to strengthen its customer services training in order to serve those with disabilities. Indeed, regardless of how well an establishment has been designed to accommodate people with disabilities or how well policies have been formulated to cater to the needs of disabled travellers, it will be of little value if the staff employed are uncomfortable and ill-prepared serving guests with disabilities.

Comprehensive programmes should include policy setters and managers as well as front-line staff and should be extended at all educational levels, especially within tertiary level hospitality management programmes.

The availability of specialized tour guides is another important factor for people with disabilities, especially those with sight and hearing impairments to enable them to enjoy tourism activities. Efforts should be made to develop and strengthen appropriate specialized tour-guiding courses in training curricula on tourism management and related tourism services.

Priority Areas for Promotion of Barrier-free Tourism

Notwithstanding the number of initiatives already pursued by countries in the region to make tourism barrier-free for people with disabilities, there are three key issues that require immediate attention.

One key area is the formulation and implementation of related legislation in order to protect the right of persons with disabilities to accessible facilities and environment.

Countries should be encouraged to continue developing such legislation as well as introduce new amendments in keeping with changes in the tourism sector, including travel conditions, and the specific situations of different disability groups. While it is essential that legislation needs to be reviewed in a continuous manner, it is imperative that members of the tourism industry be informed of their obligations and operational implications in order to protect not only their interest, but also the interests of the people with disabilities. Of equal importance is the role of the various disability bodies and organizations, which must begin to work closely with the tourism industry to improve existing practices. The organizations are well acquainted with and knowledgeable about various disability issues. They should assist the tourism industry in introducing the necessary changes required under the legislation and to assist in the organization of related staff training programmes.

Education and training on awareness and sensitivity to disability issues is another top priority area in the promotion of accessible tourism. The education sector should be encouraged to include in their training curricula on tourism management and related tourism services courses on "disabled persons' right to access" as well as "customer services to, and relations with, people with disabilities". Here again, the close collaboration between the disability organizations and the tourism industry along with the education sector would facilitate the development of required training programmes. It would also help in the publication of training material, such as facilitative guide, student handbook and audiovisual training support, for wider distribution amongst the tourism industry.

Provision of accessible facilities is by far the most important area of concern for achieving a barrier-free tourism for people with disabilities. Taking into consideration that it is highly unrealistic to presume that the situation would change overnight, owing to cost and time limitations, what is required in the short-term is that the tourism sector strives to achieve a reasonable level of accessibility, which balances disabled users' needs, the constraints of existing conditions and the resource available for such adjustments. In many cases, this relates to the issue of physical access, such as main hotel entrance access, appropriate access ramp, reception counters, disability friendly rooms, access to and location to all public areas. In the long-term, the approach will be to encourage major restructuring and/or refurbishment of hospitality establishments and tourism sites.

Attracting Tourism and Hospitality Industries

The Indian tourism and hospitality industry is on a roll, driven by the huge surge in both business and leisure travel by domestic and foreign tourists. The country's travel and tourism industry is expected to generate approximately US$ 100 billion in 2008, rising to Rs. 15 US$ 275.5 billion by 2018 over the next ten years, as per the latest Tourism Satellite Accounting (TSA) research released by the World Travel and Tourism Council (WTTC) and its strategic partner Accenture.

The growth of tourist inflow into India was well above world average, leading to a rise of India's share in World arrivals from 0.37 percent in 2001 to 0.53 percent in 2006. Also, as noted by UN World Tourism Organisation (UNWTO), the growth of Indian tourism industry was instrumental in the 'emergence' of South-Asia as a tourist destination.

Further, tourism is an important industry in Indian economy contributing around 6.8 percent of the Gross Domestic Product and providing employment to over 41 million persons. According to a research University of New South Wales (UNSW), Australian School of Business (ASB), India and China will be the new global players competing for a huge chunk of tourists, transforming the geopolitical landscape.

Inbound Tourists

The flow of foreign tourist arrivals has been recording phenomenal growth rates. The number of arrivals has increased from 3.9 million in 2005 to 4.4 million in 2006 and 4.95 million in 2007, recording a growth rate of 13.5 percent in 2006 (over 2005) and 11.9 percent in 2007 (over 2006).

Alongside, there has been a concomitant rise in the foreign exchange earnings. Total earnings from foreign tourists has shown an annual growth rate of 19.2 per in 2006 and 33.8 percent in 2007 to garner US$ 7.49 billion in 2005, US$ 8.93 in 2006 and US$ 11.96 billion in 2007.

Continuing the foreign tourists' interest in the country, the first four months of 2008 recorded a growth rate of 11.9 percent (in tourist arrivals) over the corresponding period in 2007, receiving 2.02 million in foreign tourist arrivals. Simultaneously, foreign exchange earnings grew by a much faster rate at 28.9 percent in 2008, against 20 percent during corresponding period in 2007. Total foreign exchange earnings totalled US$ 4.84 billion, against US$ 3.76 billion in 2007.

Significantly, while India's share in world arrivals was about 0.5 percent, its share in revenue generated from tourism worldwide was over 1 percent.

India, with its diverse landscape, offers huge scope for various theme-based travel like Medical Tourism, Adventure tourism, Heritage tourism, Wellness tourism, Pilgrimage tourism, Golf tourism, Ecotourism, Wildlife tourism among others. India's growing reputation as a major medical tourism destination is attracting more and more foreign visitors. In fact, Indian hospitals are fast becoming the first choice for foreign patients owing to easy access to visa facilities coupled with the best emerging medical infrastructure which will help India earn to an extent of US$ 1.86 billion in foreign exchange by 2012. Currently India's earnings through medical tourism annually is an estimated US$ 821.40 million. In fact, according to the World Travel and Trade Council, Indian tourism demand will continue to grow at a rapid pace. It estimates the demand to grow at an average of 8.8 percent between 2004 and 2013, making India the world's third fastest growing tourist market. The boom in the Indian tourism industry has cascaded to the rural areas as well. India continues to attract tourists owing to its splendid historical architecture and rich culture along with beautiful beaches, rural tourism or what now is called 'responsible tourism' is also fast gaining popularity with travellers flocking to discover the best in rural arts and heritage.

Outbound Tourists

With the economy growing consistently at over 9 percent, increasing disposable incomes, a change in the spending habits, liberalization of exchange controls, increasing affordability due to numerous holiday packages and cheaper air fares, outbound tourist traffic has been growing at a rapid pace.

Outbound tourist market has been growing at an annual average growth of around 25 percent. In 2007, an estimated 8 million Indian tourists ventured abroad. Moving ahead, the United Nations World Tourism Organisation (UNWTO) estimates the figure to reach about 50 million by 2020.

Along with the rise in the number of Indians travelling abroad, both the total and per capita expenditure spent abroad has been increasing. For example, according to the European Travel Commission, average spend per trip of Indian outbound tourists has increased from US$ 611 in 2000 to US$ 822 in 2006. Similarly, Euromonitor International estimates the outgoing tourism expenditure from India to grow to US$ 21 million by 2011, representing a growth rate of over 25.7 percent between 2006 and 2011.

Hospitality

The booming tourism industry has had a cascading effect on the hospitality sector with an increase in the occupancy ratios and average room rates. While occupancy ratio is around 75-80 percent, the average increase in room rates has been hovering around 22-25 percent.

And with the continuing surge in tourist inflow, this sector is likely to offer tremendous opportunity for investors. For example, while the estimated number of required hotel rooms is around 240,000, the current availability is just 90,000 rooms-leaving a shortfall of 150,000 rooms to be provided.

With such a huge potential available in this segment, several global hotel chains like the Hilton, Accor, Marriott International, Berggruen Hotels, Cabana Hotels, Premier Travel Inn (PTI), Inter Continental Hotels group and Hampshire among others have all announced major investment plans for the country.

The Government's move to declare hotel and tourism industry as a high priority sector with a provision for 100 percent foreign direct investment (FDI) has also provided a further impetus in attracting investments in to this industry.

It is estimated that the hospitality sector is likely to see US$ 11.41 billion in the next two years, with around 40 international hotel brands making their presence in the country by 2011. Simultaneously, international hotel asset management companies are also likely to enter India. Already, US-based HVS International has firmed up plans to enter India, and industry players believe others like Ashford Hospitality Trust and IFA Hotels & Resorts among others are likely to follow suit.

Government Initiatives

To unlock the huge potential in this sector, the Government has taken various initiatives for the development of this sector.

- Launch of Incredible India campaign to promote tourism both in domestic and international markets.
- Recognition of spare rooms available with various house owners by classifying these facilities as "Incredible India Bed and Break fast Establishments"', under 'Gold' or 'Silver' category.
- A new category of visa, "Medical Visa" ('M'-Visa), has been introduced which can be given for specific purpose to foreign tourists coming into India.
- Guidelines have been formulated by Department of AYUSH prescribing minimum requirements for Ayurveda and Panchkarma Centres.
- Ministry of tourism has tied up with United Nations Development Programme (UNDP) to promote rural tourism.

International Recognition

Along with the growth of this industry, international accolades have been pouring in, rising India's appeal as a leading global tourist destination.

- India has been elected to head the UN World Tourism Organisation (UNWTO), the highest policy making world tourism body represented by 150 countries.
- The world's leading travel and tourism journal, "Conde Nast Traveller", ranked India as the numero uno travel destination in the world.
- The Association of British Travel Agents (ABTA) has ranked India as No.1 amongst the top 50 places for 2006.
- The "Incredible India" campaign has been ranked as the Highest Recall Advertisement worldwide by "Travel and Leisure".

- India was adjudged Asia's leading destination at the regional World Travel Awards (WTA).
- India's Taj Mahal continues to figure in the seven wonders of the world.
- Bangalore-based Leela Palace Kempinski has been rated as the favourite business hotel in the world in a Readers' Choice Awards by Conde Nast Traveller.

The Travel Channels: Tourism and Hospitality Industries are Changing to Meet the Demands of Experience-Hungry Travellers

Consumers today are in constant pursuit of new experiences. They want an escape from a busy, demanding life, to be moved and inspired emotionally and spiritually. They respond to messages that evoke feelings and fantasy rather than those that outline a function. In short, they are dream chasers.

In the travel, tourism and hospitality industry in particular, companies that want to stay competitive must therefore define their unique value proposition—the "experience" only they can provide. The experience must be authentic, not contrived, and built on strong values. This means building an emotional connection with consumers, something that's never been so easy and so difficult at the same time.

Says Iris Brouwer, founder of Barcelona, Spain-based Silk Marketing: "Customers are more informed, more travelled and experienced than in the past. Not only have they become independent, demanding and self-sufficient, they are also more savvy. They know how to enjoy life; they are looking for experiences, feelings, pampering—and they know where to find it. Innovation in communication is key to keeping up with the market. This means working with the latest and most effective media." One example of packaging a feeling is a new campaign for tourism in Slovenia, which is actively promoting itself as a hot new destination. Seizing on opportunities offered by its entry into the European Union and its position as EU chair from January to June 2008, it launched a new marketing campaign called "I Feel Slovenia." The campaign invites travellers to "feel" and experience the many wonders of the country.

"We are proud that our country has the word love in its name, and we can use this to communicate stories, a love story, about

Slovenia, our unique cultural heritage and the pristine nature of our country," says Rok Klancnik, director of the Slovenia Tourist Office based in Brussels, Belgium.

Yet Slovenia is realistic and doesn't try to compete on the level of mature destinations such as France and Spain (respectively the world's top destinations in terms of international tourist arrivals, according to the U.N. World Tourism Organization's "Tourism Highlights, 2007 Edition"). Instead, Slovenia is committed to being the "best-kept secret in Europe" and to preserving the authenticity of the experience. Says Klancnik: "Slovenia should and will stay on the path of sustainable tourism development. If we ruin the beauty of our nature, old traditions and culture, we'll lose tourism as well, not only our national identity. It's not about quantity [of tourists]. Tourism of tomorrow is about quality and emotions, both for visitors and for the locals who work and live in tourism."

Delivering on the Promise

"Travelling today is not always easy, between security checks and long waits in transit," says Marco Ferrari, vice president and director of external communication at Starwood Hotels & Resorts for Europe, Africa and Middle East. "When guests arrive at their destination, we must deliver on our promise. We are lucky enough to sell dreams, experiences, emotions and sensations. We must represent the dream, and we must surpass expectations and stand for the promise of our brands."

Starwood Hotels & Resorts has been creative in using a mix of offline and online communication tools to engage with their guests before, during and after their experience. For example, Starwood Preferred Guest TV (SPG TV) is a "new means of communicating directly with guests in 300-plus hotels in Europe, Middle East and Africa," Ferrari explains. It features compelling reports of off-the-beaten-track experiences, such as the best restaurants, secret discoveries, romantic rendezvous, art exhibits and secluded beaches. Produced entirely by Starwood, SPG TV also features interviews with guests, who share their personal stories and tips. "SPG TV has now obtained 86 percent viewership of guests," says Ferrari.

The Customer as Storyteller

While the message focuses on "fantasy" and "experiences," the means to deliver that message is changing rapidly. In travel,

Trip Advisor has led the way by giving customers the chance to post reviews and recommendations of their travel experiences and hotel stays, and its success was immediate: Trip Advisor claims that "85 percent of consumers trust recommendations from other consumers" over brand web sites and advertising.

This trend is being watched carefully by hotels that seek to be the first source for customer information and sales. So far, hotels have offered pull techniques on their web sites such as "best rate guarantees" and benefit-loaded customer loyalty programs. How can hotels use new social media tools to their advantage? According to a September 2007 report from Hospitality Sales & Marketing Association International, "This new consumer behavior applies as much to travel as it does to industries as different as electronics, books, automobiles and financial planning.... According to a recent TIA/Ypartnership Travel Horizons study, two-thirds of online adult leisure travellers consume online video and audio clips; four in 10 read blogs, share photos and take virtual tours; and one in four posts responses to blogs and participates in social networks."

Emotional Connections

Marriott International is another hospitality industry leader when it comes to embracing social media tools.

Chairman and CEO Bill Marriott launched his blog, "Marriott on the Move," on 16 January 2007. "Blogging will allow me to do what I've been doing for years—on a global scale," Marriott wrote. "Talking to the customer comes easily to me. I visit 250 hotels around the world every year."

According to Marriott, the blog fulfills several goals:

* To be a part of the growing conversation online and to speak more directly with customers without a filter.
* To embrace innovative communications and be an early adopter among non-tech companies.
* To communicate to a new generation of travellers the way they prefer to communicate.

Every couple of days, Bill Marriott posts a blog entry and a recorded voice message with a new story or anecdote—everything from the latest Marriott hotel opening to his recommendations for great books or films. Whether personal or professional musings, each "Marriott on the Move" conveys the values of the company as personified by Bill Marriott himself. "Our guests are very loyal to our brand, and this blog builds on that loyalty and gives customers a better insight into our company and its values, such as community service and saving the environment, as represented by Mr. Marriott," says Marriott International's John Wolf, senior director of public relations.

By focusing on the experience-sharing stories and promising fantasy and unique experiences—all tourism suppliers can make an emotional connection with their guests. Says Iris Brouwer: "Through the story, a destination transforms itself from an asset, 'a place to stay,' into 'a place to experience,' with a value proposition that no other destination can possibly match." The same holds true for any industry and any business looking to capture the hearts and minds of its stakeholders.

Related Article: The Middle East 'Experience': Close-up on Dubai

Tourism in the Middle East is growing fast, particularly in the Gulf States, and especially in Dubai, United Arab Emirates. Dubai already offers an astounding array of "experiences," with more resorts and attractions under construction. The builders of "Dubailand," a 3 billion-square-foot development, claim it is "the world's most ambitious tourism, leisure and entertainment project, designed to catalyse the position of Dubai as an international hub of family tourism."

Universal Studios is set to run a large theme park in Dubailand, while Jumeirah, the Dubai-based luxury hospitality group, plans to build a waterpark complete with a hotel in the shape of a ship.

According to Hotels magazine's February 2007 feature "EMEA's Next Generation," "No Middle East market can outshine Dubai, but Oman and Qatar are carving out a niche of the tourism pie." Dubai's neighbor Abu Dhabi, the capital of the United Arab Emirates, has set a target of more than doubling annual visitor numbers from 1.35 million in 2006 to more than 3 million by 2215.

Like the Eiffel Tower in Paris, Jumeirah's iconic Burj Al Arab Hotel has become the symbol of Dubai. This hotel is a spectacular edifice built in the shape of a ship's sail and is known by a collection of superlatives: "the world's tallest hotel," "the most luxurious hotel in the world" and "the world's only seven-star hotel." The

Burj Al Arab Hotel is part of Jumeirah's collection of properties that "are regarded as among the most luxurious and innovative in the world."

Jumeirah is also a master at offering a different experience, with a promise to guests that at Jumeirah they will "Stay Different." Among the innovative communication tools that support the "Stay Different" promise is JCast, a podcast service launched in May 20o6 to deliver to guests all around the world the latest news and property videos of Jumeirah.

"JCasts can be accessed at the user's convenience, to deliver a virtual, personal ized experience of Jumeirah," explains Kristie Willmott Coshow, group director for Jumeirah e-business and consumer development. "These technologies can transform the value we deliver to our guests and make our properties more accessible. Our goal is to enhance our guests' overall experience and engagement with us." Jumeirah produces new podcasts every two weeks and features news on its individual properties and amenities. The initiative is a hit with guests, many of whom use iPods. It allows them to share their Jumeirah experiences with friends and family worldwide, thereby growing Jumeirah brand awareness while building customer loyalty and attracting new guests

Consumers today are in constant pursuit of new experiences. They want an escape from a busy, demanding life, to be moved and inspired emotionally and spiritually. They respond to messages that evoke feelings and fantasy rather than those that outline a function. In short, they are dream chasers.

In the travel, tourism and hospitality industry in particular, companies that want to stay competitive must therefore define their unique value proposition—the "experience" only they can provide. The experience must be authentic, not contrived, and built on strong values. This means building an emotional connection with consumers, something that's never been so easy and so difficult at the same time.

Says Iris Brouwer, founder of Barcelona, Spain-based Silk Marketing: "Customers are more informed, more traveled and experienced than in the past. Not only have they become independent, demanding and self-sufficient, they are also more savvy. They know how to enjoy life; they are looking for experiences, feelings, pampering—and they know where to find it. Innovation in communication is key to keeping up with the market. This means working with the latest and most effective media."

One example of packaging a feeling is a new campaign for tourism in Slovenia, which is actively promoting itself as a hot new destination. Seizing on opportunities offered by its entry into the European Union and its position as EU chair from January to June 2008, it launched a new marketing campaign called "I Feel sLOVEnia." The campaign invites travellers to "feel" and experience the many wonders of the country.

"We are proud that our country has the word love in its name, and we can use this to communicate stories, a love story, about Slovenia, our unique cultural heritage and the pristine nature of our country," says Rok Klancnik, director of the Slovenia Tourist Office based in Brussels, Belgium.

Yet Slovenia is realistic and doesn't try to compete on the level of mature destinations such as France and Spain (respectively the world's top destinations in terms of international tourist arrivals, according to the U.N. World Tourism Organization's "Tourism Highlights, 2007 Edition"). Instead, Slovenia is committed to being the "best-kept secret in Europe" and to preserving the authenticity of the experience. Says Klancnik: "Slovenia should and will stay on the path of sustainable tourism development. If we ruin the beauty of our nature, old traditions and culture, we'll lose tourism as well, not only our national identity. It's not about quantity [of tourists]. Tourism of tomorrow is about quality and emotions, both for visitors and for the locals who work and live in tourism."

Delivering on the Promise

"Travelling today is not always easy, between security checks and long waits in transit," says Marco Ferrari, vice president and director of external communication at Starwood Hotels & Resorts for Europe, Africa and Middle East. "When guests arrive at their destination, we must deliver on our promise. We are lucky enough to sell dreams, experiences, emotions and sensations. We must represent the dream, and we must surpass expectations and stand for the promise of our brands."

Starwood Hotels & Resorts has been creative in using a mix of offline and online communication tools to engage with their guests before, during and after their experience. For example,

Starwood Preferred Guest TV (SPG TV) is a "new means of communicating directly with guests in 300-plus hotels in Europe, Middle East and Africa," Ferrari explains. It features compelling reports of off-the-beaten-track experiences, such as the best restaurants, secret discoveries, romantic rendezvous, art exhibits and secluded beaches. Produced entirely by Starwood, SPG TV also features interviews with guests, who share their personal stories and tips. "SPG TV has now obtained 86 percent viewership of guests," says Ferrari.

The Customer as Storyteller

While the message focuses on "fantasy" and "experiences," the means to deliver that message is changing rapidly. In travel, Trip Advisor has led the way by giving customers the chance to post reviews and recommendations of their travel experiences and hotel stays, and its success was immediate: Trip Advisor claims that "85 percent of consumers trust recommendations from other consumers" over brand web sites and advertising.

This trend is being watched carefully by hotels that seek to be the first source for customer information and sales. So far, hotels have offered pull techniques on their web sites such as "best rate guarantees" and benefit-loaded customer loyalty programs. How can hotels use new social media tools to their advantage? According to a September 2007 report from Hospitality Sales & Marketing Association International, "This new consumer behavior applies as much to travel as it does to industries as different as electronics, books, automobiles and financial planning.... According to a recent TIA/Ypartnership Travel Horizons study, two-thirds of online adult leisure travellers consume online video and audio clips; four in 10 read blogs, share photos and take virtual tours; and one in four posts responses to blogs and participates in social networks."

Emotional Connections

Marriott International is another hospitality industry leader when it comes to embracing social media tools.

Chairman and CEO Bill Marriott launched his blog, "Marriott on the Move," on 16 January 2007. "Blogging will allow me to do what I've been doing for years—on a global scale," Marriott wrote. "Talking to the customer comes easily to me. I visit 250 hotels around the world every year."

According to Marriott, the blog fulfills several goals:

* To be a part of the growing conversation online and to speak more directly with customers without a filter.
* To embrace innovative communications and be an early adopter among non-tech companies.
* To communicate to a new generation of travellers the way they prefer to communicate.

Every couple of days, Bill Marriott posts a blog entry and a recorded voice message with a new story or anecdote—everything from the latest Marriott hotel opening to his recommendations for great books or films. Whether personal or professional musings, each "Marriott on the Move" conveys the values of the company as personified by Bill Marriott himself.

"Our guests are very loyal to our brand, and this blog builds on that loyalty and gives customers a better insight into our company and its values, such as community service and saving the environment, as represented by Mr. Marriott," says Marriott International's John Wolf, senior director of public relations.

By focusing on the experience-sharing stories and promising fantasy and unique experiences—all tourism suppliers can make an emotional connection with their guests. Says Iris Brouwer: "Through the story, a destination transforms itself from an asset, 'a place to stay,' into 'a place to experience,' with a value proposition that no other destination can possibly match." The same holds true for any industry and any business looking to capture the hearts and minds of its stakeholders.

Related Article: The Middle East 'Experience': Close-up on Dubai

Tourism in the Middle East is growing fast, particularly in the Gulf States, and especially in Dubai, United Arab Emirates. Dubai already offers an astounding array of "experiences," with more resorts and attractions under construction. The builders of "Dubailand," a 3 billion-square-foot development, claim it is "the world's most ambitious tourism, leisure and entertainment project, designed to catalyse the position of Dubai as an international hub of family tourism." Universal Studios is set to run a large theme park in Dubailand, while Jumeirah, the Dubai-based luxury hospitality group, plans to build a waterpark complete with a hotel in the shape of a ship.

According to Hotels magazine's February 2007 feature "EMEA's Next Generation," "No Middle East market can outshine Dubai, but Oman and Qatar are carving out a niche of the tourism pie." Dubai's neighbor Abu Dhabi, the capital of the United Arab Emirates, has set a target of more than doubling annual visitor numbers from 1.35 million in 2006 to more than 3 million by 2215.

Like the Eiffel Tower in Paris, Jumeirah's iconic Burj Al Arab Hotel has become the symbol of Dubai. This hotel is a spectacular edifice built in the shape of a ship's sail and is known by a collection of superlatives: "the world's tallest hotel," "the most luxurious hotel in the world" and "the world's only seven-star hotel." The Burj Al Arab Hotel is part of Jumeirah's collection of properties that "are regarded as among the most luxurious and innovative in the world."

Jumeirah is also a master at offering a different experience, with a promise to guests that at Jumeirah they will "Stay Different." Among the innovative communication tools that support the "Stay Different" promise is JCast, a podcast service launched in May 20o6 to deliver to guests all around the world the latest news and property videos of Jumeirah.

"JCasts can be accessed at the user's convenience, to deliver a virtual, personal ized experience of Jumeirah," explains Kristie Willmott Coshow, group director for Jumeirah e-business and consumer development. "These technologies can transform the value we deliver to our guests and make our properties more accessible. Our goal is to enhance our guests' overall experience and engagement with us." Jumeirah produces new podcasts every two weeks and features news on its individual properties and amenities. The initiative is a hit with guests, many of whom use iPods. It allows them to share their Jumeirah experiences with friends and family worldwide, thereby growing Jumeirah brand awareness while building customer loyalty and attracting new guests.

Trend Watch

"Most travel suppliers have invested substantial sums in the development and promotion of their web sites. And for good reason: The Internet is now cited as the exclusive source of information when planning both business and leisure travel by over two-thirds of all active travellers."

At Eurocomm

The IABC 2008 EuroComm Conference will be held 4-5 February in Barcelona, Spain, with Silk Marketing's Iris Brouwer speaking on social media in tourism.

Popular Destination

"In the Middle East, international tourist arrivals have risen by 9 percent... in fact most of the destinations in the region continue to report remarkably good results."

Based in France, native Californian Summer Jauneaud is a communication and marketing consultant specializing in the international tourism and hospitality industry.

3

The Economic Significance of Tourism

Today, tourism is one of the largest and dynamically developing sectors of external economic activities. Its high growth and development rates, considerable volumes of foreign currency inflows, infrastructure development, and introduction of new management and educational experience actively affect various sectors of economy, which positively contribute to the social and economic development of the country as a whole.

Most highly developed western countries, such as Switzerland, Austria, and France have accumulated a big deal of their social and economic welfare on profits from tourism.

According to recent statistics, tourism provides about 10% of the world's income and employs almost one tenth of the world's workforce. All considered, tourism's actual and potential economic impact is astounding. Many people emphasize the positive aspects of tourism as a source of foreign exchange, a way to balance foreign trade, an "industry without chimney" — in short, manna from heaven. But there are also a number of other positive and negative sides of tourism's economic boom for local communities, which not always considered by advocates of tourism perspectives. Therefore in this paper I will consider the main social and environment impacts of tourism at the country level.

The Positive and Negative Social and Environmental Impacts of Tourism

Socially tourism has a great influence on the host societies. Tourism can be both a source of international amity, peace and understanding and a destroyer and corrupter of indigenous cultures, a source of ecological destruction, an assault of people's privacy, dignity, and authenticity.

Here are possible positive effects of tourism:

- Developing positive attitudes towards each other
- Learning about each other's culture and customs
- Reducing negative perceptions and stereotypes
- Developing friendships
- Developing pride, appreciation, understanding, respect, and tolerance for each other's culture
- Increasing self-esteem of hosts and tourists
- Psychological satisfaction with interaction.

So, social contacts between tourists and local people may result in mutual appreciation, understanding, tolerance, awareness, learning, family bonding respect, and liking. Residents are educated about the outside world without leaving their homes, while their visitors significantly learn about a distinctive culture. Local communities are benefited through contribution by tourism to the improvement of the social infrastructure like schools, libraries, health care institutions, internet cafes, and so on. Besides, if local culture is the base for attracting tourists to the region, it helps to preserve the local traditions and handicrafts which maybe were on the link of the extinction.

For example in Uzbekistan, particularly in such famous regions as Samarqand, Buhara, and Horezm tourists contribute significantly to the preservation of traditional handcrafting wood carving, hammered copper work, handmade silk and carpets, and of course to preservation and maintenance of architectural and historical monuments.

Since Uzbekistan proclaimed its independence in 1991 many museums and monuments were renovated or opened to promote the national culture and traditions. Growing interest in this culture makes the local people proud of their way of life.

On the other side tourism can increase tension, hostility, and suspicion. Claims of tourism as a vital force for peace are exaggerated. Indeed there is little evidence that tourism is drawing the world together (Robinson 1999). In this context economic and social impacts on the local community depend on how much of the incomes generated by tourists go to the host communities. In most all-inclusive package tours more than 80% of travellers' fees go to the airlines, hotels and other international companies, not to local businessmen and workers. On the other hand large hotel chain restaurants often import food to satisfy foreign visitors and rarely employ local staff for senior management positions, preventing local farmers and workers from reaping the benefit of their presence. Tourism has the power to affect cultural change. Successful development of a resource can lead to numerous negative impacts. Among these are overdevelopment, assimilation, conflict, and artificial reconstruction. While presenting a culture to tourists may help preserve the culture, it can also dilute or even destroy it. The point is to promote tourism in the region so that it would both give incomes and create respect for the local tradition and culture.

There are also both negative and positive impacts of tourism on the local ecology. Tourism often grows into mass-tourism. It leads to the over consumption, pollution, and lack of resources.

However, from the ecological point of view tourism is often more acceptable and preferable than any other industrial production, as it is environmentally friendlier. The problem is that it is not easy to change the traditional way of life of the local communities. It often creates pseudo conflicts. Undoubtedly in some regions or countries the alternative industries are even more harmful to the environment than tourism.

Besides that in many countries of Asia and the Pacific, for example in Cook Islands, Samoa and others, tourism is the main source of income or the friendliest to the environment. It is at least better than chopping down the forests or destroying coral reefs.

Thus, the preceding paragraphs show that the impact of tourism on local communities can be both positive and negative, whether it comes to economic, social, or environmental effects. It depends to which extent tourism is developed in a particular region. Every region has its bearing capacity, that is to say the limit of the incoming influence that does not harm the host community.

The combined effects of major expenditures on investments in infrastructure and the associated influx of visitors mean that tourism can have significant impacts, both positive and negative, on an economy, on its culture, and on the environment (Brown, 1998). In practice, the dominant motive for the development of tourism is economic (improvements in employment, incomes and exports), but the very process of developing tourism will impose costs elsewhere. If governmental and non-governmental organisations are to make sensible and rational decisions with respect to the current and future development of tourism, they must have reliable information on its costs and benefits (Fletcher, 1989). Without such information, there is the risk that significant investment opportunities may be missed, that key infrastructure developments may be starved of funds, or that developments may take the wrong form or take place in the wrong location.

While recognising the variety of different impacts that tourism may have, this discussion will focus particular attention on the economic impact of tourism. Economic benefits are probably the main reason why so many countries are interested in the development of tourism and the contribution of tourism to the world economy is considerable. The purpose of this discussion is to examine the main economic costs and benefits associated with tourism and to highlight the difficulties associated with their measurement. Having highlighted the potential economic contribution of tourism, we will then examine the role played by tourism satellite accounts in providing a consistent and reliable source of information on the economic dimensions of tourism. Finally, the use of economic impact modelling techniques will be introduced to present an integrated framework for the evaluation of the economic impact of tourism.

The Economic Benefits of Tourism

Before discussing the various economic benefits of tourism in detail, it is perhaps appropriate to clarify the current position of tourism in the world economy. Arguably, tourism is the second largest industry in the world; estimates from the World Travel and Tourism Council (WTTC) suggest that it generates around 200 million jobs world-wide and accounts for 10% of global GDP (WTTC, 2003). Although there may be debates about the precise scale of tourism's impact on the world economy, few would argue with the view that it does make a major contribution. The scale of that contribution will vary considerably across countries partly because the extent of domestic tourism will vary and partly because the numbers and spending of international visitors will also vary. Relatively speaking, the impact of international visitors is probably greater than the impact of domestic tourists, although the importance of the latter should not be underestimated and for many large countries (eg US, Brazil, India), domestic tourism is often of far greater economic significance than international tourism.

Businesses and public organizations are increasingly interested in the economic impacts of tourism at national, state, and local levels. One regularly hears claims that tourism supports X jobs in an area or that a festival or special event generated Y million dollars in sales or income in a community. "Multiplier effects" are often cited to capture secondary effects of tourism spending and show the wide range of sectors in a community that may benefit from tourism.

Tourism's economic benefits are touted by the industry for a variety of reasons. Claims of tourism's economic significance give the industry greater respect among the business community, public officials, and the public in general. This often translates into decisions or public policies that are favourable to tourism. Community support is important for tourism, as it is an activity that affects the entire community. Tourism businesses depend extensively on each other as well as on other businesses, government and residents of the local community.

Economic benefits and costs of tourism reach virtually everyone in the region in one way or another. Economic impact analyses provide tangible estimates of these economic interdependencies and a better understanding of the role and importance of tourism in a region's economy.

Tourism activity also involves economic costs, including the direct costs incurred by tourism businesses, government costs for infrastructure to better serve tourists, as well as congestion and related costs borne by individuals in the community. Community decisions over tourism often involve debates between industry proponents touting tourism's economic impacts (benefits) and detractors emphasizing tourism's costs. Sound decisions rest on a balanced and objective assessment of both benefits and costs and an understanding of who benefits from tourism and who pays for it.

Tourism's economic impacts are therefore an important consideration in state, regional and community planning and economic development. Economic impacts are also important factors in marketing and management decisions. Communities therefore need to understand the relative importance of tourism to their region, including tourism's contribution to economic activity in the area. A variety of methods, ranging from pure guesswork to complex mathematical models, are used to estimate tourism's economic impacts. Studies vary extensively in quality and accuracy, as well as which aspects of tourism are included. Technical reports often are filled with economic terms and methods that non-economists do not understand. On the other hand, media coverage of these studies tend to oversimplify and frequently misinterpret the results, leaving decision makers and the general public with a sometimes distorted and incomplete understanding of tourism's economic effects.

How can the average person understand these studies sufficiently to separate good studies from bad ones and make informed choices? The purpose of this bulletin is to present a systematic introduction to economic impact concepts and methods. The presentation is written for tourism industry analysts and public officials, who would like to better understand, evaluate, or possibly conduct an economic impact assessment. The bulletin is organized around ten basic questions that either are asked or should be asked about the economic impacts of tourism.

Ten Questions about the Economic Impacts of Tourism;

1. What is an economic impact analysis?
2. What questions does an economic impact assessment answer?
3. What economic impacts does tourism have?
4. What are multiplier effects?
5. How are tourism's economic impacts measured?
6. What are the typical approaches for an economic impact assessment?
7. What are some examples of economic impact assessment approaches in tourism?
8. What are the steps for conducting a tourism economic impact study?
9. What are some questions to ask when evaluating or interpreting a tourism economic impact study?
10. What will an economic impact study cost?

What is an Economic Impact Analysis?

A variety of economic analyses are carried out to support tourism decisions. As these different kinds of economic analysis are frequently confused, let's begin by positioning economic impact studies within the broader set of economic problems and techniques relevant to tourism. These same techniques may be applied to any policy or action, but we will define them here in the context of tourism. Each type of analysis is identified by the basic question(s) it answers and the types of methods and models that are appropriate.

Types of Economic Analysis

Economic impact analysis — What is the contribution of tourism activity to the economy of the region?

An economic impact analysis traces the flows of spending associated with tourism activity in a region to identify changes in sales, tax revenues, income, and jobs due to tourism activity. The principal methods here are visitor spending surveys, analysis of secondary data from government economic statistics, economic base models, input-output models and multipliers. (Frechtling 1994a)

Fiscal impact analysis – Will government revenues from tourism activity from taxes, direct fees, and other sources cover the added costs for infrastructure and government services?

Fiscal impact analysis identifies changes in demands for government utilities and services resulting from some action and estimates the revenues and costs to local government to provide these services.

Financial analysis – Can we make a profit from this activity?

A financial analysis determines whether a business will generate sufficient revenues to cover its costs and make a reasonable profit. It generally includes a short-term analysis of the availability and costs of start-up capital as well as a longer-range analysis of debt service, operating costs and revenues. A financial analysis for a private business is analogous to a fiscal impact analysis for a local government unit.

Demand analysis – How will the number or types of tourists to the area change due to changes in prices, promotion, competition, quality and quantity of facilities, or other demand shifters?

A demand analysis estimates or predicts the number and/or types of visitors to an area via a use estimation, forecasting or demand model. The number of visitors or sales is generally predicted based on judgement (Delphi method), historic trends (time series methods), or using a model that captures how visits or spending varies with key demand determinants (structural models) such as population size, distance to markets, income levels, and measures of quality & competition.

Benefit Cost analysis (B/C) – Which alternative policy will generate the highest net benefit to society over time?

A B/C analysis estimates the relative economic efficiency of alternative policies by comparing benefits and costs over time. B/C analysis identifies the most efficient policies from the perspective of societal welfare, generally including both monetary and non-monetary values. B/C analysis makes use of a wide range of methods for estimating values of non-market goods and services, such as the travel cost method and contingent valuation method.

Feasibility study – Can/should this project or policy be undertaken?

A feasibility study determines the feasibility of undertaking a given action to include political, physical, social, and economic feasibility. The economic aspects of a feasibility study typically involve a financial analysis to determine financial feasibility and a market demand analysis to determine market feasibility. A feasibility study is the private sector analogue of benefit cost analysis. The feasibility study focuses largely on the benefits and costs to the individual business or organization, while B/C analysis looks at benefits and costs to society more generally (Warnell 1986).

Environmental Impact assessment – What are the impacts of an action on the surrounding environment? An environmental assessment determines the impacts of a proposed action on the environment, generally including changes in social, cultural, economic, biological, physical, and ecological systems. Economic impact assessment methods are often used along with corresponding measures and models for assessing social, cultural and environmental impacts. Methods range from simple checklists to elaborate simulation models.

Benefit cost analysis and economic impact analysis are frequently confused as both discuss economic "benefits". There are two clear distinctions between the two techniques. B/C analysis addresses the benefits from economic efficiency while economic impact analysis focuses on the regional distribution of economic activity. The income received from tourism by a destination region is largely offset by corresponding losses in the origin regions, yielding only modest contributions to net social welfare and efficiency. B/C analysis includes both market and non-market values (consumer surplus), while economic impact analysis is restricted to actual flows of money from market transactions.

While each type of economic analysis is somewhat distinct, a given problem often calls for several different kinds of economic analysis. An economic impact study will frequently involve a demand analysis to project levels of tourism activity. In other cases demand is treated as exogenous and the analysis simply estimates impacts if a given number of visitors are attracted to the area. A comprehensive impact assessment will also examine fiscal impacts, as well as social and environmental impacts.

Be aware that an economic impact analysis, by itself, provides a rather narrow and often one-sided perspective on the impacts of tourism. Studies of the economic impacts of tourism tend to emphasize the positive benefits of tourism. On the other hand environmental, social, cultural and fiscal impact studies tend to focus more on negative impacts of tourism. This is in spite of the fact that there are negative economic impacts of tourism (e.g., seasonality and lower wage jobs) and in many cases positive environmental and social impacts (e.g., protection of natural & cultural resources in the area and education of both tourists and local residents).

An economic impact assessment (EIA) traces changes in economic activity resulting from some action.

An EIA will identify which economic sectors benefit from tourism and estimate resulting changes in income and employment in the region. Economic impact assessment procedures do not assess economic efficiency and also do not generally produce estimates of the fiscal costs of an action. For many problems economic impact analysis will be part of a broader analysis. Environmental, social, and fiscal impacts are often equally important concerns in a balanced assessment of impacts.

What Questions does a Tourism Economic Impact Study Answer?

An economic impact analysis will assess the contribution of tourism activity to a region's economy. The basic questions an economic impact study usually addresses are:

- How much do tourists spend in the area?
- What portion of sales by local businesses is due to tourism?
- How much income does tourism generate for households and businesses in the area?
- How many jobs in the area does tourism support?
- How much tax revenue is generated from tourism?

An economic impact analysis also reveals the interrelationships among economic sectors and provides estimates of the changes that take place in an economy due to some existing or proposed action. The most common applications of economic impact analysis to tourism are:

- To evaluate the economic impacts of changes in the supply of recreation and tourism opportunities. Supply changes may involve a change in quantity, such as the opening of new facilities, closing of existing ones, or expansions and contraction in capacity. Supply changes may also involve changes in quality, including changes in (a) the quality of the environment, (b) the local infrastructure and public services to support tourism, or (c) the nature of the tourism products and services that are provided in an area.
- To evaluate the economic impacts of changes in tourism demand. Population changes, changes in the competitive position of the region, marketing activity or changing consumer tastes and preferences can alter levels of tourism activity, spending, and associated economic activity. An economic impact study can estimate the magnitude and nature of these impacts.
- To evaluate the effects of policies and actions which affect tourism activity either directly or indirectly. Tourism depends on many factors at both origins and destinations that are frequently outside the direct control of the tourism industry itself. Economic impact studies provide information to help decision makers better understand the consequences of various actions on the tourism industry as well as on other sectors of the economy. For example, increased air pollution standards have been opposed in some regions due to the predicted economic consequences of the closing of plants that cannot meet the new standards. Tourism interests counter these arguments with estimates

of the potential gains in income and jobs in tourism industries that depend on good air quality and visibility.

- To understand the economic structure and interdependencies of different sectors of the economy. Economic studies help us better understand the size and structure of the tourism industry in a given region and its linkages to other sectors of the economy. Such understandings are helpful in identifying potential partners for the tourism industry as well as in targeting industries as part of regional economic development strategies. Issues such as economic growth, stability, and seasonality may be addressed as part of these studies.
- To argue for favourable treatment in allocation of resources or local tax, zoning or other policy decisions. By showing that tourism has significant economic impacts, tourism interests can often convince decision-makers to allocate more resources for tourism or to establish policies that encourage tourism. Tax abatements and other incentives frequently given to manufacturing firms have also been granted to hotels, marinas and other tourism businesses based on demonstrated economic impacts in the local area.
- To compare the economic impacts of alternative resource allocation, policy, management or development proposals. Economic impact analyses are commonly used to assess the relative merits of distinct alternatives. The economic contribution of expanded tourism offerings may be compared for example with alternatives such as resource extraction activities (mining, timber harvesting) or manufacturing. Impacts of alternative tourism development proposals may also be evaluated, e.g., tourism strategies that emphasize outdoor recreation, camping development, a convention facility, or a factory outlet mall.

What Economic Impacts does Tourism have?

Tourism has a variety of economic impacts. Tourists contribute to sales, profits, jobs, tax revenues, and income in an area. The most direct effects occur within the primary tourism sectors — lodging, restaurants, transportation, amusements, and retail trade. Through secondary effects, tourism affects most sectors of the economy. An economic impact analysis of tourism activity normally focuses on changes in sales, income, and employment in a region resulting from tourism activity.

A simple tourism impact scenario illustrates. Let's say a region attracts an additional 100 tourists, each spending $100 per day. That's $10,000 in new spending per day in the area. If sustained over a 100 day season, the region would accumulate a million dollars in new sales. The million dollars in spending would be distributed to lodging, restaurant, amusement and retail trade sectors in proportion to how the visitor spends the $100. Perhaps 30% of the million dollars would leak out of the region immediately to cover the costs of goods purchased by tourists that are not made in the local area (only the retail margins for such items should normally be included as direct sales effects). The remaining $700,000 in direct sales might yield $350,000 in income within tourism industries and support 20 direct tourism jobs. Tourism industries are labour and income intensive, translating a high proportion of sales into income and corresponding jobs.

The tourism industry, in turn, buys goods and services from other businesses in the area, and pays out most of the $350,000 in income as wages and salaries to its employees. This creates secondary economic effects in the region. The study might use a sales multiplier of 2.0 to indicate that each dollar of direct sales generates another dollar in secondary sales in this region. Through multiplier effects, the $700,000 in direct sales produces $1.4 million in total sales. These secondary sales create additional income and employment, resulting in a total impact on the region of $1.4 million in sales, $650,000 in income and 35 jobs. While hypothetical, the numbers used here are fairly typical of what one might find in a tourism economic impact study. A more complete study might identify which sectors receive the direct and secondary effects and possibly identify differences in spending and impacts of distinct subgroups of tourists (market segments). One can also estimate the tax effects of this spending by applying local tax rates to the appropriate changes in sales or income. Instead of focusing on visitor spending, one could also estimate impacts of construction or government activity associated with tourism.

There are several other categories of economic impacts that are not typically covered in economic impact assessments, at least not directly. For example:

- Changes in prices — tourism can sometimes inflate the cost of housing and retail prices in the area, frequently on a seasonal basis.
- Changes in the quality and quantity of goods and services – tourism may lead to a wider array of goods and services available in an area (of either higher or lower quality than without tourism).
- Changes in property and other taxes – taxes to cover the cost of local services may be higher or lower in the presence of tourism activity. In some cases, taxes collected directly or indirectly from tourists may yield reduced local taxes for schools, roads, etc. In other cases, locals may be taxed more heavily to cover the added infrastructure and service costs. The impacts of tourism on local government costs and revenues are addressed more fully in a fiscal impact analysis.
- Economic dimensions of "social" and "environmental" impacts-There are also economic consequences of most social and environmental impacts that are not usually addressed in an economic impact analysis. These can be positive or negative. For example, traffic congestion will increase costs of moving around for both households and businesses. Improved amenities that attract tourists may also encourage retirees or other kinds of businesses to locate in the area.

Direct, Indirect and Induced Effects

A standard economic impact analysis traces flows of money from tourism spending, first to businesses and government agencies where tourists spend their money and then to :

- other businesses — supplying goods and services to tourist businesses,
- households – earning income by working in tourism or supporting industries, and
- government — through various taxes and charges on tourists, businesses and households.

Formally, regional economists distinguish direct, indirect, and induced economic effects. Indirect and induced effects are sometimes collectively called secondary effects. The total economic impact of tourism is the sum of direct, indirect, and induced effects within a region. Any of these impacts may be measured as gross output or sales, income, employment, or value added.

Direct effects are production changes associated with the immediate effects of changes in tourism expenditures. For example, an increase in the number of tourists staying overnight in hotels would directly yield increased sales in the hotel sector. The additional hotel sales and associated changes in hotel payments for wages and salaries, taxes, and supplies and services are direct effects of the tourist spending.

Indirect effects are the production changes resulting from various rounds of re-spending of the hotel industry's receipts in other backward-linked industries (i.e., industries supplying products and services to hotels).

Changes in sales, jobs, and income in the linen supply industry, for example, represent indirect effects of changes in hotel sales. Businesses supplying products and services to the linen supply industry represent another round of indirect effects, eventually linking hotels to varying degrees to many other economic sectors in the region.

Induced effects are the changes in economic activity resulting from household spending of income earned directly or indirectly as a result of tourism spending. For example, hotel and linen supply employees, supported directly or indirectly by tourism, spend their income in the local region for housing, food, transportation, and the usual array of household product and service needs. The sales, income, and jobs that result from household spending of added wage, salary, or proprietor's income are induced effects.

By means of indirect and induced effects, changes in tourist spending can impact virtually every sector of the economy in one way or another. The magnitude of secondary effects depends on the propensity of businesses and households in the region to purchase goods and services from local suppliers. Induced effects are particularly noticed when a large employer in a region closes a plant. Not only are supporting industries (indirect effects) hurt, but the entire local economy suffers due to the reduction in household income within the region. Retail stores close and leakages of money from the region increase as consumers go outside the region for more and more goods and services. Similar effects in the opposite direction are observed when there is a significant increase in jobs and household income. Final demand is the term used by economists for sales to the final consumers of goods and services. In almost all cases, the final consumers of tourism goods and services are households. Government spending is also considered as final demand. The same methods for estimating impacts of visitor spending can be applied to estimate the economic impacts of government spending, for example, to operate and maintain a park or visitor centre.

Regional Economic Models

An input-output model (I-O model) is a mathematical model that describes the flows of money between sectors within a region's economy. Flows are predicted by knowing what each industry must buy from every other industry to produce a dollar's worth of output. Using each industry's production function, I-O models also determine the proportions of sales that go to wage and salary income, proprietor's income, and taxes. Multipliers can be estimated from input-output models based on the estimated re-circulation of spending within the region.

Exports and imports are determined based upon estimates of the propensity of households and firms within the region to purchase goods and services from local sources (often called RPC's or regional purchase coefficients).

The more a region is self-sufficient and purchases goods and services from within the region, the higher the multipliers for the region.

Input-output models make a number of assumptions. The basic ones are that:

- All firms in a given industry employ the same production technology (usually assumed to be the national average for that industry), and produce identical products.
- There are no economies or diseconomies of scale in production or factor substitution. I-O models are essentially linear —double the level of tourism activity/production and you double all of the inputs, the number of jobs, etc.
- The model doesn't explicitly keep track of time, but analysts generally report the impact estimates as if they represent activity within a single year.
- One must assume that the various model parameters are accurate and represent the current year.

I-O models are firmly grounded in the national system of accounts, which relies on a standard industrial classification system (SIC codes) and various federal government economic censuses, in which individual firms report sales, wage and salary payments and employment. I-O models will generally be at least a few

years out-of-date, although this isn't usually a major problem unless the region's economy has changed significantly. An I-O model represents the region's economy at a particular point in time. Tourist spending estimates are generally price adjusted to the year of the model.

Multiplier computations for induced effects generally assume that jobs created by additional spending are new jobs, involving new households in the area. Induced effects are computed assuming linear changes in household spending with changes in income. Estimates of induced effects may be inflated due to the

violation of these assumptions. Induced effects tend to account for the vast majority of the secondary effects of tourism, and therefore should be used with caution.

What are Multipliers and Multiplier Effects of Tourism?

Multipliers capture the secondary economic effects (indirect and induced) of tourism activity. Multipliers have been frequently misused and misinterpreted in tourism studies (Archer 1984) and are a considerable source of confusion among non-economists. Multipliers represent the economic interdependencies between sectors within a particular region's economy. They vary considerably from region to region and sector to sector. There are many different kinds of multipliers reflecting which secondary effects are included and which measure of economic activity is used.

For example;

The Type I sales multiplier = direct sales + indirect sales direct sales.

The Type II or III sales multiplier = direct sales + indirect sales + induced sales direct sales.

Multiplying a Type I sales multiplier times the direct sales gives direct plus indirect sales. Multiplying a Type II or III sales multiplier times the direct sales gives total sales impacts including direct, indirect and induced effects. The multipliers defined above are called ratio type multipliers as they measure the ratio of a total impact measure to the corresponding direct impact. Comparable income and employment ratio type multipliers may be defined by replacing sales with measures of income or employment in the above equations. Ratio multipliers should be used with caution.

A common error is to multiply a sales multiplier times tourist spending to get total sales effects. This will generate an inflated estimate of tourism impacts. The problem is that tourism spending or sales is not exactly the same as the "direct effects", appearing in the multiplier formula. Tourist purchases of goods (vs. services) are the primary source of the problem.

To properly apply tourist purchases of goods to an input-output model (or corresponding multipliers), various margins (retail, wholesale and transportation) must be deducted from the "purchaser price" of the good to separate out the "producer price". In an I-O model, retail margins accrue to the retail trade sector, wholesale margins to wholesale trade, transportation margins to transportation sectors (trucking, rail, air etc.) and the producer prices of goods are assigned to the sector that produces the good.

In most cases the factory that produces the good bought by a tourist lies outside of the local region, creating an immediate "leakage" in the first round of spending and therefore no local impact from production of the good. Before applying a multiplier to tourist spending, one must first deduct the producer prices of all imported goods that tourists buy (i.e. only include the local retail margins and possibly wholesale and transportation margins if these firms lie within the region). Generally, only 60 to 70% of tourist spending appears as final demand in a local region. While all tourist purchases of services will accrue to the local region as final demand, only the margins on goods purchased at retail stores should be counted as local final demand. The ratio of local final demand to tourist spending is called the capture rate.

Capture rate = local final demand / tourism spending in local area.

The distinction between Type II and Type III multipliers involves a technical difference in how the induced effects are computed. Type II approaches include households as a sector of the economy and invert the technical coefficient matrix including the household sector, while Type III approaches treat households as exogenous.

Capture rates, like multipliers, will vary with the size and nature of the region as well as the kind of tourist spending included.

One must therefore be cautious in taking a multiplier or capture rate cited in one study and using it in another.

Another way of calculating a multiplier (generally the preferred approach among economists) is as a ratio of income or employment to sales. This kind of multiplier is sometimes called a Keynesian multiplier or response coefficient.

Type III Income multiplier = Total direct, indirect, and induced income direct sales Type III Employment multiplier = Total direct, indirect, and induced employment direct sales This income (employment) multiplier produces total income (employment) impacts when multiplied by the direct sales. One must still be careful in distinguishing between tourism spending/sales and direct sales effects. Some studies may embed the capture rate in the multiplier, expressing the ratio in terms of tourism spending rather than direct sales.

How are Tourism's Economic Impacts Measured?

The economic impacts of tourism are typically estimated by some variation of the following simple formula:

The formula suggests three distinct steps and corresponding measurements or models:

Estimate the change in the number and types of tourists to the region due to the proposed policy or action.

Estimates or projections of tourist activity generally come from a demand model or some system for measuring levels of tourism activity in an area. Economic impact estimates will rest heavily on good estimates of the numbers and types of visitors. These must come from carefully designed measurements of tourist activity, a good demand model, or good judgement. This step is usually the weakest link in most tourism impact studies, as few regions have accurate counts of tourists, let alone good models for predicting changes in tourism activity or separating local visitors from visitors from outside the region.

Estimate average levels of spending (often within specific market segments) of tourists in the local area.

Spending averages come from sample surveys or are sometimes borrowed or adapted from other studies. Spending estimates must be based on a representative sample of the population of tourists taking into account variations across seasons, types of tourists, and locations within the study area. As spending can vary widely across different kinds of tourists, we recommend estimating average spending for a set of key tourist segments based on samples of at least 50-100 visitors within each tourism segment. Segments should be defined to capture differences in spending between local residents vs. tourists, day users vs. overnight visitors, type of accommodation (motel, campground, seasonal home, with friends and relatives), and type of transportation (car, RV, air, rail, etc.). In broadly based tourism impact studies, it is useful to identify unique spending patterns of important activity segments such as downhill skiers, boaters, convention & business travellers.

Multiplying the number of tourists by the average spending per visitor (be careful the units are consistent) gives an estimate of total tourist spending in the area. Estimates of tourist spending will generally be more accurate if distinct spending profiles and use estimates are made for key tourism segments. The use and spending estimates are the two most important parts of an economic impact assessment. When combined, they capture the amount of money brought into the region by tourists. Multipliers are needed only if one is interested in the secondary effects of tourism spending.

Apply the change in spending to a regional economic model or set of multipliers to determine secondary effects.

Secondary effects of tourism are estimated using multipliers or a model of the region's economy.

Multipliers generally come from an economic base or input-output model of the region's economy. In many cases multipliers are borrowed (often improperly) or adjusted from published multipliers or other studies. One should not take a multiplier estimated for one region and apply it in a region with a quite different economic structure.

Generally, multipliers are higher for larger regions with more diversified economies and lower for smaller regions with more limited economic development. A common error is to apply a statewide multiplier (since these are more widely published) to a local region. This will yield inflated estimates of local multiplier effects.

Multipliers can also be used to convert estimates of spending or sales to income and employment. Simple ratios can be used to capture how much income or jobs are generated per dollar of sales. These ratios will vary from region to region and across individual economic sectors due to the relative importance of labour inputs in each industry and different wage and salary rates in different regions of the country. Be aware that job estimates are generally not full time equivalents, making them difficult to compare across industries with different proportions of seasonal and part time jobs. Income or value added are generally the preferred measures of the contribution of tourism to a region's economy.

What are the Typical Approaches for an Economic Impact Assessment?

At the simple, "quick and dirty" end of the spectrum are highly aggregate approaches that rely mostly on judgement to determine tourism activity, spending and multipliers. Such estimates can be completed in a couple hours at little cost and rest largely on the expertise and judgement of the analyst. At the other extreme are studies that gather primary data from visitor spending studies and apply the spending estimates to formal regional economic models for the area in question. In between are a wide range of options that employ varying degrees of judgement, secondary data, primary data, and formal models.

Different levels of detail and corresponding expense (time and money) and accuracy are possible for each of the three steps — estimating tourist volume, spending, and multiplier effects. Four typical approaches illustrate the levels of detail that are possible and the associated methods.

1. Subjective estimates that rely mostly on expert opinion
2. Secondary data in aggregate form, adapting existing estimates to suit the problem
3. Secondary data in disaggregate form, permitting finer adjustment of data to fit the situation
4. Primary data and/or formal models, usually involving visitor surveys and regional economic models.

Summary

The economic significance of tourism has been subject to considerable debate. Resolving this debate requires reliable and rigorous information on the precise nature of tourism spending and its impact on different sectors of the economy. One problem which has always faced those seeking to analyse the economic contribution of tourism is that tourism simply does not exist as a distinct sector in systems of national accounts. There are sectors which are characteristic of tourism, such as transport, hotels and accommodation, but tourists spend their money across a range of different sectors and national accounts do not track this spending. These difficulties can be resolved through the construction of Tourism Satellite Accounts which provide an internationally recognised and standardised method of assessing the scale and impact of tourism spending and its links across different sectors. Although costly, investment in the construction of satellite accounts provides policy makers with information on the economic contribution of tourism and the ability to analyses its effects economy wide. Such information is the prerequisite to efficient and effective policy decisions to guide the future development of tourism. Moreover, satellite accounts provide a foundation for more sophisticated analyses of the impact of tourism and the assessment of different policy regimes using techniques such as computable general equilibrium modelling. These general equilibrium techniques do require significant investment, but are increasingly being utilised because of the benefits they generate in terms of understanding the extent and diversity of tourism's impact on an economy.

One can employ different levels of aggregation in visitor segments, spending categories, multipliers, and economic sectors to finely tune the data and models to a particular application and also yield more detailed information about the economic impacts. For example, spending data from previous surveys may be adjusted over time using consumer price indices (CPI). If spending is itemized in several categories, distinct CPI's may be used for food away from home, lodging, or gasoline. If not, an aggregate CPI, which may not reflect the mix of goods that tourists purchase, must be used. Data for distinct tourism market segments is also valuable in tailoring secondary data to a particular application. For example, separate estimates of the average spending for day users and overnight visitors allows one to adjust the spending estimate to reflect a given mix of day users and overnight visitors.

Tourism Growth Factors

A number of factors are responsible for the rapid growth and development of the tourism industry in the Asia Pacific region. These include the strong economic growth, increase in income, breakdown of political barriers, easing of travel restrictions, liberalization of air transport, and focused marketing campaigns.

These factors are expected to accelerate the growth of tourism over the next decade.

Economic Growth

The rapid growth of the tourism industry is a reflection of the region's booming and diversified economies. Economic growth has ranged between an average of 6% to 9% in the last decade, in contrast to 3% to 4% growth achieved by the rest of the world. Only the industrialized countries of Australia, Japan, and New Zealand show a lower rate of growth than the rest of the region. China, which has achieved double-digit growth over the last 5 years, is poised to become one of the world's largest economies and surpass Japan in the next decade. The region is expected to maintain its growth at a rate between 6% to 8% over the next decade (IMF 1996b).

Strong economic growth in Asia is attributed to a focus on market reforms, export oriented industries, stable currencies, diversification of the economy, and massive injection of foreign capital. Billions of dollars are being poured into the tourism infrastructure to accommodate a burgeoning Asian tourism industry. This has intensified trade, investment, and travel within the region and with the rest of the world. Asian governments have also sought to avoid extremes of inflation and unemployment, and are keeping budget deficits small or running surpluses. It is no wonde.

4

The Measurement of Tourism

Managing Change: Performance Measurement for Destination

Management Organizations

In recent years, tourist destinations managers have been criticized because of their inability to reinvent themselves in face of the radical changes in the external environment. The tourism industry is in a state of unprecedented change. Indeed, the first few years of the new millennium have brought extraordinary change and transformation. War, terrorism, political upheaval, the spread of infectious diseases, airline restructuring and the advancement and use of technology are just a few of the events that are having a profound impact on destinations' performance around the world. It appears, however, that many DMO executives are unable to manage change and find it increasingly difficult to determine the impact these events are likely to have on the destination and on destination management organizations. The pressure exerted by competition is compelling international, national, state, and local governments to re-evaluate the existing tourism resources and to capitalize on them in order to attract more visitors (Fayos-Sola, 1996). As King (2002) points out, "nothing short of a reinvention of destination marketing organizations (DMOs) will ensure they are able to keep abreast of and capitalize upon the revolution taking place". In a highly competitive tourism market, it is increasingly important to understand the role each destination plays in relation to other competitive destinations.

The strategic responses to these developments are essentially decisions on whether to proactively shape or reactively adapt to the crisis. Deciding on which strategic orientation to choose in response to current developments is essentially a decision on whether to shape or adapt to the crisis.

Mapping your Strategy and Measures

Organizational effectiveness depends on the ability of the organization to adapt to its environment, which is in turn influenced primarily by the strategic management of the organization. An effective monitoring of external forces should help identify not only emerging opportunities and threats, but also the organization's strengths and weaknesses for meeting these opportunities and threats. Organizations are shaped by their performance measure. Performance measures play a critical role in formulating corporate strategies, evaluating accomplishments, and compensating organizational members. Performance measures and outcomes are predetermined methods for assessing whether the aforementioned goals and objectives are achieved.

Lebas and Euske (2002) provide a good definition of performance as "doing today what will lead to measured value outcomes tomorrow." Business Performance Measurement (BPM) then is concerned with measuring this performance relative to some benchmark, be it a competitor's performance or a preset target. Business performance, which reflects the perspective of strategic management, is a subset of the overall concept of organizational effectiveness.

A specific measure can be compared to itself over time, compared with a preset target or evaluated along with other measures. Since a measure is used for the purpose of comparison, it need not represent an absolute value. Following Simmons (2000), measures can be objective or subjective. Objective measures can be independently measured and verified. Subjective ones cannot. Measures are also typically classified as financial or non-financial. Financial measures are typically derived from or directly related to the chart of accounts and found in a company's profit and loss statement or balance sheet, such as inventory levels or cash on hand. Non-financial measures are measures not found in the chart of accounts, such as customer satisfaction scores or product quality measures. Measures are also leading or lagging. Lagging measures give feedback on past performance, such as last month's profit, and typically do not provide insight into future performance. Leading indicators, in contrast, are designed to measure future performance, and more often than not, future financial performance.

It is important to note that performance measurement itself has no consequence: simply knowing that there is scope for improvement in an organization because you have measured some aspect of its performance will not, in itself, lead to any improvement. So in order to get some improvement as a result of performance measurement, the organization needs to do something in the light of this information. The issues associated with 'doing something in the light of performance measurement data' are covered by the more general topic of *performance* management.

Perspectives of Performance Measurement

The field of performance measurement has evolved rapidly in the last few years with the development of new measurement approaches, frameworks and methodologies, such as the economic value added, shareholder value added, activity based costing, cost of quality, competitive benchmarking and balanced scorecard. Each framework purports to be unique and appears to claim comprehensiveness, yet each offers a different perspective on performance.

Developed by the Stern Stewart Corporation as an overall measure of financial performance, economic value added (EVA) is both a specific performance measure and the basis for a larger performance measurement framework (Otley, 1999). According to its creators, EVA is a financial performance metric that is most directly linked to the creation of shareholder value, over time. EVA is net operating profit less an appropriate charge for the opportunity cost of all capital invested in an enterprise. However, using EVA alone can cause managers to invest in less risky, cost-reducing activities rather than in growth activities and as a pure financial model, EVA cannot serve as a vehicle for articulating a strategy. Shareholder value frameworks incorporate the cost of capital into the equation, but ignore everything (and everyone) else.

Activity-based costing (ABC) was developed to provide better insight into how overhead costs should be allocated to individual products or customers. ABC links expenses related to the resources supplied to the organization with the activities performed within the organization. Expenses flow from resources to activities and then to products, services and customers. Both activity based costing and cost of quality, on the other hand, focus on the identification and control of cost drivers (nonvalue-adding activities and failures/nonconformances respectively), which are themselves often embedded in the business processes. But this highly process focused view ignores any other perspectives on performance – such as the opinion of shareholders, customers and employees. Conversely, benchmarking tends to involve taking a largely external perspective, often comparing performance with that of competitors or other 'best practitioners' of business processes.

Kaplan and David P. Norton in 1992, balanced scorecards have found widespread adoption in varied industries. Initially focused on finding a way to report on leading indicators of a business's health rather than traditional accounting measures which are lagging indicators, the balanced scored was refocused to measure the firm's strategy. Instead of measuring anything, firms should measure those things that directly relate to the firm's strategy. The balanced scorecard is broken down into four sections, called perspectives: The financial perspective relates to the strategy for growth, profitability and risk from the shareholder's perspective. The customer perspective relates to the strategy for creating value and differentiation from the perspective of the customer.

The internal business perspective relates to the strategic priorities for various business processes that create customer and shareholder satisfaction. The learning and growth perspective relates to the priorities to create a climate that supports organizational change, innovation and growth. The balanced scorecard, with its four perspectives, focuses on financials (shareholders), customers, internal processes, plus innovation and learning. In doing so it downplays the importance of other stakeholders, such as suppliers and employees. By combining these different perspectives, the balanced scorecard helps managers understand the interrelationships and tradeoffs between alternative performance dimensions and leads to improved decision making and problem solving. The characteristic feature of '*balance*' is supposed to be guaranteed by considering short-long term/financial and non-financial/lagging and leading indicators, concerning four perspectives.

One might reasonably ask, how can multiple, and seemingly inconsistent, business performance frameworks and measurement methodologies exist? They can exist because they all add value.

They all provide unique perspectives on performance. They all furnish managers with a different set of lenses through which they can assess the performance of their organizations. Firms adapt these frameworks for a variety of reasons, but chiefly to improve control over the firm in ways that traditional accounting systems have not allowed. If the organization wishes to implement a major change in its strategy, a BSC scheme may be embarked upon first and then the missing elements can be captured with the help of other frameworks. Using this approach, companies get insights into profitable and profitless activities based on a customer or a product viewpoint.

However, organizations in some industries have also modified the balanced scorecard in order to fit their business models.

Benefits of Performance Measurement

Measurement plays a crucial role in translating business strategy into results (Lingle & Schiemann, 1996). Performance measures or indicators are measurable characteristics of products, services, processes, and operations the company uses to track and improve performance. The measures or indicators should be selected to best represent the factors that lead to improved customer, operational, and financial performance. A comprehensive set of measures or indicators tied to customer and/or company performance requirements represents a clear basis for aligning all activities with the company's goals. Through the analysis of data from the tracking processes, the measures or indicators themselves may be evaluated and changed to better support such goals. Numerous researchers have discussed the link between strategy, measurement and success. Those that measure gain agreement on the strategy, clarity of communication, focus and alignment and organizational culture advantages. Strategy and performance measurements need to be intertwined, and as such are likely to be unique for each organization. Organizations should measure how parts of their value chain actually fit together for an overarching advantage instead of relying on process-byprocess metrics (Porter, 2002).

Measuring results facilitates early identification and correction of problems at the source, before they require correcting from the outside. A key attribute for the BSC and other BPM frameworks is the support for identifying and communicating causal linkages between components of the business that fulfill the strategy.

Identifying the causal linkages may be a bottleneck. If data show a drop in success, a quick diagnosis can identify the reasons and suggest immediate remedies. At the most basic level, metrics tell us what is working and what is not. DMOs can provide better service to its stakeholders while avoiding the necessity of having remedies imposed from the outside.

Performance Measurement Systems

The level of performance a business attains is a function of the efficiency and effectiveness of the actions it undertakes. This not only identifies two fundamental dimensions of performance, but also highlights the fact that there can be internal as well as external reasons for pursuing specific courses of action (Slack, 1991).The mechanics of performance measurement are complex and the development and deployment of the process painful. Typically many measures will be reported and tracked before a key set will emerge. Many choices will be driven by industry best practices measures so that a competitive benchmarking program can be established. Many will be reported in order to establish a baseline well before a target improvement value is established. A balance between breath, completeness and complexity and competitive comparison must be developed. Business Performance Measurement/Management can be done at two distinct levels: strategic and operational. The balanced scorecard is an example of a strategic BPM. Operational BPM help managers with specific operational process control issues that may or may not be directly related to the strategy however are crucial to develop the organizations BSC and hence contribute to the overall success of the organization. The key to successful performance measurement is to identify and collect meaningful performance measures that can or actually will be used.

Once a firm becomes large enough that a single manager cannot sense the firm's current state and cannot control its behavior alone, the firm must use performance measurement and control systems to replace the eyes and ears of the beleaguered manager. Over the past few decades, firms have used information technology to provide this "sense and control" capability. Performance measurement system is a widely applied management tool which can be used to assess an organization's progress towards achieving its predefined goals, which include the efficiency with which resources are transformed into goods and services, the quality of these goods and services, the results of a program activity compared to its intended purpose and the effectiveness of operations in terms of their specific contributions to the organization's objectives. The system tools can leverage the latest advancements in data and application integration approaches, web-based charting and reporting, statistical analysis, artificial intelligence, machine learning and expert system technology.

Implementing a performance measurement system can significantly enhance an organization's capacity to successfully leverage information and data. More importantly, this can help an organization foster a culture that is largely focused on strategy, learning, and continuous improvement through monitoring and measuring its own performance. It is crucial that performance measures will provide an organization with tools to examine and formulate their strategies. This entails measures that are indicative of procedures, processes, and strategies of investing in and building long-term resources, facilities, and infrastructure as needed to adapt to the fast pace of today's changing environments.

At the lowest level of analysis lies measurement of human performance and the overall organizational performance is the ultimate level of evaluation. In between the overall organization effectiveness and the individual lie other layers, such as the functional or service group, workgroup or team and the business activity. Performance Measurement systems are often designed to be a vehicle for strategic dialog within the firms. System tools enable individuals to record and discover discrepancies between stated goals and actual performance creating a favourable learning environment which in turn facilitates organizational change. Technology allows storing and retrieving relevant actual performance information for future comparison and decision making.

Performance Measurement Systems can help provide this firmwide coherency and enable decision makers to bundle measures based on their cognitive understanding and knowledge of the organizational environment. These systems facilitate coherence of performance metrics and scorecards scattered horizontally and vertically across an organization, so that the conversations between people about the strategy is consistent and all the different measurement units contribute to the performance of the organization as a whole.

Future of Performance Measurement in Tourism

Traditionally, the tourism industry has used visitor satisfaction studies, conversion studies, and economic impact models as indicators to evaluate the performance of a destination. However, these measures do not provide a clear understanding of the impacts on the destination performance generated by the efforts of the DMO. As a result, CVBs would sometimes find themselves limited in their ability to systematically and credibly articulate their contribution to the destination. To address this problem *A Handbook for CVBs* is published by the Destination Marketing Association International formerly, International Association of Convention and Visitor Bureaus (IACVB). The association represents nearly 600 destination management organizations in over 30 countries. The Performance Measurement Team (PMT) recently created by the Destination Marketing Association International has recommended bureaus use a standard business return-on-investment formula to quantify the financial impact on its local community for convention and leisure travel. By using the standard corporate business valuation model, PMT has developed a definitive Return on Investment (ROI) formula for bureaus to apply.

IACVB claims that with the adoption of these industry standards, a CVB will have recognized benchmarks to utilize for assessing internal performance, as well as a means to accurately compare performance with other CVBs. It is IACVB's intent that the handbook on performance reporting (IACVB, 2005) will aid the decision making process for resource allocation, sales and marketing campaign development, as well as staff training and development. IACVB continues to build on its long-standing commitment to provide strategic and operational guidance to convention and visitor bureaus (CVBs). Through the development of standards, best practices and systematic approaches to organizational functions, CVBs are able to employ comparative analytical tools in identifying organizational strengths, weaknesses, and opportunities.

In addition to internally reviewing their operations, CVBs are often required, due to their unique funding sources, to undergo external performance reviews by various stakeholders within their local communities. At times, these external audits/reviews may be done by firms lacking CVB knowledge and experience. As a result,

CVBs' achievements were underreported and misunderstood, a circumstance potentially damaging to the relationship between the CVB and its stakeholders. Most bureaus are classified as independent, not-for profit organizations, but some are part of city or county governments while others have special legal authority. Further, because bureaus vary in terms of their structure, scope, size, geographic location and type of management the standard measures might sometimes be misleading if these differences are not taken into consideration.

The IACVB's standard measures fail to recognize that the external environment, often referred to as the organizational environment, are different for all CVBs. The external environment consist of all elements outside the boundary of the organization and includes elements of competition, resources, technology, economic conditions and other elements that may in some way be related to the performance of the organization. As all DMOs belong to the same tourism industry they are likely to select some measures that are similar (mainly process measures), but they also need to identify a number of measures that are unique to each one of them and are a reflection of differences in their long-term goals and in the specific issues they face, despite being in the same industry.

Smart-Perform for Destination Management Organizations

Incremental strategic change may be successful in fairly stable environments. However, in order to survive in the dynamic environment DMOs need to establish relationships with all important partners and prove that they know what they are doing. Understanding the link between environmental characteristics and performance has several important implications for the way in which DMOs plan for the future. In order to facilitate this, the National Laboratory of Tourism & eCommerce at School of Tourism and Hospitality Management, Temple University is developing a performance

measurement system, SMART-PERFORM, specially catering to the DMOs. This system is designed to address the increasing information needs by integrating historical, present (near real time) and future (forecasts) data which is critical for the design and implementation of a DMOs marketing/communication programs or campaigns. Based upon the information, the system will help bureaus establish a series of performance criteria with which to evaluate their marketing efforts and resource based/ capacity building aspects of the organization. More specifically, the system will benefit the bureau in terms of:

- Systematic performance appraisals;
- Useful, timely and credible market information;
- Improved visitor satisfaction;
- Fostering accountability and responsibility;
- Improved managerial decision making; and,
- More meaningful and easy-to-understand information that can be presented to stakeholders.

In the process of adopting and implementing the bureau will go through a process to outline their measures and set up baseline measures (the first measure taken) of a current processes, work output or organizational outcome results which could then be used for benchmarking against other like programs or CVBs. As a performance measurement system, Smart-perform involves the collection, synthesis, delivery, and display of information related to the measurement of productivity output and accomplishment, as well as in-process parameters that affect productivity. If the results differ from goals and objectives, the bureau members can analyse the gaps in performance and make adjustments. A model for measuring the bureau's performance will help all members-customers, suppliers, employees, and community understand and evaluate their contributions and expectations.

Performance measurement is an evolving, iterative challenge. The Perform system developed especially for each participating DMO will help the bureau executives to make decisions regarding critical organizational issue such as depth/quality of strategic planning, indicators of partnerships and alliances, anticipating and preparing for changes in the environment, and investments in new markets and technologies. This will be an efficient and effective management tool which will empower managers to both monitor past performance and stimulate future action.

The Development and Planning

The delivery of quality products and services, within international tourism and hospitality, reflects an increasing focus on intangibles and the role of what can be styled the "human factor". Companies struggle to create clear distinction and consumer recognition of added value on the basis of physical product differentiation (Balmer and Baum, 1993) except within a relatively limited band of the market. Airline brand relaunches (new first-and business-class products) and the executive floor products, within the hotel sector, represent a small proportion of the global market and trends in this direction are counter-balanced by the growing strength of budget or economy products (hotels and no-frills airlines) in Europe and North America, catering for both the leisure and business customer. There is considerable evidence to support the notion that there has been a merging of the tourism experience, in physical product terms, across the range of designated quality levels. The introduction of "Business First" products by airlines offers consumers what is claimed to be a first-class environment for business-class price, while budget to mid-range hotel rooms offer a range of facilities which are not significantly different from some products in the four-star range. This trend is one which has, in part, created the need to focus on service delivery as an alternative differentiator in the marketplace. The Marriott empowerment series of advertisements is a good example of recognition of this focus by a major hospitality corporation.

A "people" focus, within tourism and hospitality, is by no means new and successful organizations such as Disney, British Airways, Singapore Airlines, Marriott and Ritz Carlton have developed strong reputations for their recognition of the role which their staff play in meeting customer expectations within their sector. As a consequence, this is an area which has been studied and analysed in considerable depth, and the literature represents a significant collection of empirical research, good practice case-studies and rather polemical "how to wow the customer" pieces. The focus of such work is at the level of the firm and much of it builds on the work of major corporations such as those identified above. Best practice, in the area, appears to recognize that quality service delivery is not the outcome of an isolated service enhancement training programme, but has to do with change in organizational culture from top down and is a complex process which impacts on all areas of the organization and its systems (Mahesh, 1994). It is also a process which is rather more commonly taken aboard within the context of larger organizations. Small to medium-sized enterprises (SMEs), which have the advantage of simple internal communication systems, face other challenges reflective of their resource structures, expertise and nature of their workforce. There is little doubt that consumer experience of "human value added" through service is varied within and between the hospitality sectors of most countries. In part, this is a reflection of the eclectic nature of customer expectations which may demand very different things from the same service delivery situation. It is also a factor of the number of human interactions (moments of truth) which most customers experience within any one hospitality purchase-these may or may not be within the one organization and thus the ability to "control" the customer's experience may not lie within the organization, which suffers through lost business. In many respects, a customer's assessment of hospitality will be based on the total destination experience.

This article develops the argument that human resource management is more than a strategic and operational concern for companies competing within the hospitality marketplace. It considers human resource management as a strategic dimension within the wider enhancement of quality and market positioning of tourism at the level of organizations, specific destinations, regions within countries or whole nations. The main thesis advanced is that the tourism and hospitality industry, from the perspective of all its stakeholders (public sector, private sector, visitors and host community), benefits from the close integration of human resource, labour market and education policies, with those policies relating to, and impacting on, the tourism and hospitality sector. This thesis is developed by reporting key findings from two research projects which address aspects of the relationship between these two areas of policy. The first is concerned with the identification of key future policy priorities for human resource development in tourism and hospitality, while the second addresses the structures and policy formulation environment necessary for creation of effective linkages between tourism and hospitality, on the one hand, and education, training and development on the other.

Human Resource Policy Issues in Tourism and Hospitality

The tourism and hospitality sector, in all locations, has a close relationship with the labour market environment from which it draws its skills and consequently depends on its workforce for the delivery of service and product standards to meet existing and anticipated demand from its visitor marketplace. This relationship is, on the one hand, one of dependency in that the make-up of the local workforce (or that which can be introduced into the local environment) has a direct influence on the standards and character of the tourist offering which can be prepared and presented to visitors-if local art and craft skills are not developed within the education system or at community level, it will not be possible to offer this dimension to visitors. On the other hand, tourism and hospitality, for many communities, provides a major and growing sector of the economy and, with it, employment opportunities which other traditional and declining sectors of the economy may not provide.

This is true in an industrial, urban context where cities such as Glasgow (now the second most visited urban centre in the UK) have developed tourism in the wake of the decline of its traditional heavy industrial sector. It is an equally valid scenario in locations where the exploitation of natural resources no longer provides the same level of employment opportunity as it did in the past-the decline of the North Atlantic fishery has seen island locations, such as the Faroes, Iceland, Greenland and Newfoundland, focus on tourism as part of wider economic diversification strategies. As one of the studies reported in this article illustrates, the two-way relationship between tourism and hospitality, and human resource development and management is not always recognized in a holistic and policy-focused manner by public or private sector concerns.

Writing in 1993, Baum identified a number of what were described as "universal themes": issues which literature and practical experience identified as the major human resource concerns faced by tourism and hospitality at both a practical, operational level and in the context of wider strategic and policy-oriented discussion. These were:

Demography and the shrinking employment pool resulting in labour and specific skills shortages. This is primarily a developed country phenomenon found in Western Europe, North America and "tiger economy" countries of the Far East. However, labour shortage is also a concern elsewhere when it is recognized that the specific skills which tourism demands (technical, cultural, communications) may be in short supply within many, less developed destination areas. Demographic and other forms of structural change within the labour market demand responses which take tourism recruitment beyond its traditional youth pool into consideration of mature worker alternatives (those returning to work; seeking a career change; retirees) and this, in turn, has major implications for relative remuneration, working conditions, employment security and related issues.

For many subsectors in tourism and hospitality, and in most developed countries, the negative employment image of the sector is a major issue and barrier to the recruitment and retention of quality and well educated employees (Choy, 1995). Wood (1995) argues that "both industry employees and wider society view hotel and catering labour as relatively low status, mainly because of the personal service nature of the work involved". This poor image is the result of a cocktail of historic and contemporary factors-the origin of hospitality work within domestic service and its consequent associations with servility; links, in some countries, between hospitality employment and colonial legacy; widespread use of expatriate labour in many developing countries, creating the perception that the sector is one offering only limited opportunity for promotion and progression; widespread exposure to work in the sector as a first working experience, resulting in generalized assessment based on limited exposure; and the reality of antisocial working conditions and casualized remuneration.

In some respects, the negatively-held perceptions are not wholly justified by the reality of work for major airlines, international hotel groups, theme parks or within heritage organizations. In other regards, the perceptions are a mirror of the reality of work within an industrial sector dominated by small and medium-sized enterprises (SMEs) and the impact of irregular demand. The effect of these perceptions is to impose a barrier to employment and employment choice among school and college leavers, parents and career guidance teachers which has been very difficult to counter. However, the situation, in some developing countries, is rather different in that international tourism offers a high status and secure employment environment when compared to alternatives in both the primary and manufacturing sectors.

In some contexts, cultural and traditional perceptions may also militate against the recruitment of the best able and qualified recruits into the tourism and hospitality sector. Religious barriers, for example, may exclude some groups from participation, notably women. As already indicated, the rewards and benefits structure of the tourism and hospitality industries can act as a barrier to the recruitment and retention of quality employees. This is a concern of particular focus within hospitality but perceptions regarding working conditions, hours and pay extend more generally across the tourism-related service sector. There is a clear and unavoidable reality, within tourism and hospitality, that the demand cycle is antisocial and falls out with "normal" nine-to-five working parameters. Aircraft fly at night, hotel guests expect services at weekends and theme parks reach peak demand during public holidays. In terms of remuneration, the sector faces challenges in common with other labour-intensive service areas and in many countries has seen pressures for increased productivity alongside deskilling in many areas of work. At a policy level, the sector is influenced greatly by legislative intervention, for example European initiatives with respect to minimum wage levels, duration of the working week and unsociable working times.

Notwithstanding national and sub-sectoral diversity within tourism and hospitality, a combination of reality and perceptions gives an overall negative gloss to the image of many areas of the industry. As we have already suggested, this acts as a major barrier to the recruitment of quality personnel into work in the area. Many entrants to work in the sector do so with expectations of impermanence-this reflects reality in terms of the demand cycle (seasonality and fluctuations as a result of instability within the business cycle in general) whereby longer-term and sustained opportunities are not available to those who take employment in hotels, as resort couriers or ski instructors. It is also reflective of short-termism within many tourism and hospitality businesses which may be unwilling to seek long-term commitment in return for reciprocal long-term investment in the recruit.

As a consequence, many entrants to the sector do so with assumptions of impermanence-this is work to be undertaken on the way to somewhere else, a first exposure to the demands of the workforce but one to be shed when better opportunities arise elsewhere in the economy. Furthermore, as Riley (1996) shows, the sector is one of unconstrained access to most of its working positions and one which, therefore, benefits from unrestrained recruitment to most of its positions but, conversely, also suffers because the skills it engenders in its workforce are in considerable demand within other areas of the service economy. Thus, while entry is open, so is the opportunity to move out elsewhere, both within tourism and hospitality, and to other employment areas. Staff turnover, therefore, can be very high, especially in tight and competitive labour markets, and is a major inhibitor for organizations and destinations seeking to achieve overall enhancement of service and product quality.

A key issue, relating to recruitment, is that of specific skills shortages in key technical and some managerial areas. In part, this is an extension of the concerns addressed above-image, conditions, remuneration-but is also linked to a reluctance, within some industry sectors and businesses, to invest in the skills development of their key personnel. The Irish tourism industry, throughout a period of sustained growth from the mid-1980s onwards, has experienced acute shortages of key technical personnel, particularly chefs, despite levels of national unemployment considerably above the European Union average (Walsh, 1993).

Contrary trends, however, also raise important issues with respect to recruitment and retention. The combined impact of technology and product substitution in the workplace; centralization of key management functions (finance, information analysis, marketing); standardization of product and service delivery; and delayering of management structures in many developed tourism economies means that opportunities for meaningful and developmental careers in skilled craft or managerial areas have been reduced. Reduced opportunity, in turn, impacts on perceptions of the sector and the likelihood of young people, in particular, opting for tourism/hospitality as their career choice.

A changing tourism and hospitality industry environment is, in a sense, complemented but also complicated by changing social expectations of work (Linney and Teare, 1991) and an increasingly diverse profile of employees (Christensen, 1993). Diversity provides the opportunity to create new working environments and conditions, but demands comprehensive review of traditional practice. A good example of this is the present reluctance of many employees to accept split-shift working and the consequent need for employers to reorganize their work environment accordingly.

Education, training and development, for tourism and hospitality is also, in part, a recruitment issue in that providers of educational and training programmes, particularly within the college and university sector, are influenced by the same perceptual factors as the industry itself. Recruitment standards to vocational programmes for the sector are lower than those to equivalent courses in related professional areas, for example business. Tourism studies are, in a sense, somewhat different from hospitality in this respect in that vocational outcomes are less clearly defined and graduate choice is likely to be rather more eclectic. There are clear opportunities to use such educational programmes in a rather more general education sense rather than facing clear vocational channelling (Baum, 1996). Ritchie (1993) argues that one key issue is a lack of tourism sector consensus as to the need for sector-specific educational provision. Commitment to ongoing career development of existing employees, within tourism and hospitality, varies greatly and is influenced by the sub-sector and the size of the enterprise (Cooper, 1993). The presence of career development opportunities, however, is likely to exert a considerable influence on the retention of ambitious employees, with potential, within the sector.

Recognition remains relatively limited that human resource development is an important contributor to the delivery of quality products and service, within tourism and hospitality, and that this, in turn, impacts on the level of both new and repeat business achieved by businesses and destinations. This situation has altered significantly in recent years and the business advantage achieved, through a people focus, by companies such as British Airways, Singapore Airlines, Marriott and Ritz Carlton, has been an important contributory factor. However, many small businesses do not have the resources or skills to focus on their human capital. Given that tourism destinations have images that are only as strong as their weakest link, it is important to strive to ensure that the visitor's experience is positive throughout the full range of contact with the providers of goods and services.

Human resource development is, frequently, addressed as a reactive concern within tourism and hospitality, and rarely in a proactive and planned sense. Product and market shifts and developments may be the target of strategic analysis and preparation, but it is not common, within the sector, to find enterprises or wider destination communities putting in place recruitment, education and training in support of such change, whether quantitative (in the sense of increased arrivals numbers) or qualitative (in the sense of new market segments) in advance. Recognition of the lead-time needed to achieve benefit from human resource investment is also limited at both corporate and national levels. The above points represent a complex and inter-related series of issues and concerns which have greater or lesser applicability according to the specific corporate or destination context. What is clear is that these issues feature in an assessment of human resources, within tourism and hospitality, wherever such analysis is undertaken, and that the response to them is frequently fragmented and limited by lack of co-ordination and policy direction. These issues are addressed in the context of two research studies reported here.

An Assessment of the Human Resource Demands of the Tourism and Hospitality Industries

This section is based on the work of Spivack (1997). Her study, using Delphi methodologies, sought to identify and measure gaps between the skills and wider human resource requirements of the tourism and hospitality industries, and the provision made by education and training providers in support of the sector. In addition, the study looks to the future and attempts to identify the educational and training priorities for tourism and hospitality in response to changes within the sectoral and wider socio-economic and political environment. The approach of the study was:

To develop a qualitative methodology, through a consensus model approach, for determining gaps between the output of education and training delivery systems and the current and future needs of employers. Inherent in the premise is a falsifiable theory: there is no relationship between education and training system outputs and the delivery of quality service (Spivack, 1997).

This study brings together two areas of applied policy development which impact significantly on the development of a wider and cogent policy framework for human resource development within tourism and hospitality: first, that of quality service attainment as central to a successful tourism and hospitality sector, and, second, that there is a role which public education and training can play in achieving such quality.

Spivack's study consisted of two components, employing similar methodologies but working with distinct groups in order to verify the approach and to test outcomes in different contexts. The first global survey was based on a sample drawn from international tourism interests, from both the public and private sector, and representing a wide range of sub-sectoral interests and geographical regions. The second component involved a localized study, employing a similar approach and located in a region of Spain. Modified Delphi methods were used for both components, recognizing both the benefits that this approach brings to a qualitative study but also its clear limitations (Witt and Moutinho, 1989). Its advantages include the potential breadth of the study, its internal anonymity the manner in which it permits reflection time for participants and the ability of the approach to tackle complex issues in a balanced manner. Problems relate to the sampling process-the rationale for Delphi is that it draws on expert contributors, but there can be difficulties in defining and identifying appropriate expertise; in maintaining response levels over a number of survey rounds; and in the time commitment demanded of participants.

The global study commenced with 100 participants, drawn on a controlled formula basis from both sectoral and geographical populations to ensure minimum representation within each category. The criteria used for inclusion of participants required that panellists exhibit some or all of the following:

- hold upper-level management positions within their field;
- serve in leadership positions in professional associations related to their field;
- demonstrate familiarity with many different career levels within their sector;
- demonstrate leadership and decision-making skills;
- articulate trends impacting their industry;
- possess familiarity with tourism education and training in their world region.

Selection of the sample was based on access to various databases and directories of international tourism. While there must be clear limitations to this process, the final sample met representation criteria in terms of both sectoral and geographical considerations. Communication was by mail and fax. The response rate to the two rounds of the study showed expected levels of drop-out so that the first round was completed by 66 percent of the 100-member sample and the second round by 44, representing a 44 percent participation rate from the original sample. The local study, based on the Castilla-La Mancha region of Spain, employed the same approach but saw some significant modifications to suit local conditions. Participation criteria were modified to reflect the different level of responsibility of tourism sector leaders at a regional level and, as a result, included rather more members with direct line management responsibility for enterprises or tourism agencies. Geographical considerations related to representation of the five provinces within the region, while the sectors were modified to reflect the structure of the local industry. The sample was 160 and the three rounds of the survey were conducted: first, by face-to-face personal interview; second, using a telephone survey based on a questionnaire resulting from analysis of the first-round outcomes; and, finally, through panel workshops in each of the five provinces, requiring panellists to prioritize the outcome issues relevant to their specific area and to develop regional action plans. Participation in the three rounds was as follows:

- Round 1: 160.
- Round 2: 140, representing a 13 percent drop-off.
- Round 3: 39, representing a 76 percent drop-off from the original sample.

The outcomes of the two studies identified a number of key gaps with respect to the human resource requirements, as articulated by the respondents (both public and private sector) and the skills and knowledge of those recruited into the tourism sector, whether from specialist vocational programmes or through the general education process. The main area of deficiency related to what Baum (1990) describes as soft competences within the sector, those relating to communication (with customers, colleagues and in various languages other than the mother tongue), information (technology-derived, but also analysis and interpretation) and service (marketing-related, understanding customer needs), all of which are attributes which are generic to the sector and, indeed, to services in general.

By contrast, technical ability deficiencies were identified as far less significant within both surveys-there is growing recognition that the diminishing technical demands of the sector (as identified above) can readily be met within the workplace by larger employers, provided soft competences and attitude dimensions are in place. However, the skills requirements of SMEs remains an issue and it is noteworthy that the local study gave a rather less clear-cut endorsement of this assessment than did the global survey representing larger organizations and interests. In policy terms, this central finding affirms previous research at a more localized level and within the context of specific subsectors and suggests the need for review of public education and training provision for the tourism and hospitality sector in terms of curriculum and, indeed, wider focus and purpose.

The global study also gives an indication of future education and training priorities for tourism and hospitality. Spivack (1997) reports a number of what she calls "skills development issues" derived from anticipated changes within the tourism and hospitality sector, and which the panel consensus process prioritized as central to education and training needs in the future. These were, in rank order:

1. Managers will need to develop more skills in human resource management, particularly in knowing how to build an enthusiastic workforce.
2. With continued internationalization of business, all levels of management will need more training, especially in interpersonal and multicultural skills.
3. Environmental awareness and conservation techniques will become an essential part of tourism education at all levels.
4. The expansion of franchises among transnational firms will accelerate the need for international-level quality of service and skill standards.
5. Public health issues, such as AIDS, that relate to the delivery of tourist products and services will become an essential part of tourism education at all levels.
6. Supervisors will need to learn more high-level management skills such as forecasting and strategic planning.

The local study did not generate significantly different responses from those presented above, with the main emphasis on the growing importance of environmental awareness, business acumen and the enhanced role of enterprises in the education and training of the workforce.

On the basis of this assessment, the study also considered and prioritized key training issues for the future. At an education and training level (Spivack, 1997), these were:

1. Schools of tourism and hospitality management will need to strengthen their curriculum content that deals with business administration skills.
2. Managers will need more training to direct a growing contract-based, part-time and possibly job-sharing workforce.
3. With continued technological change, alternative methods of training and education (such as distance learning, multimedia interactive training, etc.) will markedly replace traditional education.
4. In the future, industry will itself assume increasing responsibility for in-house training of employees at all levels, and rely less on formal education.
5. Employees with formal education in tourism and hospitality management studies generally perform better than colleagues who lack such education.
6. Companies will increasingly encourage and pay for continuing education for their employees to ensure employee commitment and retention.
7 International employee exchange programmes at all levels of employment will become commonplace.

With respect to wider personnel issues, a number of priorities were also identified (Spivack, 1997):

1. Industry will favour hiring employees who have a combination of on-the-job training and formal education.
2 Performance standards, rather than other criteria, will increasingly determine employee compensation and benefits.
3. Groups that have been traditionally been under-represented at management levels in the tourism workforce, such as women, will have a greater role in the future.
4 Changing family lifestyles will require companies to incorporate practices such as work-at-home employees (the virtual office) that lead to a more flexible workforce.
5 Employees will be required to adjust their expectations regarding promotion time-frames, entry-level positions and pay.

6. Corporations downsizing will slow the advancement of employees within their own organizations.
7 To increase the quality of service and better compete in the marketplace, employee incentives, for example, stock options, will become standard for companies.

Spivack's study points to a future which is, in part, already here in that some of the indicators and priorities are already recognized by some sectors of the tourism and hospitality industry, and responses are clearly emerging in the light of such recognition. British Airways' planned reorganization of its personnel base, with a shedding of low-skills employees and the recruitment of a flexible, technology-and language-literate workforce in its place, is one example of this recognition. However, the situation is far from even; while some businesses are in a transition stage and moving towards the future painted by this research, others, especially SMEs are locked in the past in their human resource policies and practices, unable or unwilling to face up to the consequences of the issues addressed earlier in this article.

If the human resource environment predicted by Spivack's study is taken to be a reasonable prognosis for the future, there are significant implications for both tourism enterprises and the wider communities within which they exist. What is implied is the need for a significant mind-shift by those providing leadership within the tourism sector, both public and private, but it also points clearly to the need for changes, at a policy and practice level, within the environment controlled by the wider public sector, both tourism-related and that within the provenience of education, training, employment or other labour market authorities. This leads to the second research study addressed in this article.

Worlds in Different Orbit? Policy Dimensions of Tourism and the Labour Market

At a practical level, tourism education, training and development within the firm and beyond as part of public or private institutional provision, is relatively mature in most developed countries and is an evolving area of activity to communities and countries for which tourism and hospitality activity is rather more new. There is, however, ongoing and, at times, acrimonious debate between providers of tourism and hospitality education and those who see themselves as clients of the system, the industry itself, regarding the relevance, level and focus of education and training (Amoah and Baum, 1997; National Liaison Group for Higher Education in Tourism, 1995).

One of the difficulties for tourism and hospitality education is that it is expected to dance to the tune of a fragmented and heterogeneous sector where there are few commonly defined needs at a technical or knowledge level. The requirements of major airlines, hotel companies or heritage sites are diverse in themselves but are also significantly different from the needs of SMEs across the sector. The sector also draws in players from areas of activity which may, at best, acknowledge a tenuous association with tourism and hospitality and, at worst, fail to see their responsibilities in this area at all-such areas can include national parks, leisure and recreational interests, the finance sector, the security services and parts of the retail sector. One of the consequences of a fragmented public and private sector interest in tourism and hospitality is that there is rarely a clear, single authority with responsibility for the management and direction of education, training and development initiatives in support of the sector. In reality, there is frequently a range of organizations and agencies which have some involvement but also have loyalties and interests which lie out with the domain of tourism and hospitality. Such organizations and providers may include:

- the various industry subsectors and their representative associations;
- national, regional or local tourism development agencies, generally public but also in the private domain;
- public sector agencies or government authorities responsible for areas such as heritage, the environment, marine and other water resources, agriculture, national parks, etc.;
- national or provincial education providers;
- private education providers;
- specialist training agencies, public and private;
- national employment, labour or manpower agencies and their respective government departments;
- social partner organizations such as trade unions.

What is frequently seen as a practical issue, in that education providers may or may not be delivering appropriate curricula to meet industry's needs, is also an issue of policy concern and, in many respects, it is policy shifts that will be required to provide the lead, and assist the sector and the wider community to face up to predicted changes within tourism and hospitality in the future. Amoah's (1997) study is one which seeks to establish the extent to which policy formulation in the area of tourism and hospitality evolves in tandem with, or in isolation from, that applicable within the education, training and development domain. While based on empirical work in Western Europe and similar developed-country contexts, the findings appear to be considerably more widely applicable.

Amoah's study is based on a series of national case studies which were the outcome of local interviews and policy analysis. Amoah postulates that effective linkages between policy formulation and implementation in the tourism and the education/labour market environments are an important building block towards meeting the human resource challenges which Spivack identifies. She argues that this outcome is most effective where specific tourism education policies are articulated and put in place as a result of the convergence of the two supporting policy areas. Amoah has articulated this convergence process through presentation of a conceptual model which places tourism and education/training within a policy conceptual framework (Amoah and Baum, 1997), and identifies some of the key linkages which need to be in place for the effective delivery of tourism education, a delivery which can be fully responsive to the range of future needs identified earlier.

In practice, Amoah's research suggests that few, if any, national or sub-national jurisdictions fully acknowledge the policy linkages which the framework proposes. Indeed, the reality, in many cases, is that the two key policy domains of tourism and education (where both are clearly identifiable) can operate in either virtual isolation or on the basis of dependency and adaptation where tourism and hospitality are required to respond to or accommodate, within policy and practices driven by education and training, priorities developed without specific sectoral reference. It is arguable, for example, that the NVQ/GNVQ vocational education framework which was developed in the UK in the early 1990s was done so without specific sectoral consideration or recognition of policy priorities within tourism and hospitality. As a consequence, the structural and content focus does not fully meet tourism and hospitality industry needs. That said, it is difficult to fully verify this argument at a policy level because the UK, in common with many jurisdictions, has little more than embryonic components of a national tourism policy.

Amoah's research points to approaches at a provincial level in parts of Canada and at a national level in the Republic of Ireland as representative of environments where policy convergence is most in evidence and most effectively implemented. In both situations, this policy convergence is achieved under the auspices of a national or provincial co-ordination agency. While commencing life as public sector bodies, a number of the Canadian models-for example, the Alberta Tourism Education Council (ATEC)-have been moved out of the public sector and now operate as private bodies. The Irish model, through CERT:

> ...is unique (in Europe) in that it provides by far the most comprehensive approach to co-ordinating the inputs of education and the tourism industry into a unified system and, through CERT, operates through total coordination and the identification of training and development needs at both macro and micro levels (Baum, 1995).

What these models have in common is a starting point within identified national and provincial tourism and hospitality policy priorities and the interpretation of these within the context of the education, training and development environment. As a result, modification of the latter is possible and takes place to accommodate sectoral needs. In Ireland, specific tourism and hospitality programmes, operating within different parameters and with divergent objectives to those found in other vocational areas, were developed in the mid-1980s to provide career access within the secondary school system. This initiative, in turn, influenced the structure and focus of a wider system of vocational provision across other curriculum areas-in other words, tourism and hospitality policy requirements impacted on and gave direction to wider vocational educational policy within the country.

5

Modern Trends in Tourism

Hospitality Industry: Hotels Business Current and Future Trends

Hospitality has Long been Synonymous with the Hotel Industry

have wide scale implications on an otherwise diverse industry. What might be an opportunity for a traveller can be a matter of survival for hotels? It will not be an oversimplification to suggest that the emerging concepts in hotel industry reveal an atmosphere of stiff competition. Here is a look at a few major issues:

Is Green better?

Amid growing concern over environment friendly services, a majority of travellers now prefer Green and Eco lodgings. Recent surveys by trade associations such as Partnership Travel Industry Association and online retailers like Yahoo revealed that nearly seventy percent of the tourists are willing to pay extra when it comes to environmental friendly lodgings. These surveys further revealed that these guests will pay anywhere from nine to ten percent premium on the already advertised prices.

What can be stated as a welcome relief for the educated traveller might pose real challenges for the hotel business. To better understand the scenario, it should be noted that hotels are presently facing severe shortages in occupancy rates which are at their lowest since 1971. Such a crisis and lack of funds can definitely hamper any efforts to install appliances that comply with the LEEDS standards (Leadership in Energy & Environmental Design). Some experts agree that a trade off may lead hotels into removing free amenities that include little bottles of shampoos, jams and free basket of fruits; all of which are the hallmark of these eco lodgings.

Where are the Workers Gone?

The hotel industry gives employment at a very large proportion of part time workers, who after gaining substantial experience, leave for other lucrative jobs at restaurants and outdoors. Low wages in the hotel industry is one of the primary reasons for low retention rates.

Hotel industry Gurus are already thinking of ways to attract and retain qualified workers by increasing the pay scales and by reducing the long working hours. The top management is now devising constructive methods that will retain the existing workers by sponsoring education and creating attractive career paths.

Mega Hotels

The rising cost of construction and a struggling real estate has prompted hoteliers to deploy the prefabricated and cost effective solution in the construction of new hotels. In fact they are fighting back by producing highly efficient designs that utilize a greater proportion of space for revenue generating purpose. Future trends in the hotel construction will seek to maximize the use of building areas by constructing a multi purpose facility that will include Casinos, shopping outlets and Theatres. The stand alone hotel concept is likely to vanish as the new properties will be constructed as a mixed use development to provide guests with facilities such as Church, Hospitals and Theme Parks. Such a variety will ensure that guests remain at one spot which will help generate revenue for the entire hotel complex.

The Evolution of Savvy Traveller

The evolution of internet has given rise to a phenomenon where travellers are becoming ever more demanding. Industry professionals suggest that an increase in a trend, to review properties online, will make travellers less forgiving as they are able to post their travel experiences. Such an overemphasis on web may even lead to stiff competition and price reduction strategies where only large players may be able to survive.

To ward of such threats, the small business owner is now turning towards opening a boutique establishment as an alternate to 70,s style motels. Such niche properties are popping up everywhere by advertising a more personalized "home away from home" kind of experience. The introduction of such boutique properties has also given rise to the popular and widely accepted theme of modern hostels. These hostels are keen to provide a clean and safe environment for budget conscious travellers. Their goal is to wipe out the myths associated with cheap motels and dingy guesthouses.

Whatever may be the case, one thing is for sure that constant remodelling of the hotel industry has made it more functional and practical not only for the guests but also for the hotel owners.

Disaster Management Plan for the Hospitality Industry

The idea behind India's 9/11 was to do a Marriott at the Taj, i.e. like the Marriott was reduced to rubble in Islamabad, the same was expected to be done at the Taj... To reduce India's symbols of economic strength, even as the country struggles with a slowing economy... To hit hard the visible symbols of pride of the country, which the historic Taj was... To create an atmosphere of insecurity in the country: a visit to the grocer maybe as safe/dangerous as that to the Taj. Terrorism is a reality in India, today. The Indian tourism industry, considered to be amongst the world's top three performers (behind China)-defined as countries set to grow fastest over 2007 and the decade to come – will be negatively impacted as tourists prefer to visit safe destinations. However, history shows that there are other popular tourist destinations such as New York, London, Madrid and Bali that have also suffered from terrorist attacks. These places and their countries have recovered from the sudden downturn in image that had a correspondingly negative effect on the international tourism industry and the country's economics. There are lessons to be learnt from the experiences of others. While Spain used a 'business as usual' approach in recovering from its terrorist attacks, Tunisia used 'counter messages' inviting tourists to create peace. Essentially, in due course and with correct marketing the image can be changed to a favourable one. It is our belief that there would be a recovery in due course as every destination at some time of its existence faces a threat from either a natural disaster or one through malevolent human action, as was the case in Mumbai.

Perhaps the need of the hour is the formulation of a framework for disaster management for the hospitality industry. A previous disaster that visited the hotel industry was the 2004 Indian Ocean tsunami when coastal resorts/ hotels were wiped out or greatly damaged and most literature pertaining to disaster management in this industry deals with such scenarios. However, crises do not emerge just out of natural conditions. To start with, what is a crisis/disaster? Perhaps the best accepted definition is by Selbst who defines a crisis as 'any action or failure to act that interferes with an organisation's ongoing functions, the acceptable attainment of its objectives, its viability or survival, or that has a detrimental personal effect as perceived by the majority of its employees, clients or constituents.' In relation to tourism, Faulkner considers the principal distinction between what can be termed a 'crisis' and a 'disaster' to be the extent to which the situation is attributable to the organisation itself, or can be described as originating outside the organisation. Thus, a 'crisis' describes a situation 'where the root cause of an event is, to some extent, self-inflicted through such problems as inept management structures and practices or a failure to adapt to change', while a 'disaster' can be defined as 'where an enterprise... is confronted with sudden unpredictable catastrophic changes over which it has little control'. The incidents at the Taj and Oberoi certainly classify as disasters. And there is a need to learn from these disasters and not allow them to strike the death knell for the Indian hospitality industry.

There is a need to capture the experiences of the hotel staff and the measures they employed in guiding their guests through this dark hour. Hotel staff displayed tremendous courage and India's famed hospitality in the truest sense even at this hour. Scores of tales have emerged of unnamed workers hiding guests, feeding them, barricading doors, tending the vulnerable and issuing orders. A hotel worker, identified only as Mr. Rajan, put himself between one of the gunmen and a family, taking the bullets in his own abdomen. Another example is that of a general manager who was seen assisting guests out of the hotel within the initial hours of the attack, but unable to save his own family. The staff of the hotel has emerged as heroes, reaffirming our faith in humanity, which had been stripped by the terrorists' remorseless and indiscriminate firing. There are many lessons to be learnt through this tragedy and the brave contributions of those who have put their own safety at risk to save others should not go in vain.

Hotels-especially those vulnerable to such motivated violence as that witnessed at the Taj and Oberoi-should incorporate crisis management planning into their overall sustainable development and marketing/management strategies to protect and rebuild their image of safety/attractiveness, to reassure potential visitors of the safety of the area, to reestablish the area's functionality/attractiveness, and to aid local travel and tourism industry members in their economic recovery. These lessons should include the following:

Security would obviously be the most important element of this disaster management plan and guests at five-star hotels should expect to be checked along with their baggages. The way luggage is scanned through x-ray machines in airports, it should be also done in hotels. The screening should start at the very entrance where minimum damage can be done. Since this iconic bastion of hospitality has been stormed, hospitality too should sit up and be hospitable to guests who do not abuse their name and premises and threaten their very existence. The terrorists were met with ill-equipped and thus inadequate initial resistance when they stormed in. Hotels, thus, need to have their own effective security systems and intruder deterrents in place so that they can react immediately to the situatior. before essential time is lost in calling for help from external agencies. The security, especially, at the entry points and perimeters needs to be strengthened so that an easy walk in like at Mumbai is not replicated in future. Security should be supported by latest technology, for example a sensor like system by way of which the general manager would know that the security had been breached and immediate action may be initiated before being faced with terror at such close quarters. Since it was the National Security Guard (NSG) commandos who eventually evacuated the hotel, it maybe prudent to get them on board and learn from their experiences while formulating such guidelines.

Knowledge of hotel layout and who has this knowledge is critical as the recent crisis has shown. The NSG commandoes at the press conference clearly enunciated that the terrorists had a clear advantage as they knew the layout of the hotel well and were able to move about freely creating much destruction. On the other hand, the NSG were disadvantaged as they did not know the layout of the hotel and had to go room-to-room. In such crucial situations where knowledge is power, hotel blueprints should be available with the disaster management team so they can readily brief the security forces/rescuing agency. At the same time, care should be taken to secure them so that they do not fall into wrong hands. Moreover, like emergency fire exits, multiple contingency plans for exit of hotel guests in case of terrorist attacks should be in place. There may even be a need to take this reality into account when constructing new hotels.

A sophisticated communication system needs to be in place. Even though the cable network to the rooms where the terrorists were holed in was cut, they had access to updated information with mentors through satellite phones.

A superior communication system that could perhaps jam the links of the terrorists and give hotel staff the upper hand in their communication with guests and external coordinating agencies needs to be evolved. The hotel must at all times have access to the most recent communication system. While technology can be made available it is important to practice it in dummy situations for enhanced effectiveness.

A coordinated, team approach is required to be developed, given the range of private and public sector organisations directly and indirectly involved. While in the Mumbai case the hospitality sector was the target, terrorism may be faced by any sector. Thus, it is incumbent to have a well coordinated security cover with a specified person 'incharge' and more importantly 'responsible and thereby accountable'.

The government response and guidelines and the regulatory framework to provide the resources need to be put in place. A case in point is the obligation on the Telecom industry to provide the specified inputs to the security agencies. The security agency by itself has to have a person 'by name' made responsible to avoid having a typical fallout of passing the buck.

International security standards and guidelines that are well defined and internationally accepted should be evolved at this juncture by the international community. A case in point is the ISO 27001 and 27002, which are the international best practice information security management standards, defining and guiding Information Security Management System (ISMS) development. These will provide the necessary benchmarking for individual users to know the type of cover and the responsibilities that are defined and provided by that institution for its guests. Most importantly, training, to staff needs to be regularly imparted in dealing with such

Modern Tourism and the Third World

Tourism fulfills a human need for rest and recreation. People normally set out to see other places and meet other people. Other people, meanwhile, extend their hospitality to their guests-a national trait worthy of praise.

But tourism also satisfies the thirst for profit. Big business, hungry for megabuck profits, resort to gross commercialism and imposes unsuitable development programs.

In the process, people get trampled upon, cultures erode and eco-systems deteriorate. Third World nations, main recipients of these 'development programs,' usually end up the losers.

Alternative Tourism, as a counter trend, seeks to right these abuses by challenging the profit structure and commercial premise of the tourism industry. Alternative Tourism works to redefine tourism back to its original spirit of exchange and solidarity among peoples.

A Billion Dollar Industry

Tourism has increased rapidly since the end of the Second World War as improved mass transportation provided people with cheaper and faster ways of getting to other places. It also enabled them to go to farther and farther destinations and meet more people.

From around 70 million people who spent a few billion dollars in 1960, the number of tourists rose to half a billion, spending some $324 billion, in 1993. With a yearly average increase of 7%, the number of international tourists is expected to reach 956 million by the end of 2000.

The tourism industry employs 74 million people and domestic and international tourism receipts account for 9.3% of GNP worldwide.

The hotel and airline industries control the bulk of the tourist business, as tourist spending goes mainly to the carrier and to accommodation. A good part of the earnings also goes to the tour and travel operators. These transnational companies, either affiliated with each other or subsidiaries of larger conglomerates, earn billions of dollars from the tourist money spent on holiday travel, rest and recreation, and even business and convention activities. Transport industry suppliers such as the shipbuilding and train industries also rake in a good profit. The construction industry, likewise, profits from hotel and resort building contracts.

Tourism in the Third World

Many Third World nations in the early 1970s embraced tourism as a quick recipe for development. Staggering from high unemployment rates and heavy indebtedness, many governments saw tourism as a source of foreign exchange to fund balance of payments deficits and service their foreign debts. Tourism also promised a viable source of investments for their backward economies and a source of quick livelihood and employment for their unskilled workers.

With encouragement from the United Nations (UN) and the IMF-World Bank, this tourism-development strategy paved the way for the entry of TNCs and other investments in hotel and resort development, foreign-funded government infrastructure and other tourism-related projects and tourism programs. Bilateral and multilateral loans poured in to finance these projects.

Too poor to resist and not given much choice, many Third World countries soon adapted the strategy. Bilateral and multilateral loans poured in to finance these projects. Various aid organizations like the UNDP, WTO, ESCAP, JICA and the ADB lent their 'expertise' in supporting and promoting tourism or tourism-related projects in Southeast Asia, South America, the Caribbean and the Pacific islands.

People from industrialized countries were treated to cheap, exotic and unspoiled destinations in the Third World. In the process, the social, economic and cultural life of many third world countries were opened up to widescale tourism exploitation and their natural resources displayed for despoiling.

Whatever initial financial relief Third World countries had was eventually lost in the form of repatriated profits or debt service money.

Tourism's negative impact on the third world countries and their peoples is staggering. Self-sufficient economies get smothered, social relations break, cultures eroded and environments are laid waste. The list is long and well-documented: Self-sufficient agricultural economies giving way to tourism-reliant economies;

women and children being forced into prostitution to service sex-tours and pedophiles; fishermen turning into waiters; and urban poor and indigenous communities domains giving way to golf courses and large hotels.

Alternative Tourism

Alternative tourism emerged from the Third World as a reaction to the negative effects tourism heaped on its countries.

Alternative tourism came in different names and various models. All tried to stop the onslaught and improve the situation. Backyard tourism, for instance, sought 'to preserve the original rural appeal' of the tourist destination. It also relied on the services of small local enterprises while rejecting the development of modern resorts.

Endemic tourism, on the other hand, used the 'special characteristics of individual communities which attracted tourists' and the 'great value of the cultural characteristics of communities' as tourism assets.

Increasing global concerns for the environment, meanwhile, produced ecotourism which tried to 'shy away from commercial destinations and focused on environmental themes.' Sustainable tourism is yet another new form of alternative tourism that is led by an 'empowered and gender-sensitive community' that 'protects and enhance ecological resources.'

The Philippine Experience

The Philippine experience remains a classic case of what tourism has done to a third world country. Tourism's impact on our society, culture, economy and environment already gives a perfect picture of what the Third World has gone through in its adoption of tourism-development.

Sex-tourists and pedophiles walking hand-in-hand with women and children is a common site in the red-light districts of Manila, Cebu and Davao. Golf courses, hotels and large shopping malls are continually displacing peasants in CALABARZON and urban dwellers in the poor districts of Metro Manila. Indigenous tribes like the Mangyans and Igorots are turned into tourist attractions. And who will forget the former US military bases in Subic and Pampanga. These monuments to tourism left thousands of Amerasians fatherless and hooked on drugs and prostitutes dying of AIDS while awaiting the promised return of his 'sailor boy.'

Early attempts at alternative tourism in the country dates back to the mid-1970s when residents of Puerto Galera in Mindoro built cottages for 'back pack' tourists searching for the ambience of nature and warm smiles of the local people. The residents also employed family members to serve drinks and wash the clothes of these tourists.

These family-owned enterprises, soon to be known as backyard tourism, were at first modestly successful as they managed to do away with the expensive accommodations offered by hotels and the degrading work of serving foreign owners.

Foreign tour operators, however, learned to adjust to the negative image of tourism and soon began building their own cottages and not touching the natural ambience of the place. Soon backyard tourism became another adjunct of the mainstream tourism industry as foreigners took over management and ownership of the local cottages.

Other types of alternatives to tourism came out through the eighties and nineties still in reaction to the worsening negative effects of tourism. These models also tried to adjust to the failures and co-optation of the earlier models by working on broader concerns and action plans.

People's organizations, cause-oriented groups and NGOs began promoting their own type of 'exposure programs' to interested and 'concerned' foreigners. These groups offered an alternative tourism hinged on a much broader nationalist program that directly challenged the profit motive of tourism and worked for a 'real empowerment for the people as masters of their fate' and ready to reject imposed development models on them.

PGX and Alternative Tourism

The People's Global Exchange (PGX) is one of many NGOs that started alternative tourism programs in the mid-80s.

PGX has long been hosting foreigners active in the solidarity movement for the Philippines. Its Development-Education program served to deepen the circle of friends already familiar with Philippines realities and active in solidarity work by immersing them in the day-to-day lives and struggles of the different sectors.

Soon it was hosting 'walk-ins' and other visitors unfamiliar to Philippine realities, but who were otherwise interested to learn from an 'exposure' program and possibly do 'concrete things' upon return to their countries.

Working with a broad network of people's organizations and organized communities, PGX began promoting alternative tourism as a new program and concept for the unfamiliar but interested people from industrialized nations.

A 1992 PGX paper says alternative tourism is 'an educationally-oriented' and 'non-commercial' program. It also 'promotes a socially and ecologically responsible' tourism that is 'people-centered.' Most important, it 'creates a venue for initiating friendships and solidarity between peoples.'

Since the late 1980s, PGX has hosted more than a thousand visitors who came individually or in groups. It even managed to host boatloads of Japanese 'tourists' belonging to Peaceboat, a Japanese NGO also active in alternative tours, in 1991, 1992, 1997 and 1998. These exposurees numbered more than three-hundred per boat-load and were divided into groups of fifty or more people who then went to different communities.

With its partners, PGX offers a range of programs aimed at promoting sectoral issues as well as broader concerns. Sectoral issues range from peasant landlessness to poor working conditions in factories to demolitions of squatter families to evictions of tribal groups. Similarly, the accompanying struggle of said sectors are highlighted and their calls for solidarity extended to the visitors.

Broader concerns, notably ecological problems (poisoning of rivers and lakes), women issues (prostitution, wife battering), children (pedophiles, drugs) have gained increasing interest on the visitors' part.

Exposure programs usually last from seven-day mini-exposures to 2-year internships. Visitors come from different groups: students, academics, factory workers, homemakers and even children.

These alternative programs seem to pay off as many exposurees, upon returning to their countries, have taken up Philippine issues and linked-up with Philippine support groups. Some have even influenced their families and friends to try the same exposure they have gone through. A few have formally joined and became active in solidarity groups.

Prospects

Concerned groups and individuals have taken many alternatives and paths in facing the issues of tourism. Some proved effective for some time but eventually failed. Others were co-opted by big business interests who have learned to adjust to changing perceptions of tourism. Others remained and, in their own way, continued trying to change the system by testing new models.

More than three decades of experience suggests that true alternative tourism is one that is not subject to the profit motives of big business interests. Alternative tourism also work for an empowered community that can and will reject development impositions on their lives.

6

New Directions in Tourism for Third World Development

Globalization-Tourism the New Imperialism

Aside from war, tourism is the single most destructive global force unleashed by man. Tour companies, for their image, often claim to adhere to a code of conduct, on the ground they rarely even bother to pay lip service.

Tourism is the fastest growing global industry. In 1996 tourism revenue amounted to $423 billion, the number of tourist arrivals clocked in at 592 million. By the year 2000, if not before, tourism is expected to be the world's largest industry.

1 in 4 Brits now travel abroad on a package holiday. This is an industry that has grown from nothing not long after the Second World War. The early operators were viewed in the same light as second hand car dealers, the way the travelling public is still treated little has changed. The growth in the package holiday business has destroyed much of the Mediterranean and the tour operators are now looking further afield for places to despoil. Majorca, population 700,000, has 6 million tourists each year, 2 million of them Brits. It has brought in a lot of money and taken the local people on a journey to hell.

Tourism is having a massive global impact, not just on the global economy. Airports are seizing vast tracts of land. Residents living near airports are having their lives made a misery. Aircraft are rapidly becoming the number one global polluter, the effect is made all the more dramatic as the pollutants are emitted at high altitude where they have the maximum effect. Local cultures are being destroyed. In Tenerife local bars serve English beer and pander to English tourists, in Cyprus local Cypriot bars make way for karaoke nights and moronic English DJs. Hotels and tourist resorts need land and water. In Cyprus water is rationed to ensure a plentiful supply to hotel resorts. It is in the Third World that tourism is having the maximum impact.

Hotels, Tourist Resorts, the Supporting Infrastructure Needs Land

In Akamas, an area of outstanding natural beauty in the West of Cyprus, there is pressure to open it up for development and tourism.

In Malaysia, 29 local shops were destroyed to make way for a tourist development project.

Tourists like to be on prime coastal sites. These sites are often important fishery grounds, places where turtles come ashore to lay eggs.

Tourist Resorts Need Water

The villagers of Sinquerim (Goa) were denied piped water and have to rely on a well. Water is piped through the village to the nearby Taj Holiday Village and Fort Aguada complex.

Golf courses consume vast tracts of land. 350 new golf courses every year. The golf courses demand large volumes of water for irrigation; the pesticide, fertiliser, and herbicide run-off effects local water courses bringing damage to fisheries, polluting drinking water.

In Thailand the health of many local people has been damaged through eating fish poisoned by pesticide run-off from golf courses.

In Bali local people were forced from their land to make way for a golf course and hotel complex by shutting off the water that irrigated their fields.

Not everywhere are local people compliant. In Vietnam when Daewoo (one of the biggest exploiters in Vietnam) planned a £93 million golf course near Hanoi local villagers set up barricades and refused to budge. They were offered a paltry £125 per family to move.

Tourism is Destroying the Environment

Tenerife is rapidly becoming one big building site. The pleasant green Orotava valley in the north of Tenerife will soon have disappeared under concrete. Inter-island high speed ferries are killing whales and dolphins. In the south of Tenerife the sheer mass of whale watching trips is harassing whales and dolphins to death.

UK tour companies have codes of conduct on protecting the environment. These same tour companies are promoting whale watching trips, inter-island day trips that use high speed ferries.

Tourist feet trample across sacred religious sites, showing no respect to the indigenous cultures. Native people are often expected to perform sacred rituals on demand

In Peru, Yagua indians were forced from the remote Upper Amazon region to more accessible areas to enable tourists to see them perform their sacred rites. Viewing stations were built for the voyeurs.

In Hawaii many tourist complexes have been built on sites sacred to indigenous Hawaiians. Many burial grounds have been destroyed.

Tourism Directly and Indirectly Supports and Finances Human Rights Violations

Burma is one of the world's most repressive regimes. In scenes reminiscent of the Japanese occupation, forced labour is being used to prepare infrastructure and resort complexes. On one railway project alone, it has been estimated that 200-300 people have died through illness and exhaustion. On other similar projects the death rates are reported as averaging one a day. 30,000 forced labourers helped to construct the new airport at Bassein, when cholera broke out they received no medical care. Hundreds of thousands of people have been forced from their homes and lands to make way for tourist projects.

Like Burma, Turkey is another country with an appalling human rights record. Tourists who rarely venture beyond their air-conditioned hotel complexes fail to see the squalor or abuses. Hard currency earned from the tourists is used to buy military hardware to continue the repression against the Kurds and the illegal occupation of northern Cyprus.

Sexploitation is a growing sector of the tourist trade, with many tour companies offering special package tours to the best sex spots. Favoured destinations are Sri Lanka, the Philippines, Thailand, Brazil, with Eastern Europe rapidly developing its sex market-all perversions well catered for. Many children are forced to work as prostitutes in brothels. In Sri Lanka a survey showed that 86% of children had their first sexual experience with a foreign tourist, for the majority of the children they were aged between 12 and 13 years old at the time.

There is no such thing as a cheap holiday. The price is bought on the back of some one else's pain.

Tourism is often offered as a model to Third World countries as a means to earn hard foreign currency. Like many other models forced on the Third World, it tightens the shackles, for which only the West has the keys.

Third World countries are encouraged to build their tourist sector as a means of earning hard foreign currency. The reality is somewhat different. The holiday will be run by a foreign tour company, foreigners build, own and manage the tourist complexes, food and capital equipment is imported. What little is paid to local people will be marginally higher than the local wage rate thus ensuring the destruction of local industry. The few crumbs that trickle down to a handful of local people do not make up for the destruction of their environment and culture.

Zanzibar has a fragile eco-and social system dependent upon agriculture and fishing. Villagers are being evicted from their coastal villages and placed in compounds, their beautiful coral cottages left to rack and ruin. All inclusive tourist compounds surrounded by razor wire and protected by armed guards are built on the vacated land. Fish bought from local fisherman for the tourist compounds drives up the price reducing local people to a diet of boiled rice.

In Cuba dollar tourism is destroying the country its people and its culture. Two internal markets are developing-the dollar market and the pesos market. The real Cuba is discovered by visiting local people in their homes, not interacting with dollar prostitutes who work the tourist trade. Fidel Castro should hang his head in shame for turning his beautiful country into a dollar whore. Air transport is the fastest growing transport sector, with a consequential effect on global pollution. Air travel is the most energy intensive, polluting mode of travel.

Air transport has been growing at a rate of about 10% a year. Emissions from aircraft account for about 3% of global emissions, but because these emissions take place at high altitudes their significance and impact on climate change is considerably higher than the figure would suggest (aircraft have more than half the global warming potential of road traffic). Aircraft emissions are currently exempt from the Kyoto protocol under the climate convention. The aviation industry enjoys many tax concessions, including duty free fuel. Within the EU alone, the externalised costs are estimated at 4.6% of EU GDP, 16.4 billion euros/year.

Knock on effects include large infrastructure demands, noise, generation of road traffic etc.

Does Tourism Benefit the Third World?

Third World governments invariably justify the promotion of tourism as a driving force for economic development. *Anita Pleumarom* questions this claim and says that it is time to stop treating tourism as a holy cow to be protected and nurtured at all costs.

Tourism discourses are full of high-sounding rhetoric, liberally peppered with such terms as 'poverty reduction', 'sustainability', 'fair trade', 'participation', 'good governance', 'corporate social responsibility', and 'peace-building'. Moreover, concepts of 'new tourisms', such as community-based ecotourism, are projected as ways forward to reform mass tourism, which is increasingly dreaded because of its negative impacts.

But what about the reality behind the glossy rhetoric? What can be observed is, the more tourism leaders vow to protect ecosystems and natural resources in destinations, the more the environment gets thrown out of balance due to the continued frenzied construction of tourism facilities. The more we are told about tourism as a force for peace and understanding, the more the world is affected by the 'war on terrorism', and human-rights-abusing dictatorships like Burma use tourism to prop up their bad image.

The more decision-makers parade tourism policies for poverty elimination, the more the gap widens between the rich and the poor among and within nations, due to aggressive and unfair economic liberalisation. While people in rich countries drown in conspicuous consumption thereby destroying their own and others' life bases, communities in less and least developed countries only receive the crumbs from the wealth that capitalist growth produces.

A Global Business

Like other big industries, tourism is characterised by unhealthy mass concentrations of people, mass production, and mass activities. Today, it is common for people to criss-cross the globe to search for an exotic paradise, go shopping, attend a conference, play golf, cheer at a big sporting event, gamble in a casino, get thrilled in a theme park, relax in a spa resort or have medical or cosmetic surgery in a five-star hospital. En route, the travelling consumers can satisfy their needs and desires in the same fast food chains, supermarkets and designer brand shops like at home.

Tourism is a truly global business that turns everything on Earth-even the most sacred domains-into commodities. Most travellers would not want to wake up to the fact that they are just feeding a multi-billion-dollar industry and contributing to unsustainable patterns of consumption and production. And there is little awareness that as always, it is the poor who have to pay for the social and environmental costs of excessive tourism.

Governments emphasise tourism as a driving force for economic development. The latest World Tourism Barometer released by the United Nations World Tourism Organisation (UNWTO) indicates that international arrivals will amount to 880 to 900 million by the end of 2007, which points to a continuation of the sustained growth rate experienced over the past years. The Asia-Pacific region is the acknowledged motor behind the global tourism growth, with China and India representing the fastest-growing markets. According to the World Travel and Tourism Council (WTTC), travel and tourism presently employs approximately 231 million people and generates over 10.4% of the world's GDP.

Illusory Picture

However, the positive statistics offered by the WTTC and UNWTO project an illusory picture of the contribution of tourism particularly to the Third World.

These data often serve to justify expensive infrastructure developments that primarily benefit the top echelons in travel and tourism. Many of the projects are based on external borrowings, deepening the financial debt crisis for poor nations, and many of the supplies and equipment used in the development of these projects are imported and the personnel involved in construction engaged from abroad. Meanwhile, governments increasingly neglect the basic needs of local communities. Following the earthquake/tsunami disaster on Boxing Day 2004, for example, Thailand, Sri Lanka and India spent huge amounts of aid and taxpayers' money to help the tourism industry back on its feet, while fishing and agricultural communities were displaced; and until today, poor tsunami victims are lacking adequate housing, water supply, social services and opportunities to rebuild economic livelihoods.

'Leakages'

Tourism is a big money-spinner, but local residents do not get a fair share because most of the tourism revenue is siphoned away by urban-based and foreign investors. The tourism sector is notorious for causing financial 'leakage' (due to high import content, repatriation of profits by foreign-owned tourism companies, etc.), and unbalanced and inequitable distribution of income. According to current statistics compiled by the UN Conference on Trade and Development (UNCTAD), leakages in the tourism sector total up to 85% in some African least developed countries (LDCs), more than 80% in the Caribbean, 70% in Thailand and 40% in India.

Globalization has only worsened the economic conditions for poor countries. Tourism services negotiations under the World Trade Organisation (WTO)'s General Agreement on Trade in Services (GATS) as well as bilateral and regional free trade agreements (FTAs) have been used particularly by the US and European Union to increase pressure on governments of developing countries to abolish restrictions on foreign ownership and to allow a high degree of self-regulation by transnational corporations in the sector. As a result, tourism-related industries in developing countries are experiencing unprecedented mergers and acquisitions, squeezing local businesses that are ill-equipped to face the cut-throat competition favouring giant foreign firms.

New policies for tourism development as part of Special Economic Zones (SEZ) just add to the increasing inequality and asymmetry. The establishment of SEZs often involves the selling or leasing out of vast tracts of land to private developers and allows massive unregulated exploitation of natural and human resources for tourism purposes.

In recent years, however, tourism has as never before been highlighted as a dependent and high-risk industry. Frequent natural and man-made disasters, oil price hikes, exchange rate fluctuations and political turmoil have shown up the extreme vulnerability of the industry. Unexpected events such as the 11 September attacks in the US (2001), the Bali bombings (2002), the outbreaks of the SARS and avian flu epidemics (2003-04) and the tsunami disaster (2004) have all been the cause of major tourism slumps.

Ironically, the worsening climate crisis, to which the tourism industry itself has contributed significantly, is now ticking like a time bomb for the industry as many tourist attractions may be irreversibly destroyed by the impacts of climate change. Particularly threatened are low-lying coastal regions and small island developing states (SIDS). Many SIDS have developed tourism monocultures, with tourism receipts constituting up to 90% of services exports in the Bahamas, the Dominican Republic and the Maldives; in Antigua and Barbuda, tourism contributes directly and indirectly to over 75% of the GDP, according to the UNWTO.

While large tourism companies have responded quickly to impending emergencies by sponsoring high-tech disaster-warning systems and anti-terror security schemes, urgent mitigation and adaptation measures to enable poor communities to cope with any impending catastrophe are often delayed due to governments' lack of funding and other shortcomings.

Employment Effects

Tourism is seen as a boon in terms of employment for people in developing nations. But in fact, tourism-related jobs are uncertain, seasonal and part-time, with a high turnover of staff.

The loss of livelihoods through tourism-e.g., in agriculture and fisheries-has rarely been subjected to research. But the high out-migration of locals from tourist centres is a clear indication that tourism destroys more jobs than it creates.

Despite the tourism leaders' new affection for 'corporate social responsibility' (CSR), exploitation of tourism workers remains rampant. Worldwide, the industry is taking advantage of migrant workers who provide the cheapest labour, endure the harshest working conditions and are least likely to organise in trade unions.

Women in tourism are found to have the most dehumanising and the worst-paid jobs. Tourism has an infamous reputation of boosting the sex industry wherever it takes root. Efforts to make industry comply with the Code of Ethics promoted by the UNWTO have not helped to curb trafficking in women and girls for sex work in tourist destinations, which in many cases deprives the victims of their fundamental human rights and exposes them to health risks such as HIV/AIDS.

Industry self-regulation has proven an utterly inadequate tool in tourist centres, such as Pattaya in Thailand, Cancun in Mexico or Johannesburg in South Africa, where the sex, drugs and crime, gang violence, mafia-style politics and corruption are out of control.

The erosion of culture and traditional values is visible in all tourist destinations driven by over-commercialisation. Even many of the UN Educational, Scientific and Cultural Organisation (UNESCO)'s World Heritage sites are not properly protected from privatisation and 'Disneyfication'.

Tourism-including 'ecotourism'-also exploits indigenous and local communities and their cultures, turning them into mere exhibits for tourists' entertainment. The ugliest creations are 'human zoos' as set up by tour operators in the borderlands of Burma and Thailand to feature women from the Kayan ethnic group, also known as 'Long Neck' people because they wear rings that elongate their necks.

Many indigenous peoples' rights groups are therefore condemning tourism as a form of development aggression. Highlighting incidents of land rights violations and biopiracy, they have raised serious concerns about the rigorous approach of the 'ecotourism' industry that threatens indigenous peoples' sovereignty and aggravates conflicts and tensions in their communities in tourism-related processes at the UN (e.g., at the Commission on Sustainable Development, meetings of the Convention on Biological Diversity and the International Year of Ecotourism 2002).

Environmental Impacts

Tourism as 'sustainable development' is a myth as it continues to wreak havoc on land and marine ecosystems and biodiversity. Despite the industry's 'greenwash' attempts, fertile agricultural lands are still being cleared, forests cut down, mountains flattened, beaches dug up, and coral reefs destroyed to provide resources for more and more monstrous tourism complexes.

Moreover, tourism accelerates unhealthy urbanisation processes and contributes to traffic congestion, noise and air pollution and the dumping of waste and untreated sewage. The depletion and degradation of scarce water resources, particularly due to mushrooming golf courses and spa businesses, aggravates the water supply crisis in many communities. According to a UN study, the average tourist consumes as much water in 24 hours as a Third World villager requires to produce rice for 100 days.

High energy consumption in tourism facilities and greenhouse gas emissions linked to transportation, especially the explosive growth in air travel, contribute significantly to climate change.

Given all these serious impacts, tourism must no longer be treated like a holy cow that is protected and nurtured at all costs. Particularly in these times of looming social and environmental crises, governments and inter-governmental agencies like the UN should prioritise people's basic needs, particularly food security. Decision-makers should take a more responsible approach to tourism, by establishing strong legal and regulatory frameworks and ensuring the enforcement of these rules and regulations on the industry.

Corporate-driven voluntary initiatives, such as guidelines, codes of conduct and accreditation schemes, are not the key to effectively tackling tourism-related problems. What is needed instead is a people-centred approach to development that is aimed at reversing the negative impacts of globalization and restoring the values of justice, democracy and self-determination in development-an approach that allows local communities to reclaim land and resources that have been unfairly taken away, to rehabilitate the environment that greedy capitalists have ravaged and to revive traditions and cultures that have been distorted and exploited for profit-making purposes.

Internet Use in Tourism Industry

The Hospitality and Tourism industry was one of the earliest to go online. Since travel had few geographical boundaries, and, thanks to the widespread adoption of e-tickets, which airlines aggressively pushed, the airlines faced none of the logistical issues of online product retailers such as shipping and variable tax-collection schemes, the travel industry was uniquely suited for the Web. As the travel industry took off in the late 1970s and early 1980s, five major components came to comprise what this report will call the travel supply chain: Providers, Distributors, Travel Agents, Charge Card companies, and Travellers.

Providers-airlines, hotels and transportation companies; these entities invested in products (planes, properties, vehicles) and services for travellers.

Distributors-Computer Reservations Systems (CRSs); technology companies that consolidated supplier information, inventory and pricing data, and provided a way to electronically search, book and issue tickets and documents.

Travel Agents – Using CRSs, provided leisure and business travellers with one-stop shopping guidance and pricing and schedule advice to make reservations, issue tickets and provide ancillary services such as passport processing or currency conversion.

Charge Card companies-Played a role by making purchasing more convenient and secure for consumers, and by providing corporate buyers consolidated transaction data about their company's activities, which helped them with purchasing decisions and policy tracking.

Travellers – The end-user or customer, who may be leisure and/or corporate traveller, or a travel planner who books trips for an employee to take.

In addition, there are many matters involved in the selection and organisation of a holiday: gathering tour information, preparing the holiday package, confirming holiday information, actually having the holiday (including shopping for things and paying for them – not always easy in a foreign country), and sharing the holiday experience with other people during the holiday and once arriving back home.

Thus, it might be very difficult to manage all the people and matters precisely, and much of this potential complexity is about interaction through or using *information*; information management becomes an important consideration. One can deduce that information management will be important in the tourism industry, especially when one anticipates the consequences of the Internet – the most recent innovation in conveying information and sharing information between different parties.

We consider that it is necessary to combine the world of business and the world of technology in the tourism industry. In particular, information is interacting between tourism service providers and tourists.

The Online Travel Market

Use of the Internet by travellers to plan and book their trips continues to grow at a rapid rate. In the United States, according to the Travel Industry Association (TIA 2007), more than 75 million online travellers used the Internet in 2006 to get information on destinations or to check prices and schedules. From 1999 to 2006, online booking showed a remarkable double-digit growth for four consecutive years, with a spectacular 58% growth in 2001, followed by a 25% growth in 2002. While growth of the online traveller market has slowed, the number of online travellers who actually use the Internet to plan trips has remained relatively stable. A majority (67%) of online travellers say they consult the Internet to get information on destinations or to check prices or schedules.

Not surprisingly, nearly all online travel planners say that some of the trips planned on the Internet in the past year were for pleasure, vacation, or personal purposes. Three in ten say some of the trips planned on the Internet were for business or convention purposes. For online travel planning, online travel agency websites (such as Microsoft Expedia, Travelocity, or Priceline), search engine websites, and companyowned websites (airlines, hotels, etc.) are the most popular types of websites used. A majority of online travel planners also use destination websites.

Online travel planners do a variety of trip planning activities on the Internet. The most popular are searching for searching for airfares/schedules, maps or driving directions, and looking for places to stay.

While the growth in the number of Americans planning trips online has remained relatively stable, there has been strong growth in online travel booking. Indeed, four in ten (41%) online travellers are booking or making travel reservations online. This may include booking an airline ticket, hotel room, rental car or package tour online. Nearly all of those who make travel reservations online say they made reservations for pleasure, vacation, or personal purposes. About three in ten say they made reservations for business or convention purposes.

Among those who have booked travel online, the most popular item to purchase online is airline tickets. A majority of online travel bookers have reserved overnight lodging accommodations, and over one-third have made rental car reservations. The most popular types of websites used to book travel are online travel agency sites such as Microsoft Expedia, Travelocity or Priceline and company websites, such as airline, hotel, or rental car companies that sell directly to consumers. More than one-third of online travel bookers pay for or make their reservations

There is another important aspect and it is concerning the use of Internet While Travelling. Portable electronic communication devices such as cell phones, laptops, and personal digital assistants help people stay connected while away from home or office. In fact, large majorities of business travellers and pleasure travellers said that they brought cellular telephones with them on a trip taken in the past year. One in four business travellers brought a laptop computer with them on a trip, but only about one-tenth of pleasure travellers did so.

With the advent of wireless technology, portable devices are now being used to access the Internet for information, including travel information. Whether using a computer, cell phone, or PDA, four in ten business travellers say they have gone online while away from home. One in five pleasure travellers alsoclaim to have accessed the Internet while on a past-year pleasure trip.

Computer Reservation System (CRS) – Global Distribution System (GDS)

Deregulation meant that airlines that had previously operated under government-set fares which ensured they at least broke even now needed to improve operational efficiency to compete in a free market. While there were many aspects to this, one of the earliest changes was the development of the Airline Reservations System (ARS), its evolution into and proliferation of the Computer Reservations System (CRS), and then into Global Distribution System (GDS).

There are a few issuses about the use of CRS, like:

" *CRS are expensive for small and medium agencies to maintain and so Internet booking may be a more cost-effective medium;*

" *CRS do not always provide agents with improved business levels unless used to their full;*

" *The airlines have to pay fees to have a presence in CRS;*

" *There are new forms of technology that are overtaking CRS in some market segments (etravel agencies).*

The GDS took the place of CRS by the end of 1990s. The GDS operators collaborated with a variety of travel service providers such as airlines, cruise operators, hotels, railway companies and car rental companies, in addition to accepting special meal requests, managing seat allocation and performing backoffice accounting functions for travel agents.

There are about a dozen major GDSs worldwide. Amadeus had become the world leader after merging with SystemOne, achieving a 27 percent market share; Galileo and Sabre followed, each with 22 percent.

After these came Worldspan, formed by Delta, Northwest and TWA, with a 10 percent share, and Abacus and Infini, the dominant CRSs in Asia, with a combined share of 9 percent.

The GDS technology developed with four functional components that, while integrated and interdependent, would later serve as points of differentiation when Internet providers entered the market and pulled apart the links of the supply chain. They were: inventory management and display; pricing-and fare-search engines; ticketing and document generators; and database reporting engines.

Use of the Internet by the Travel Agencies

Many travel agencies have developed an Internet presence by posting a website, with detailed travel information. Full travel booking sites are often complex, and require the assistance of outside travel technology solutions providers such as Travelocity. More and more tourists use the Internet websites to book and/or get useful informations.

These companies use travel service distribution companies who operate Global Distribution Systems (GDS), such as Sabre Holdings, Amadeus, Galileo and Worldspan, to provide up to the minute, detailed information on tens of thousands of flight, hotel, and car rental vacancies. Some online travel sites allow visitors to compare hotel and flight rates with multiple companies for free. They often allow visitors to sort the travel packages by amenities, price, and or proximity to a city or landmark.

Travel agents have applied dynamic packaging tools to provide fully bonded (full financial protection) travel at prices equal to or lower than a member of the public can book online. As such, the agencies' financial assets are protected in addition to professional travel agency advice. All travel sites that sell hotels online work together with numerous outside travel agents. Once the travel site sells a hotel, one of the supplying travel agents is contacted and will try to get a confirmation for this hotel. Once confirmed or not, the customer is contacted with the result. This means, that booking a hotel on a travel website will not get you an instant answer. Only some of the hotels on a travel website can be confirmed instantly (which is normally marked as such on each site). As different travel websites work with different suppliers together, each site has different hotels that it can confirm instantly. Some examples of such online travel websites that sell hotel rooms are Expedia, Orbitz and Trip Advisor.

There are also Internet travel agencies. These are Web sites that expand traditional agents' offerings. In addition to selling regular travel services such as air tickets and hotel rooms, they also offer travel tips, destination information and other services. Many large traditional agencies such as American Express and Liberty Travel have extended their shops to the virtual marketplace. Portal travel sites such as AOL and Yahoo! link customers looking for travel services to sites that may appear on their portals, but generally are powered by one of the big Internet travel agencies listed below. The last category for Internet travel agencies is bidding sites, such as Priceline. There, deep discount travel is available, but the travel provider's brand (usually an airline) is hidden until the purchase is complete.

The travel category lists those sites which are related to travel and the travel industry, including publications, travel agencies, transport services/people carriers, airports, destinations, resorts, travel and locality guides and accommodation.

The rise of online retail travel is taking place at a time whent the distribution function in tourism is changing in many ways. It is growing rapidly and will undoubtedly develop and change greatly in the future. It has provided an opportunity for non-tourism organisations such as Microsoft to enter the tourism market, and in doing so, to create competition for traditional high street travel agents.

Internet Marketing and the Norwegian Tourism Industry: A National Coordinated Marketing Effort on the Internet

The growth of the WWW on the Internet has created many opportunities as well as challenges for commercial businesses and industries. One of the challenges for a small-or medium-sized business is how to be found by the potential customer. This is underlined in a recent article about international marketing in *Sloan Management Review* (Quelch and Klein, 1996). The authors state that "the potential for 'information overload' is enormous". Even though the lack of rules on the net is critical to electronic commerce (Spar and Bussgang, 1996), this is not so critical for Internet as an information source. Stephan H. Haeckel, director of strategic studies at IBM's Advanced Business Institute writes (Deighton, 1996), "suddenly, and basically without warning, the Internet became a plausible and economical solution to a huge problem that has plagued business since 1960s: integrating increasingly heterogeneous IT systems between and within organizations. The Web now offers providers and seekers of information around the globe easy access to one another that proprietary systems cannot match—but can easily benefit from".

It can be hypothesized that the net is of particular interest for the travel and tourism industry. In many countries the tourism industry has a high number of international visitors. Thus, the international travellers have a need for information. In tourism research, some scholars go even further and argue that "gathering, processing, and evaluating information can be seen as an integral part of the travel experience" (Snepenger and Snepenger, 1993. In Norway, the industry consists of many small-and medium-sized businesses. Quite often, the tourists or consumers buy an experience, a holiday-product produced by a number of independent firms. Normally, this is also true when the consumer uses a travel agent or a tour operator. Moreover, independent travel has a substantial market share. In Europe, approximately 30% of summer travel abroad in 1996 belonged to the non-prebooking category, according to the *European Travel Monitor.* Thus, travellers have an obvious need for information, and businesses, on the other hand, have an information or marketing need. According to Pitt et al., " many marketing managers have (not) yet given careful consideration to the full potential of the WWW as a marketing tool, particularly with regard to its potential to move the prospective buyer from being a passive surfer to an interactive customer" (Pitt, Berthon, and Watson, 1996).

The purpose of this paper is (1) to present the NIN project and the Norwegian Tourism Guide, a Web site launched in January 1997, and (2) to discuss interactive marketing and interactivity as a basis for further development for the ongoing Norwegian project.

The Norwegian Tourism Guide

A national initiative for building a NIN (NIN, 95) in Norway was established in 1994. A number of application areas were chosen, the tourism industry being one of them. The goal of the project was to introduce and extend the use of computer networks within the tourism industry, particularly for connecting the numerous small-and medium-sized businesses around the country. The Internet was chosen as the main network, but the project is also following the development of other international network projects, such as the EU project TIM (Maartman-Moe et al., 1994), which are using point-to-point connections through Integrated Services Digital Network (ISDN) or Asynchronous Transfer Mode (ATM) networks (TIM, 1994).

The focus of the project is twofold: using the Net as a tool for cooperation and communication within the industry, and using the Net as a marketing and sales tool. We have started with the last focus and are now building a national framework on the WWW for marketing and selling Norwegian tourism products.

The project is run by NR, the Norwegian Computing Centre, on behalf of NORTRA, the Norwegian Tourist Board. The main activities in this phase were to develop demonstrators and define concepts and strategies. During the preproject phase, we based the concept on three elements (Aanonsen, 1996): the organizational model for cooperation within the industry, the model for financing the system, and the technical solution. We chose distributed models for all three of the elements, to encourage participation of tourism businesses at all levels all over the country. During the implementation phase, user requirements became a significant part of the concept, and we included this as the fourth basic element of the solution.

National Cooperation and Strategic Alliances

To implement the solutions based on the elements we identified in the preproject phase, we made three main strategic decisions: to distribute responsibility for information to the regional level, to base the technical solution on regional Destination Information Systems (DIS), and to establish an alliance with a national ISP. The reasons for these decisions and our experiences from implementing them during the first phase is discussed in Aanonsen, 1997-1; how these related to relevant marketing and organizational theories in discussed in Tjostheim, 1997. The basic element of the organizational model is cooperation between tourist boards around the country. The Norwegian tourism business is organized as a hierarchy with NORTRA on top, then five regional tourist boards covering most of the country, a number of local tourist boards or "destination companies" on the next level, and suppliers at the bottom. Each regional tourist board is responsible for information from the region and for organizing further distribution of responsibility. The goal is to create a network where the responsibility is as close to the information source as possible.

NORTRA and the regional tourist boards are cooperating in a number of ways to promote Norway as a tourist destination on the international market. An agreement between NORTRA and these partners is already established in such areas as brochure production and participation in fairs and campaigns. The cooperation on the Internet follows the same model, and the existing agreement will be extended to include this.

The regional tourist boards play a central role in the model for cooperation in this project. The responsibility for information about each region is distributed to these partners. The tourist boards produce presentations of their regions and provide general practical information. They also supply basic information about the suppliers in their region, which may include links to presentations from each business.

The regional tourist boards are also responsible for organizing the participation of local tourist boards and destinations within their region. These partners will be responsible for producing local presentations, including practical information about their destination. These partners may also take responsibility for the basic information about local suppliers and for linking their presentations to the framework.

The Partners in the Network

The project has also established cooperation with two main technical partners—an ISP and a provider of DIS (Sheldon, 1993). The national ISP contributes technical and marketing expertise for using the application on the Net. Initially, the national ISP intended to contribute economically to the project since tourism was also part of their strategy for establishing new business on the Net. This intention changed for different reasons during the first phase of the project, and the tourism industry is taking over the costs, ownership, and responsibility for the solution. At the regional and local level, the industry may chose any partner as ISP. The other main technical partner is the provider of DIS. They are providing a system the tourist board can use for a number of their tasks, such as producing brochures and providing information to local tourist offices. The DIS also has extended routines for maintaining the quality of the information. Our main reasons for including this partner in the concept are to enable reuse of information and integrate Internet marketing in the set of tasks performed by a tourism organization. Our goal is both to increase the efficiency at the tourist boards and assure the quality of the information.

The Financial Model

The main element of the financial model is splitting costs and income between the different participants. The national tourist board is responsible for the central parts of the system, for the content at the national level, and for marketing the Web site. Their income will be from regional tourist boards and national providers of tourism products linked to the application. Regional and local tourist boards will finance the regional part of the solution and get the income from providers within their regions.

The Technical Solution

The main motivation for choosing this technical model is to enable reuse of information from regional and local tourist boards. These partners collect and distribute large amounts of information through their brochure production and daily work at the tourism offices. To make this information available on the Web, a technical solution based on their DIS was chosen. This information is combined with Web pages that profile destinations and products. The system consists of a Web application with a structure of national and regional front pages, a set of menus and icons, maps, and search functions accessing a national database. The information in this database is collected from the regional databases, which are part of DIS.

The Technical Model

The content of the Web site is based on information from brochures produced by the national and regional tourist boards. The design, layout, and structure is created for the Web and includes links, search functions, and "clickable" maps. The destination presentations are mainly created from the editorial parts of the brochures, which are designed to attract the tourist. They contain presentations of main attractions, activities, history, culture, nature, and geography. Useful practical information for travellers will also be part of a destination presentation. Presentations of products and providers will contain general information, "yellow pages" with basic information about each provider, the provider's own presentation, and direct access to main regional and national providers.

The information for the "yellow pages" is stored in the regional databases. This is in many ways the core of the system. The regional tourist boards maintain these databases for a number of purposes. By using them for Internet marketing, the tourist boards are able to reuse information efficiently. Local providers will also be able to present information about their products through these databases. The regional tourist boards offers them differentiated presentations as either simple one-line entries, standardized one-, two-or three-page presentations, or links to their own Web presentation, by including their uniform resource locators (URLs) in the database.

User Requirements

The tourist can find different types of information through this Web application. The information is divided into presentations of destinations and presentations of products and providers. The user can navigate through the information in different ways, either by geography, by product type, or through the profiling material (Aanonsen, 1997-2). These two types of presentations are also connected directly. The connection makes it possible for the users to find all products in one destination and to navigate from a presentation of a product to the presentation of the destination where the product is situated.

Modernisation of Hotel Industry

The hospitality and leisure sector is highly diverse and fragmented, consisting of organisations in gaming, attractions, golf, hotels, spa resorts, restaurants, pubs and clubs, health and fitness and holiday parks to name but a few.

Growth in Revenues – but also Costs

Over the last few years, growth in consumer spending has strengthened, providing a boost for the hospitality and leisure sector. In parallel to this growth, there has been a sharp increase in both utility and workforce costs, with increases in the minimum wage that have impacted profit margins with this growth in revenue.

The UK may well see its opt-out from the European Union working time directive phased out over the next few years, which could have a negative impact on the sector. Plans to overhaul immigration rules to attract more highly skilled workers from abroad may also add to an increasing wage bill.

Corporation tax changes will have differing affects on the industry, with hoteliers experiencing reductions in building allowances until 2011 when they will then be removed altogether. Smaller hospitality and leisure businesses face increases in the small business corporate tax rates.

The hospitality and leisure sector is extremely sensitive to consumer demand and as such is extremely susceptible to environmental, economic and market trends. Interest rate rises in 2007 are expected to dampen consumer spending growth in 2008, and expected further strong growth in the euro zone over a more subdued growth in the US suggests that the number of overseas visitors is likely to slow, further impacting the sector.

Consolidation in Wet-led

With the implementation of the smoking ban in public areas, lack of outdoor space with current pub properties and restrictions on drink promotions, the outlook for growth in hospitality and leisure industries that are 'wet-led' is looking more subdued. As a result, this may lead to a period of consolidation in this sector, although restaurants may well improve due to the smoking ban.

Internet Booking Affects Growth

Growth in direct internet booking is putting further pressure on firms in the travel and hospitality sector, with travellers searching for better deals and booking later, resulting in shorter cash flow prediction analysis. Innovative firms, such as larger hotel operators, are increasing their use of in-house Internet booking systems and customer loyalty systems to help maximise revenue.

Changes in Health and Fitness

Government focus on tackling health issues will ultimately benefit the health and fitness sector. However, it is important that services offered are correctly aligned to demographic trends, older population requirements, spending capability and busy lifestyles.

It is therefore important that the correct financial and operational metric information is available to maximise revenues and attract the correct customers.

Uncertainty in Gambling

Uncertainty around the government plans and revisions to the Gambling Act, allied to increased duty levied on casinos, will act as a deterrent to potential investors, which will dampen growth potential in this sector. This will be further exaggerated by the smoking ban referred to above.

Going for Growth

Whilst it is clear that the sector is and will continue to experience challenging times, there will be increased investment in the industry due to the successful Olympic 2012 bid, albeit predominately focused within the London region.

The winners in the highly diverse and fragmented hospitality industry will be those organisations that turn these challenges into opportunities, delivering against profit and growth targets, managing employee skills effectively and ensuring they have the right information available to them to increase the performance of their operations.

Online Travel: A Modern Trend of Tourism

eTourism is a subset of Travel technology with a particular focus on the tourism industry.

In June 2003, the United Nations Conference on Trade and Development, UNCTAD, established a Task Force on Sustainable Tourism for Development that proposes the use of the concept of e-tourism as part of a strategy to build sustainable and locally rooted tourism industries. The e-Tourism Initiative aims to promote ICT-driven growth through a participative strategy that includes networking and competitive collaboration for the tourism sector of developing countries.

7

Tourism and Developing Countries

According to estimates from the World Development Report 2000/2001, almost half of the world's 6 billion inhabitants live on less than US$2 a day, and a fifth live below the international poverty line-less than US$1 a day (World Bank, 2000a). While the number of people who live below the poverty line declined between 1987 and 1998 in some regions – most notably East Asia and the Pacific – in most developing countries the number continues to rise. Poverty is particularly acute in South Asia and sub-Saharan Africa, which are home respectively to 43.5% and 24.3% of the people in the developing world who subsist on less than US$1 a day.

While extreme income poverty persists in many developing countries, they have also experienced considerable growth in international tourist arrivals and receipts. During 1998/1999, East Asia experienced a growth rate in tourism arrivals of 11.1%, the Middle East 16.2%, Africa 7.8%, and South Asia 8.3%, all of which are well above the global average of 4.0% (WTO, 2000).

Between 1990 and 1997, tourism was either an important sector of the economy (accounting for more than 2% of GDP or 5% of exports), or growing rapidly (aggregate growth greater than 50%) in almost half of the low income countries, and in virtually all of the lower-middle income countries (Deloitte and Touche, IIED, and ODI, 1999). Tourism is significant in eleven of the twelve countries which hold 80% of the world's poor. Moreover, tourism has become the world's leading source of export earnings if international tourism receipts and international fare receipts are combined (WTO, 2000). In light of these statistics, some analysts believe that the tourism industry can play a significant role in poverty reduction.

The Viability and Sustainability of International Tourism in Developing Countries

The tourism sector is probably the only service sector that provides concrete and quantified trading opportunities for all nations, regardless of their level of development. However, it is also a sector where there is clearly an uneven distribution of benefits, which is threatening the social, economic and environmental sustainability of tourism in some developing countries. For many developing countries tourism is one of fundamental pillars of their development process because it is one of the dominant activities in the economy, while for others, particularly by islands and some small economies, it is the only source of foreign currency and employment, and therefore constitutes the platform for their economic development.

Against this background, part I presents an overview of the most important trends and features of international tourism and the most influential factors affecting the performance, efficiency and sustainability of tourism transactions in developing countries. Part II presents an overview and examples of the main issues affecting the viability of tourism in developing countries, including (a) the impact of the leakage effect which is adversely affecting them in taking advantage of commercial opportunities; and (b) the anti-competitive practices affecting tourism viability and performance in different segments of the tourism sector, as well as in other sectors closely linked to travel and tourism. Part III presents some reflections about the GATS 2000 negotiations as a possible turning point for making effective the increasing participation of developing countries in international tourism flows in a sustainable perspective. In this connection, some comments are provided on the impact of the proposed Annex on Tourism on the economic, social and environmental sustainability of tourism.

Salient Trends and Features of the Performance of Developing Countries in International Tourism

Overall Trends in International Tourism

"International tourism highlights 2000" of the World Tourism

Organization (OMT/WTO) reports that during 1998 total tourism receipts, including those generated by international fares, were the most important export revenue worldwide. Export revenue that year amounted to an estimated US$ 532 billion, surpassing all the other international trade categories. International tourism totalled to US$ 441 billion and the international transport of passengers US$ 91 billion, which corresponded to 7.9 and 1.3 percent respectively of worldwide exports of good and services. According to the OMT/WTO *Tourism Economic Report 1998*, tourism is one the five top export categories and the main source of foreign currency for at least 38 percent of them.

Tourism Spenders

The world's top tourism spender during 1998 was by far the European Union, with an over US$ 160 billion. The most important spenders among its members were Germany (2nd world ranking), US$ 46.9 billion; the United Kingdom (4th), US$ 28.8 billion; France (5th), US$ 17.8 billion; Italy (6th), US$ 17.7; and Netherlands (7th), US$ 11.0 billion. The other members' expenses during the same year ranged between US$ 8.8 and 1.8 billion. During the same year, the United States (1st in world ranking by individual countries) spent US$ 56.1 billion; Japan (3rd), 28.8 billion; Canada (8th) US$ 10.8 billion; China (9th), US$ 9.2 billion; Russian Federation (13th) US$ 8.3 billion; Switzerland (14th), US$ 7.1 billion; and Australia, US$ 5.4 billion. Also during the same year 45 countries reported more that US$ 1 billion in international tourism expenditure

Tourism Trends and best-performing Countries in Developing Regions between 1997 and 1999

Africa: The African region showed a growth rate of 7.8 percent in the number of arrivals, nearly twice the world average. There is a high concentration of international tourism arrivals in this region, bound for destinations in the north and south of the continent. The best-performing countries in terms of the increase in the number of arrivals included Morocco (18 percent), Zimbabwe (11 percent) and Zambia (26 percent), while the important tourism destinations of Tunisia (3.4 percent) and South Africa (6 percent) continued to show steady gains.

Americas: The rate of growth for the whole region 2.4 percent was lower than the world average, mainly owing to flat results for South American countries (-1 percent) and Mexico (-2.9 percent). Central America fared much better, especially Guatemala (29 percent) and El Salvador (21 percent). Results in the Caribbean were mixed, with Cuba (12 percent) and the Dominican Republic (15 percent) among the big winners and Puerto Rico (-11 percent) among the losers.

East Asia/Pacific: After two years of decreasing tourist arrivals, East Asia and the Pacific bounced back strongly in 1999, attracting nearly 10 million more tourists than the previous record, set in 1998. Growth was widespread, with especially good results in Malaysia (43 percent), Cambodia (29 percent), Viet Nam (17 percent), Singapore (11 percent), Thailand (10 percent), Republic of Korea (10 percent), China (8 percent) and Hong Kong, China (18 percent).

Europe: Overall, tourism to Europe grew by 2.7 percent in 1999, with results mixed according to region. In this region some economies in transition were affected by the Kosovo crisis and instability in the Russian market, which caused problems for mature destinations in Central and Eastern Europe such as Hungary (-14 percent), Poland (-4.4 percent) and the Czech Republic (-1.8 percent). However, emerging destinations managed to attract the interest of travellers, for example, Estonia (15 percent), Kyrgyzstan (17 percent) and Georgia (21 percent), as well as Russian Federation (17 percent) and Ukraine (21 percent).

Middle East: The Middle East is one of the world's smallest regions, receiving nearly 18 million tourists in 1999, but it also had the fastest growth rate with arrivals up by 16 percent. Egypt, which represents a quarter of the regional total, recorded a spectacular growth rate of almost 40 percent and a record number of tourist arrivals that far exceeds the totals achieved in its best year, 1997. Dubai, Lebanon and the Syrian Arab Republic also fared well, with arrivals increasing by 14, 12 and 9 percent respectively. The Libyan Arab Jamahiriya registered an increase of 25 percent.

South Asia: Tourism increased in most countries in this region, resulting in an increase of 8.3 percent over the previous year's results. India registered an increase of 5.2 percent, while arrivals in the Islamic Republic of Iran rose by 16.5 percent, in Sri Lanka by 14.4 percent and in Maldives by 8.6 percent.

International Tourism Receipts

Preliminary results processed by the OMT/WTO indicate that during 1999 tourism receipts worldwide amounted to US$ 455 billion and a further US$ 93 billion. In 59 countries the receipts amounted over US$ 1 billion.

Some Indicators about the Sustainability of International Tourism in Developing Countries

Importance and Impact of Export Revenues from Tourism for Developing Countries

During the period 1995-1998, tourism revenues were one of the five leading sources of export revenue for 69 developing countries. Among the latter, tourism revenue was the main source of foreign currency in 28 countries, its share in total exports ranging between 79 and 20 percent; in 27 countries it accounted for between 20 and 10 percent; and in the 24 remaining countries it was around 10 percent.

The contribution of export revenues to gross domestic product (GDP) was equally important and accounted for between 82.29 percent (in Maldives) and 30 percent (in Samoa). In the second group the contribution of export revenues to GDP is between 30 and 10 percent and in the remaining countries under 10 percent. One aspect to be underlined is that although the contribution of tourism revenues is important in all these countries, its contribution to GDP is declining as the economies become more diversified. The best examples of this are Mauritius, the Dominican Republic and Tunisia.

The Particular 'Situation of LDCs

Although only 0.5 percent of the world's exports of services originate in the LDCs, international services are an important part of the economies of those countries. In 1998, services accounted for 20 percent of the LDCs' total exports of goods and services. However, in 13 of the 49 LDCs services export receipts exceeded merchandise export receipts and in all but three of those the share of tourism services exports in total foreign exchange earnings was more than twice the share of merchandise exports.

The share of the LDCs in the world's exports of international tourism services was 0.6 percent in 1988 (with 2.4 million international tourist arrivals) and 0.8 percent in 1998 (5.1 million).

During the 1990s tourist flows to the LDCs increased more rapidly than tourist flows to the rest of the world. This growth was particularly strong in seven countries (Cambodia, Mali, Laos People's Democratic Republic, Myanmar, Samoa, Uganda, United Republic of Tanzania), which hosted over 1.2 million visitors in 1998, in comparison with 0.4 million in 1992. During that period, tourism growth was much slower in several LDCs, while a decrease was observed in a number of countries that suffered socio-political and economic instability.

The growth of international tourism receipts in the LDCs was also quite rapid during the 1990s: total receipts more than doubled between 1992 and 1998 (from US$ 1 billion to US$ 2.2 billion). There is a great degree of concentration in the distribution of tourism receipts among the LDCs: five countries (Cambodia, Maldives, Nepal, Uganda, United Republic of Tanzania) accounted for 51 percent of the total tourism receipts of the group in 1998. Particularly strong, over the decade, was the growth in international tourists' expenditure in Cambodia, the United Republic of Tanzania, Myanmar, Bangladesh, Samoa, Uganda and Haiti.

Tourism is the first source of foreign exchange earnings in the whole group of 49 LDCs, aside from the petroleum industry, which is concentrated in only three LDCs (Angola, Yemen, Equatorial Guinea): the combined tourism export receipts of all LDCs in 1998 accounted for 16.2 percent of the total non-oil export receipts of the LDCs, thus exceeding the second and third largest non-oil export sectors (cotton and textile products) by 39 percent and 82 percent, respectively.

Level of Performance and Sustainability of Tourism in Developing Countries

The proper functioning of the tourism economy is linked to that of many other related economic activities, which accounts for the importance of its economic, social and environmental sustainability. As a matter of fact, the extent to which the business operations of international tourism, backward and forward are linked with other sectors will determine the level of performance and profitability of tourism, the extent of multiplier and spillover effects, and the retention of value added, i.e. the leakage effect. The sectors producing goods and services are linked backwards with tourism in catering for the needs of tourists and tourism operators, e.g. agriculture and food-processing industries, and other manufacturing industries providing furniture, construction materials and other articles required by tourism establishments. Similarly, many other services, such as transport, business services, financial services, professional services, construction design and engineering, environmental services, security services and government services, also ensure the efficient performance of tourism operators. Some of these sectors are also crucial for the proper linkage of tourism with foreign markets (forward linkages) because they constitute the platforms for "taking off" and for keeping the national tourism providers fully integrated with international tourism flows.

Many developing countries have found important to improve the linking of tourism (forward and backward) with the other sectors of the economy as one of the foundations of tourism development policies, so as to capitalize on the benefits of the globalization and internationalization of markets. Successful experiences of small economies and islands that have recently become emerging tourism destinations, such as Mauritius, Maldives, the Dominican Republic and other Caribbean islands, attest to the vital importance of the proper linkage of tourism with the rest of the economy, in their capacity of retaining value added, e.g., reducing leakages. Despite developing countries efforts to develop the most suitable domestic policy environment, the economic sustainability of tourism is being undermined by external factors beyond their control, notably the predatory behaviour of integrated suppliers which enjoy a dominant position in the originating markets of tourism flows.

Key Issues with Special Impact on the Social, Economic and Environmental Sustainability of Tourism

This part presents an overview and illustration of the main issues affecting the viability of tourism in developing countries, including (a) the leakage effect produced by their structural vulnerabilities and their difficulties in taking advantage of commercial opportunities; and (b) anti-competitive practices affecting tourism viability and performance in different segments of the tourism sector, as well as those in other sectors closely linked to travel and tourism.

Leakages from Tourism in Developing Countries

As a modality of international commerce, tourism involves

not only inflows of foreign financial resources but also outflows, referred to herein as "leakages". When they exceed specific levels, these outflows can significantly neutralize the positive financial effect of international tourism. Leakage is the process whereby part of the foreign exchange earnings generated by tourism, rather than being retained by tourist-receiving countries, is either retained by tourist-generating countries or repatriated to them in the form of profits, income and royalty remittances, repayment of foreign loans, and imports of equipment, materials, capital and consumer goods to cater for the needs of international tourist and overseas promotional expenditures.

Leakages can be divided into three categories: internal leakage or the "import-coefficient" of tourism activities; external leakage or pre-leakage, depending on the commercialization mode of the tourism package and the choice of airline; and invisible leakage or foreign exchange costs associated with resource damage or deterioration.

Internal leakages can be measured by establishing "satellite accounts" within national accounting and survey procedures to detail all tourism-related economic activities. It is a normal effect present in both developed and developing countries. In principle, import-related leakages are highest where the local economies are weakest owing to sparse factor endowment or inadequate quality of goods and services. The average leakage for most developing countries today is between 40 and 50 percent of gross tourism earnings for small economies and between 10 and 20 percent for most advanced and diversified developing countries. Importantly for LDCs, tourism import-related leakages are often inferior to other economic activity leakages, including manufacturing and, in some cases, agriculture, thus confirming tourism as a choice sector of development for which they possess comparative advantages in many areas.

A first step in reducing internal leakage is to identify what levels are appropriate given the economic structure of a country and then to ensure that effective leakage remains near this objective range while strategies to build up the local supply capacity are put in place. Although restrictive trade policies can reduce the size of the market, it is important to note that import openness tends to facilitate the leakage effect unless the economy has already in place a structure capable of reacting to the competitive stimulus of imports, which is usually not the case in LDCs. External leakage or pre-leakage is much more difficult to measure and relates to the proportion of the total value added of tourism of services actually captured by the servicing country. To the extent that developing countries have limited access to commercialization channels in their target markets, they can only offer base prices to intermediaries that capture the mark-up on those services. Observed differences between paid and received prices for developing country tourism services (lodging, food, entertainment, etc.) suggest external leakage or pre-leakage levels of up to 75 percent. In some cases, base prices do not allow for the economic sustainability of projects, and normally do not contemplate replacement costs associated with resource depletion. This leads to problems of infrastructure and environmental sustainability, which tend to be overlooked in view of the short-term importance of crucial foreign exchange inflows.

As a flow variable, leakage levels do not have a static effect. They vary in time depending on:

(a) The stage or cycle point of the tourism industry. For example, a nascent tourism industry tends to require large amounts of one-time imports, whereas loan grace periods may allow for a decrease in leakage during the first few years of operation. During a maturity phase leakage may increase as large sums are invested in marketing, rehabilitation of facilities and upgrading of products provided, etc.

(b) The evolution of the economy to provide new services and products resulting from demand from the tourism sector. The import of products and services initially not available should trigger enough entrepreneurial response to enable these to be provided locally, thus allowing for a lessening of leakage. It is therefore a main objective of leakage limitation to provide and promote these links between domestic industry and tourism. For example, in the Dominican Republic leakages diminished between 1990 and 1995 as local industry became increasingly interested in servicing the tourism market. The largest companies have now created subsidiaries specifically for this purpose.

Another factor to be evaluated in identifying appropriate leakage levels is the type of tourism being promoted. High-income tourism, because it requires the provision of very high quality and high priced goods, may actually result in increased leakage in some cases despite of the higher income it may generate. Mass tourism could have higher potential for leakage than ecological or adventure tourism because the latter value and consume local resources as part of the tourism experience. However, low-leakage tourism can also equate to low-income tourism, resulting in lower total income and therefore limiting the possibilities for expansion and development by other sectors of the receiving country's economy. In order to correctly evaluate the return on investments it is necessary to carry out a cost-of-opportunity study that will establish a "leakage break-even point" as a function of the country's economic capacity to serve different types of tourism and choose the type most suitable for a project or country.

Leakage effects on tourism net income levels are nonetheless offset by increased value added or volume. As an example of the positive outlook for LDCs, value added in tourism, measured as tourism income per tourist arrival (Yt/At) has grown by over 100 percent in 21 (almost half) of the LDCs surveyed between 1998 and 1992.

Interestingly, growth in income per tourist appears to bear no clear relationship to the level of or growth in arrivals. This suggests that growth in income per tourist is not a function of volume, and has therefore grown basically because of a favourable quality/price ratio. This also confirms the enormous diversity of situations present in LDCs and their tourism industries; but, in general, as value added grows, the *potential* for leakage lessens.

To the extent that leakages lead to a definition of economic opportunities it can be useful as a strategic blueprint for further economic development. Domestic policies in developing countries against leakages from international tourism should include (i) the provision of incentives to reinvest profits and potential cash transfers that otherwise would be invested abroad; (ii) the enhancement of the capacity of tourist destinations for intensifying the production of goods and services required by the tourism sector; (iii) the provision of incentives to domestic investors to expand their participation in tourism and iv) the enforcement of domestic competition policy against anti-competitive practices by tour operators. As regards external leakages, most issues address points of discussion under the GATS Annex on tourism in the

WTO, such as (i) local and international competition policy, particularly with regard to market access issues and best business practices in relation to regulations on contractual practices; and (ii) ecological and economic sustainability and the valuation and use of non-tradable resources.

Anti-Competitive Practices Affecting Tourism Sustainability

The competition issue and the treatment of anti-competitive behaviour are at the core of the problems of efficiency, viability and sustainability of tourism in developing countries. The latter's ability to deal with those two aspects and to counter their effects is a crucial matter. Firstly, this is because anti-competitive behaviour occurs largely in developed countries, as a result of the fierce competition among a few integrated dominant players with a high market share in their own market and in all segments of tourism industry supply, notably tour operators, travel agencies, hotels etc. Secondly, the pattern of globalization, which is the driving force of many of the developments in the supply of the tourism and air transport, also mostly originates and is controlled in the two leading developed economies, namely the European Union and the United States. Consequently, what often appears to be a normal commercial relationship in a developing country may actually be the result of a network of anti-competitive practices arising from a globalized and highly integrated tourism trading environment, dominated by a few suppliers in the originating tourism markets. Moreover, other non-behaviour-related industry issues, such as the inadequacy or absence of a domestic competition legal framework in developing countries, and the lack of multilateral disciplines and mechanisms within the GATS framework, also affect the ability of developing countries to deal with or prevent anti-competitive practices in their tourism sectors.

Why and how do anti-competitive practices threaten the viability of sustainable tourism in developing countries?

The economic and social viability of tourism in developing countries depends on sustainable growth perspectives, in terms not only of absolute values, but also of their capacity for retaining more value added in their economies, i.e. smaller leakages, an even distribution of benefits in commercial operations, elimination of all barriers to tourism, particularly to commercial presence, and the movement of tourism suppliers in both origin and destination markets, and the effective implementation of provisions enumerated in Articles IV and XIX of GATS. The foundations for sustainable tourism are already in place in most developing countries as a result of the autonomous liberalization of the tourism sector itself and the progressive liberalization of many other services sectors. However, for those countries highly dependent on tourism revenue, the benefits of the liberalization of tourism are being threatened by the predatory practices of a few dominant tourism suppliers in the world tourism market. The evolution of the GATS disciplines, and the consistency of future commitments of developed countries with the economic, social and environmental sustainability of tourism in developing countries in the GATS 2000 negotiations, should mark a turning point favouring more profitable tourism for all WTO members, particularly the most vulnerable small developing countries.

The predatory practices and anti-competitive behaviour in international tourism have two main effects on the economic sustainability of the tourism of developing countries: unbalanced trade benefits, and the deepening of the leakage effect. Their combined impact minimize the positive impacts of spillover and multiplier effects inherent to tourism, and undermine the financial capacity of enterprises and the ability of countries to earmark necessary resources to maintain and upgrade basic infrastructure and quality standards in order to satisfy in an adequate way competitive conditions and international demand. Moreover, in most vulnerable and small developing economies, particularly LDCs, the foundations of tourism are threatened by unbalanced results in their business operations, which are in turn threatening the social, economic and environmental sustainability of tourism.

There is much documented evidence about the negative impact of anti-competitive behaviour of developed countries' dominant tourism suppliers on their own markets and overseas. Unfair practices, which confront developing countries' suppliers in their business operations with dominant suppliers in tourism-originating countries, are of a different nature and occur in different segments of tourism and related activities. One of the salient features that become evident in commercial relations is the uneven distribution of benefits, due to the dominant position and market power of integrated suppliers in their own markets and worldwide. These suppliers have absolute advantages, because of their control of inbound and outbound operations in their countries and overseas, which allow them to keep consumers dependent on the offer of the products and services they supply, at the expenses of imposing onerous commercial conditions on suppliers in different tourism destinations. The huge supply capacity of dominant players in all segments of tourism, including transporters, CRS/GDS, tour operators, travel agencies and hotels, allows them to prepare holiday packages and retail them through their own business networks, as well as to impose prices and conditions on suppliers in tourism destinations.

How do the business operations of tour operators and travel agencies in the originating markets of tourism affect the sustainability of developing countries' tourism?

Tourism suppliers from developing countries e.g. hotels, inbound operators and land transport companies participate in international tourism mainly through the transactions of tour operators and travel agencies from developed countries in the developed countries' originating markets. As wholesalers of tourism products and services they assemble the holiday package by negotiating with destinations and operators in third countries. They view the tour package as an attractive option with many advantages for them: (a) it ensures flows of tourists; (b) it reduces the international marketing costs of the destination; and (c) it increase the volume flow of package travellers, which is likely to increase investment by foreign construction companies, major tour operators and airline companies that wish to make the tourism product more attractive to consumers. However, tourism suppliers from tourism destinations in developing countries have very often underlined their weak bargaining position in business transactions, particularly with dominant suppliers of the most important originating tourism market from developed countries.

International Competition among Tour Operators and Travel Agencies

Tour operators in originating countries manage business operations through (a) a subsidiary of a vertically integrated firm with a number of related travel interests; (b) an entirely independent firm that specializes in putting holiday packages together and selling them; (c) a subsidiary of an airline; and (d) an operator directly linked to a travel agent. The tour operator of each major market is dominated by a small number of national firms with a relatively large market share, which compete fiercely with each other. For instance, four firms with a share of over 60 percent dominate the United Kingdom market. This results in the larger operators having a dominant position with a very little competition, because the layer of the next competitor is too small. Consequently, the travel agencies (the retailers of tourism packages) in destination markets are almost entirely dependent on their linkages with the dominant tour operators. Also, consumers become captive in their choices of tourist package offered by dominant suppliers. The effect of this supremacy of integrated tourism suppliers in their own markets is mirrored in their dominant position in commercial relations with tourism suppliers in destination developing countries.

The benefits and costs of package tours to service suppliers in developing countries depend to a large extent on the nature and terms of the contracts between them and the tour operators from the tourism-originating countries. Accordingly, the bargaining powers of suppliers from developing countries are a central issue affecting the tourism sustainability of developing countries. Some examples of how the common practices in contractual arrangements affect the sustainability of tourism in developing countries are presented below.

Use of Monopsonistic Power over Local Tourism Suppliers in Developing Countries

The contract between a tour operator from an originating country and the suppliers in the destination country involves a block reservation for a future period at a negotiated price and specifies the terms of risk sharing in the event that not all the packages are sold. The tour operator normally has the greater bargaining power during the contract negotiations; if it considers that the negotiating partner's offer is not attractive enough, it can choose another hotel in the same area or even another region of the same country. Tour operators thus often exercise a monopsonistic power over local tourism suppliers, such as local hotels, since for the latter the servicing of the package tour is a vital means of securing their occupancy rates.

The asymmetry of bargaining power is clearly revealed in the content of the contract. Often contracts last for one year or more, and the risk inherent in a long-term contract for a tour operator (e.g. uncertainty of future demands for the package) is reduced by negotiating various conditions favourable to the tour operator.

A contract frequently contains the following provisions: a substantial discount is provided on rooms after the departure of the clients; no deposit is required for the booking; payment may be made long after the departure of the customers; and the tour operator retains the right to return unfilled rooms ("release-back clause") shortly before the arrival date, without any need to pay compensation.

Anti-Competitive Practices Resulting from Vertical Integration

Vertical integration among tour operators and travel agencies, which is currently proceeding at a notable pace in Europe, threatens to reduce the actual number of tour operators in the market. As a result, a great deal of market power is being transferred to the intermediaries that direct consumers to specific destinations. The consequences of this should be a major concern to developing countries' tourism destinations.

The increase in the degree of concentration in the travel market in favour of mega-operators puts developing countries' suppliers and the other competitors in local markets at a clear disadvantage. It also opens the door to unfair practices, which directly affect tourist destinations. An example of this is the travel agent's "racking policy", which refers to the decision about which brochures to put on display. This has a crucial impact on the tourism destinations of developing countries, because for them the travel agent's display rack is almost an essential facility, and denial of access to it can severely restrict consumer exposure.

The threat of "deracking" (i.e. removing brochures from the shelves) is used by integrated suppliers in attempt to negotiate larger commissions, by pressuring tour operators not to supply independent travel agencies on better terms or by pushing their own holidays through in-house incentive schemes. The lasting impact of this practice is more restrictive in originating countries where tour operators are the main distribution channels, such as in Europe, where more than 60 percent of tour packages are sold by integrated suppliers.

Conversely, in the United States the possibility of "deracking" is lower because about 70 percent of travel agencies are independent, GDS/CRS are more important as distribution channels, and the Internet is becoming a primary source of information for consumers about tourism destinations.

International Competition among Hotels

The international hotels sector is characterized by a considerable diversity in the modalities of services provision, and by a high concentration of a very small number of large hotel groups, including hotel consortia, integrated hotel chains and tourism lodging (second homes). Their scope and focus are very often limited, either by a focus on home markets, notably through the hospitality franchising systems, or by a concentration on business travel and destinations. One important aspect to be noted is that the intensive use of the accommodation infrastructure, particularly hotels receiving international tourists regardless of the hotel's size, requires the continuous allocation of financial resources to maintain and upgrade the quality of accommodation to meet the standards of international demand.

In most developing country destinations huge investments have been made in the hospitality and accommodation sector either through investment of domestic resources or attracting foreign investors by increase of different modalities, including management contracts and franchising brand names

As in all the other segments of tourism-related activities, the importance of competition issues stems from a mix of practices through the distribution mechanisms. Anti-competitive behaviour in those mechanisms is thus most likely to have a significant effect on the ability of destinations, and of their hotel sectors, to compete effectively and to gain a fair share of the rewards of attracting tourists and travellers.

The sustainability of this sector in developing countries' tourism destinations depends on the occupancy rates (affected by seasonality) and the level of profits, which are highly influenced by the results of commercial transactions between hoteliers and tour operators from tourism-originating countries. In this connection, it has to be underlined that the accommodation sector is the one most affected by the dominant power of mega-operators, whose stringent demands in terms of quality standards are not duly compensated for with fair commercial remuneration.

Another, wider impact of this predatory behaviour in the tourism economy of receiving countries is the deepening of the leakage effect and the undermining of positive inherent multipliers effects of tourism. Depending on the magnitude of these unfair compensations from dominant tour operators, some tourism destinations in developing countries might be subsidizing tourists from originating countries.

Computerized Reservation Systems (CRS)/Global Distribution Systems (GDS)

The development of international tourism relies on the effective commercialization of tourism products to consumers at tourism-originating countries. World information and distribution networks play a decisive role in the international tourism sector since they bring the buyers and producers of tourism products into contact. CRS, GDS and the Internet are the backbone of world information networks, which provide the infrastructures and networking facilities for airlines, tour operators, travel agencies and other tourism operators to process and obtain information, make reservations and market tourism products.

CRS have been developed by large air carriers since the 1970s to process flight reservations. They later evolved and expanded to offer further services related to air transport, such as the storage of information on a worldwide basis, the issuance of tickets, marketing (by displaying information on fares, discounts and conditions attached to them) or the sale of products and services. Moreover, they cover not only services provided by airlines, but also land services supplied to tourists, such as package tours, hotels and vehicle rentals. With this enlarged range of services, they became known as global distribution systems. GDS have significantly improved the efficiency of travel agents' business operations and their use is growing rapidly. They have become the main marketing and trading tool of international tourism, as well as a major source of income for the carriers which own them. Through strategic alliances and other forms of cooperation or mergers in the most important markets, these systems minimize their costs and reduce the need for a direct commercial presence. A single GDS terminal provides immediate access to all services companies which have opted to market their products through this network.

The companies (air carriers or independent commercial companies) that control CRS and GDS either partly or entirely sell access to the system to tourism operators worldwide. There are many obstacles to and measures governing GDS networks. These include (a) unfair rights of access, (b) restrictions on display, (c) costs of services influenced by monopolistic practices,

(d) neutrality and regulations, and (e) the technology gap among users.

Access problems: Despite their major contribution to the development of tourism, GDS are frequently considered a barrier to market entry, mainly because they are controlled by the major carriers and because of the unfavourable access conditions for competitors. While some East Asian developing countries have participated in the establishment of a major GDS (Abacus, complemented by the strategic alliance with Worldspan), other developing countries have not been able to do likewise, leaving their carriers and other service suppliers without privileged access to any GDS. Additionally, countries not yet seen as attractive tourist destinations, or whose hospitality sector is underdeveloped (particularly in Africa and South Asia), tend to be poorly represented, if at all, on GDS. Therefore, access to information on their tourism products is limited, thus making it difficult for them to sell their tourism services. These difficulties have meant that many smaller carriers, especially some from developing countries, have been obliged to continue using the traditional SITA CRS, which leaves them at a competitive disadvantage compared with those what are represented in the major GDS. On the other hand, in many developing countries, particularly in Africa, GDS are present as a result of joint ventures with local partners (e.g. the national carrier) but operate within a de facto monopoly. This leads to excessive user fees and hinders their potential for developing tourism.

Display: The GDS allows a travel agent to view a wide range of information, which sometimes requires several pages on a terminal screen. In most cases, however, travel agencies only consult the information on the first page (screen); the order in which screens are displayed is thus a crucial determinant in the user's selection of products. The display may discriminate against smaller carriers which do not own a major CRS, since controllers' own flights may be better displayed on the screens than those of their competitors (this is known as "display bias"). There may also be discrimination in favour of their suppliers of land services.

Cost: The cost of having services presented GDS may be prohibitively high for SMEs, leaving them with no access to this marketing tool. Even though all service providers have to pay a fee for having their services displayed in the systems, the costs of participation for the owners of GDS are fully or partly covered by the profits generated by the systems. The cost of hardware and user fees may prevent small users from using GDS; this puts some service suppliers (particularly SMEs) from developing countries at a disadvantage compared with their larger national or international competitors.

Neutrality and regulations: In order to prevent CRS from being used as an anti-competitive tool (e.g. by charging excessive fees for reservations made for non-owner companies) and to ensure their neutrality (e.g. by prohibiting display bias), the United States, Canada and the European Union have issued regulations in recent years on GDS operations related to air services, while the International Civil Aviation Authority (ICAO) adopted a code of conduct for CRS in 1991. However, the regulations and code have not been sufficient to resolve completely the anti-competitive bias of the systems, and particularly to address the specific problems of carriers from developing countries. The ICAO code (the only multilateral one) is non-binding and therefore there are no mechanisms to ensure its enforceability. The relevant domestic regulations are binding, but only within the territories of the countries concerned. The European Union regulations apply to CRS from countries which have similar legislation to ensure neutrality. On the other hand, although CRS have been included among the "soft" air services rights included in GATS, the commitments do not deal with their anti-competitive potential.

Technology gap: Installing and maintaining a system poses a greater problem to travel agents in developing countries, owing to deficiencies in the infrastructure necessary for such an information network, and the shortage of professionals to manage, operate and maintain the system. This not only represents a technical hindrance to the use of modern technology, but also increases the associated costs, thereby putting travel agents in developing countries at a disadvantage compared with their counterparts in developed countries.

***Electronic commerce*:** The expansion of the use of the Internet and other forms of electronic communication opens up significant opportunities for developing countries to develop their tourism and air transport sectors. Their service suppliers can reach consumers around the world directly, offering both package tours and individual air and land services. They thereby cut out the costs of intermediaries (e.g. agency fees) and transaction costs and avoid the need for a direct commercial presence and its associated costs. Nevertheless, electronic marketing and trading have their own costs in terms of human and physical capital requirements. In countries where these requirements are in relatively short supply, the cost of electronic marketing and trading can be reduced if individual suppliers pool their resources. This could be coordinated, for instance, by national tourist authorities. Moreover, modern technologies are likely to be increasingly used as institutional promotion tools. If there is a minimal critical mass of information infrastructure in a given country, the new technologies can offer substantial cost savings.

Air Transport

Air access in international tourism depends on the availability and conditions of air transport connecting tourist-generating countries and destination countries (i.e. prices, frequencies, travel time, etc.). Air transport is a major factor underpinning international tourism in the vast majority of developing countries, but its importance for tourism varies considerably from one region to another. It is the means of transport used by the majority of tourists arriving in developing countries. Air transport developed as a result of the increase in demand for tourism-related travel, becoming in turn the driving force behind the development of the tourism industry. In 1998, passengers were responsible for about 75 percent of air traffic volume and for of the total operating revenues of airlines. It is estimated that up to 40 percent of air passenger travel is for business purposes (as opposed to leisure or personal travel) and that business travellers account for up to half of airlines' income. Like tourism, the world air transport industry has expanded at twice the rate of world output growth, and is expected to continue to do so in the next twenty years.

The main recent developments affecting air transport and the industry structure are the increased international ownership of airlines and their growing concentration, worldwide moves to liberalize and deregulate the sector, the privatization of airlines and the formation of strategic alliances among firms. The main benefits of the latter are the cost reductions and efficiency gains that can be achieved by rationalizing the joint use of resources (such as check-in facilities and ground personnel), creating synergies and providing "network value" (i.e. the wider coverage of points serviced by the carrier and its partners) without the need to physically expand operations. The large global alliances aim at world coverage by pooling the networks of their members. The main drawback in doing this is that the alliances can restrict competition and thus negate some of these benefits, particularly if they collectively achieve a dominant position on given routes.

How the GATS 2000 Negotiations should mark a Turning Point to make Effective the Increasing Participation of Developing Countries in International Tourism Flows in a Sustainable Perspective

How Negotiations could Support the Sustainability of Tourism Operations

The GATS 2000 negotiations mandated by the Final Act of the Uruguay Round provide developing countries with a unique opportunity to counterbalance the asymmetries imbedded in the outcome of the Uruguay Round services negotiations. In this perspective, it is the right time to take advantage of these negotiations to prepare and put forward negotiating proposals on how to make effective use of the provisions of Art IV and XIX, aimed at increasing participation of developing countries in trade in services and the expansion of their services exports including through the strengthening of their domestic services and its efficiency and competitiveness. The two-way process involves not only the refinement of offers, but also the preparation of requests from trading partners as one of the key ways to obtain substantive benefits as result of the GATS 2000 negotiations. Moreover, an active participation of developing countries in the GATS rule-making process is a contribution to building of an improved multilateral framework which would take into consideration existing asymmetries and the need for a predictable markets access for exporters of services from developing countries.

The viability of tourism, i.e. its economic, social, cultural and environmental sustainability, is at the heart of domestic policies and development concerns of developing countries. Accordingly, in the course of the present negotiations on trade in services, there is a need for similar focus on strengthening future substantive commitments on tourism by GATS members as was the case in other sector such as telecommunications and financial services. In this perspective the proposal for the Annex on Trade in Tourism

Services (WT/GC/W/372), may contribute to providing a pro-competitive framework as a complementary tool which would ensure:

(a) *An adequate coverage and consistency of commitments in all tourism activities as defined by the Satellite Tourism Account.* This aspect is of paramount importance in view of specific characteristics and diversity of transactions linked to trade in tourism services, notably the heavy reliance of tourism on air transport and travel distribution systems.

(b) *The prevention of predatory behaviour and anti-competitive practices by dominant integrated suppliers in the originating markets.* This refers to disciplines to prevent anti-competitive conduct including from air transport and travel distribution systems, and to safeguard trade in tourism services from competitive exclusions, abuse of dominant and misleading or discriminatory use of information.

(c) *The effective access and use of information on a non-discriminatory basis.* It should include provisions on access to ensuring non-discrimination, transparent, reasonable and objective criteria; compliance with Art. IV of GATS and the truthfulness of the information on tourism distributed by governments (travel warning) and through GDS; the unbundling of travel distribution systems as a measure to counter vertical integration and conflicts of interest in travel agencies and the interconnection of CRS, through the portability of reservation numbers. Submitting GDS operations to effective multilateral disciplines and dispute-settlement mechanisms would have a substantial effect on trade and anti-competitive practices.

(d) *The implementation of an adequate framework for sustainable development of tourism.* Provisions on cooperation for the sustainable development of tourism are needed in recognition of the role of tourism in economic development; its need for infrastructure and development assistance; equitable trading conditions for economic sustainability; the relevance of enforcing internationally-recognized environmental and quality standards; the need for cooperation at all levels; and the importance of providing information on technologies required for competitive provision, regulation and sustainable development of tourism and all related-activities.

(e) *To preserve the environmental sustainability of tourism and the cultural heritage.* Guiding principles for national policies and trade commitments to preserve the ecological systems, the biodiversity, cultural patrimony and traditions.

Issues for Consideration by Developing Countries in Negotiating Specific Commitments in Tourism

The liberalization under the GATS 2000 will be determined on one hand, by the level of removal of barriers in the revised horizontal commitments (which affect all sectors) and on the other, the lifting of conditions and limitations applied to each sector at sector-specific level and in the four modes of supply. Accordingly the consistency between the two types of commitment is an important issue to be addressed by developing countries, seeking to obtain commercially meaningful commitments at specific sectoral level.

Improvement of Horizontal Commitments

In preparation of their positions in services negotiations, developing countries must assess to what extent the horizontal commitments of developed countries impede the liberalization of tourism and travel and related services. The major limitation in the horizontal commitments is in the lack of significant trading opportunities in mode 4, i.e. temporary movement of natural persons, since practically no commitments in this mode were made in specific services sectors. The temporary presence of natural persons in all services sectors is undermined by the recurrence at the horizontal level to the economic needs tests, nationality and/ or residence requirement and cumbersome administrative and visa procedures to be met by foreign nationals as services providers. The existing horizontal commitments by developed countries mainly refer to limitations for the establishment of the commercial presence (mode 3) by foreign providers to carry out the commercial operations.

Specific Tourism Sector Commitments

Majority of tourism originating countries are developed countries, which have undertaking commitment to liberalize fully or partially the supply of services in different tourism subsectors and modes of supply. Still, *the impact of commitments in commercial presence* in term of market value is nullified by restrictions to the commercial presence of foreign tour operators, travel agencies, restaurants and hotels, which are not listed there. Also, the movement of natural persons engaged in the tourism supply of different services is precluded by limited horizontal commitments and the lack of specific sectoral commitments. For instance in many Members States of the EU the commercial presence of foreign tour operators from the third countries is precluded or allowed only in association with already established national firms therein. Similarly, foreigners are precluded from undertaking of the business operations in the restaurant sub-sector even for those specializing in typical national food from other countries. In addition, the level of restrictions on commercial presence is aggravated by the possibility of recourse to the economic needs test, cumbersome and discriminatory licensing requirements that foreign suppliers of tourism services must meet.

Temporary Presence of Natural Persons as Consumers and Providers of Services

It should be underlined that although the existing commitments on market access on *consumption abroad have no limitations* in the case of majority of the GATS commitments, including in the top originating countries; in real terms the freedom of movement for consumption abroad is restricted by the level of binding in other modes of supply, in particular the commercial presence of foreign suppliers in the tourism originating markets. The movement of consumers in most of the top originating markets of tourism is captive, because the existing level of binding of commercial presence consolidates the absolute advantage of the dominant mega-tour operators and other national suppliers including the travel agencies, since the exclusive right of selling directly to travellers of holiday packages in their own markets has been consolidated in the existing commitments on commercial presence. Moreover, under such commercial conditions, the consumers' choices are limited by the offers of holiday package by dominant tour operators, but not only them, also by the opportunities for suppliers from destination countries to reach consumer in the originating markets directly. In addition, the consumers' choices in these markets are restricted by unfair practices in the management of information systems and the "racking policies" by travel agencies, which are usually integrated with mega-tour operators.

To improve horizontal commitments on mode 4, developed countries should remove the application of the economic needs test with respect to the movement of professionals supplying tourism services. Not all the professions and occupations are equally important to the movement of persons in the context of trade in tourism services. For example, the possibility to have the waiver from the application economic needs test should be provided to individual tourism services suppliers involved in catering, maintenance services or in such areas where cultural affinities and close contacts with tourists may contribute to the quality of the services provided. To the extent that the remaining occupations would remain subject to the application of economic needs tests, efforts should be made to reduce the scope for arbitrary and discriminatory practices, provide greater transparency and introduce more neutral economic criteria.

The issue of transparency in respect of the application of the GATS commitments is crucial as a tool in promoting trade in tourism services. In that respect, commitments in mode 4 are closely linked to the implementation of the relevant immigration regulations, policies and procedures in a clear and transparent manner. Publishing of the legislation and implementing regulations which significantly affect ability of the foreign nationals or permanent residents move across borders to supply services is a general obligation, since this is the way to limit the room for discretionary and procedural rules. The lack of transparency, clarity in the existence, implementation and application of policy guidelines affecting application for and consideration of temporary work permits, residency requirements of visas impede market access, effectively violating key GATS provision.

While tourism is a key export for most developing countries, it is particularly important for Least Developed Countries (LDCs) and Small Island Developing States (SIDS). For more than half of SIDS, tourism receipts represent between one to three quarters of their total export revenues. For the 49 LDCs taken as a group, tourism is the first source of foreign exchange earnings and seven of them critically depend on it for revenues.

Yet, LDCs accounted for less than 1% of international tourist arrivals and less than 0.5% of international tourism receipts in 2001. The value-added of trade in tourism (measured by spent income per tourist arrival) has declined sharply in some developing regions, e.g. in the Middle East, and in several African and Asian countries.

The Forum will examine lessons learned from existing experiences on the liberalization of tourism to support export competitiveness. That includes implementation of policies to ensure spill over effects from tourism on local communities and poverty reduction. It will consider, among other things, models and schemes to develop market intelligence, areas for increased South-South tourism trade flows and possible cooperation in infrastructure-related projects.

Why Tourism is Important for Developing Countries

Tourism is probably the only services sector that provides concrete trading opportunities for all nations, regardless of their level of development. In many developing countries, tourism makes a greater contribution to foreign earnings than such other major exports as textile and clothing or agriculture, without encountering the same magnitude of trade barriers.

Trade in tourism services and tourism activities in general have the potential to become an engine for growth and economic development. Tourism can also be a driving force in efforts to combat poverty, which is one of the central objectives of the UN Millennium Development Goals.

But it is also a highly vulnerable economic activity affected by several risk factors, including global events related to international politics, health-related problems and climate changes. Creating a coherent developmental framework for trade in tourism services is a crucial issue, particularly for countries with high economic dependence on tourism. Promoting the industry's sustainability and preventing environmental degrading is also important.

A major challenge for developing countries is the growing control of a few global tourism operators and travel distribution networks over many aspects of world tourism, including organized travel, international booking, marketing and sales of tourism and related activities. This concentration of power reduces the benefits that developing countries can reap from the liberalization and expansion in world tourism.

Since the operators are based in developed countries, their anti-competitive behaviour is difficult to prevent in the absence of a legal framework governing competition and multilateral disciplines on cross-border restrictive business practices.

E-Tourism in Developing Countries: more Links, Fewer Leaks

Since 1994, the number of tourists visiting Cambodia, one of the poorest countries in the world, has multiplied six-fold, reaching the one million mark in 2004. Tourism is one of the country's leading economic sectors and was expected to generate 7.3% of gross domestic product (GDP) in 2004 and close to 400,000 jobs.

Cambodia is not an isolated case: tourism is a key sector in many of the least developed countries (LDCs), a grouping officially recognized by the United Nations in 1971. Still, their overall share in international tourism is small, accounting for less than 1% of global tourism receipts.

Over the last few years, information and communication technologies (ICT) have had a growing impact on tourism promotion, marketing and sales. With the advent of new forms of ICT, a novel type of tourism, e-tourism, has emerged that is radically transforming the international tourism industry. More and more people now prefer to search for information on tourism destinations and offers on the Internet.

But in most cases it is not developing countries that benefit from new tourism opportunities.

World tourism is mostly concentrated in a handful of rich countries, which both run the business and reap the benefits. Most information on tourism opportunities in developing countries is generated, updated and marketed online by major international service providers based in developed countries. With their obvious technological advantage, these providers carry out most of the sales transactions and absorb a large share of the profits. In African LDCs, up to 85% of total profits from the tourism industry are repatriated to developed countries. The situation is not much better in the Caribbean (80%) or Asia (70% in Thailand and 40% in India).

What can be done to reverse this trend? One solution is for developing countries to take advantage of the new opportunities offered by ICT to brand and promote their own tourism industry. Unlimited and low-cost access to world markets and information and trade networks is essential. To achieve this would require wider involvement of local small and medium-sized tourism enterprises in global ICT networks as well as innovative national ICT policies for the sector. But the challenge is worth it: e-tourism could help developing countries exploit the untapped development opportunities tourism offers and, if set up efficiently, could give them better control of their own tourism industry.

UNCTAD launched the E-Tourism Initiative at UNCTAD XI – the organization's eleventh ministerial conference – in Sao Paulo, Brazil, in June 2004.

Why? To enable developing countries to benefit more from international tourism and reduce their dependence on developed-country tour operators and markets.

It seeks to:

- Organize the local tourism industry, public and private, by creating an Internet-based network for the tourism sector to find information, book online and set up partnerships.
- Encourage local small and medium-sized enterprises and national tourist offices to market their destinations and access clients directly.
- Reduce the repatriation of tourist earnings – the so-called leakages. How? The Initiative is structured around three elements: a tool, a method and partnerships.
- *The tool:* A website generator that makes it possible to replicate e-tourism websites in different countries. By providing general information on the country and local information on tourism services, these local websites, or "e-marketplaces", will help to brand and promote tourism online. The contents of the websites are based on business plans tailored to market demand and to the countries' needs and development strategies. The sites are managed locally by public-private partnerships.
- *The method:* Training and guidelines to help countries identify information on the tourism industry, standardize it and post it on the Internet. Appropriate training and generic guides provide full directions for using the "e-marketplace".
- *Partnerships:* To build up business relations, the different sectors of the country's tourism industry (hotels, restaurants, travel agents, airlines) are responsible for their

part of the business plan. This kind of cooperation will help developing countries to improve their tourism products, launch new ones, build on their human resources and adopt state-of-the-art information technologies.

Adventure Tourism in India

India, a vast land of distinct topographical features like high mountainous regions, barren desert areas, verdant valleys, turquoise sea etc. Amalgamation of all these geographical features has made India an incredible land of natural beauties.

To exhibits all these treasures troves of nature to its guests, Indian government has started various forms of tourism within its territory. One of such forms of tourism is adventure tourism, which is still in its infancy in India.

Gradually, adventure tourism is catching up the pace and Indian government is working hard to make India, one of the best adventure tourism destinations in world.

What is Adventure Tourism?

Adventure tourism is a form of tourism that involves exploration or travel to remote or exotic areas. This form of tourism enables the tourist or adventure seekers to engage themselves in various kinds of outdoor recreational activities, which are provided to them on fee-for-service basis, with a focus on experiences associated with the natural environment.

Adventure tourism bring the tourists close to the nature, due to which it is also known as nature-based tourism.

Adventure Tourism Zones In India

India is a unique land having varied geographical features in its kitty. All these distinct features are available in various regions that are the best site for adventure tourism in India. The snow-capped mountainous region of Great Himalayas are an ideal zone for adventure tourism in our country. Jammu and Kashmir, Himachal Pradesh, Uttaranchal, Sikkim, Upper fringes of West Bengal, are all part of Himalayan mountainous region that are the finest zones of adventure tourism.

Apart from Himalayas, Goan beaches, desert area of Rajasthan, Western ghats and Eastern ghats of South India, and various wildlife sanctuaries and national parks are the excellent zones for adventure tourism in India.

Adventure Tourism Destinations in India

India has plentiful of adventure tourism destinations. Some of the popular destinations that are brim with adventure enthusiasts throughout the year such as Leh-Ladakh, Zanskar Valley, Kargil and Suru valley, Manali and Kullu valley, Lahual and Spiti valley, Dharamshala and Kangra valley, Chamba valley, Kinnaur and Sangla valley, Rishikesh, Garhwal and Kumaon valley, Darjeeling.

Even some wildlife sanctuaries and national parks such as Jim Corbett National Park, Gir National Park, Ranthambore National Park, Kaziranga National Park which are popular among the tourists for wildlife safaris and nature walks.

Adventure Activities in India

India has vast range of adventure activities which are attracting loads of vacationers and adventure seekers. Some of the best known adventure sorts of India are trekking, mountaineering, rock climbing, cycling, skiing, heli-skiing, para gliding, hangliding, river rafting. These exciting sports can be done at mountainous region of Himalayas, Sahyadri range of Western ghats etc.

Some other thrilling adventure sports are scuba diving, swimming, surfing which can be done at the vast azure Arabian sea and Bay of Bengal. Goa, a tiny coastal land which is famed for various kinds of water sports. Beside these you can also indulge yourself in some other adventure sports like desert safari, wildlife safari, elephant safari, jeep safari, nature walks at various wildlife sanctuaries and national parks of India.

A Planning Framework for Tourism

Principles of the Planning System

Tourism is an important industry. Its future development will be secured by tourism developers engaging with the planning process and by those operating the planning system recognising that importance. This section sets out the principles of the English planning system which governs all forms of development including planning for tourism.

Sustainable development is the core principle underpinning planning. At the heart of sustainable development is the simple idea of ensuring a better quality of life for everyone, now and for future generations. The planning process provides the opportunity to help to make new development more sustainable, both through the preparation of development plans and when decisions are taken on specific schemes. The outcomes should be developments which:

- provide well-designed, safe and accessible development, and create new opportunities that will improve the well being of individuals and the regeneration of communities;
- result in the more efficient use of land and bring forward sufficient land to meet a wide range of expected needs;
- provide a supportive framework for economic growth and successful business;
- create vibrant, vital and viable town centres;
- reduce the need to travel; and
- protect and enhance the natural and built environment and safeguard natural resources.

Plan-Led System

The planning system in England aims to realise these objectives of sustainable development through a 'plan-led' system of development plans prepared by regional planning bodies and local planning authorities. These plans lead the subsequent development by setting a framework which helps to provide both an overall strategy for that development and policies for the determination of individual development proposals. Where these plans contain relevant policies, applications for planning permission should be determined in line with the plan unless material considerations indicate otherwise. These plans have a number of key characteristics:

- they provide developers, businesses and communities with certainty and predictability about future development in an area;
- they are transparent so that users can readily understand them and the information and assumptions upon which they are based;
- they are flexible so that they can be adjusted to meet changing circumstances and priorities. Planning authorities must ensure that plans are kept up to date and report annually on how their plan's policies are being achieved; and
- they are drawn up with community involvement and present a shared vision and strategy of how the area

should develop to achieve more sustainable patterns of development.

Development plans should reflect and build upon the Government's statements of national planning policies.

The development plans prepared by regional planning bodies and local planning authorities are known respectively as regional spatial strategies (RSS) and local development frameworks (LDFs). Planning policy statement 11 (PPS11) provides advice on the preparation of RSS and planning policy statement 12 (PPS12) provides advice on the preparation of LDFs.

The preparation of RSS is a statutory requirement. They:

- provide a broad development strategy for the region for a fifteen to twenty year period;
- should contribute to the achievement of sustainable development;
- are locationally, but not site, specific;
- are focused on delivery mechanisms which make clear what is to be done by whom and when;
- should be well integrated with other regional strategies, including any regional tourism strategy;
- should address sub-regional issues where appropriate; and
- provide a spatial framework to inform the preparation of LDF documents, local transport plans and regional and sub-regional strategies and programmes that have a bearing on land use activities.

Local development frameworks should be:

- based on a clear understanding of the economic, social and environmental needs of the area;
- clear, succinct and easily understood by all;
- underpinned by a comprehensive and credible evidence base; and
- front-loaded', seeking consensus on issues and taking key decisions early in the process.

Development plans are expected to take a spatial planning approach which integrates land use policies with other policies and programmes. The aim should be to co-ordinate spatial plans with urban and rural regeneration strategies, regional economic and housing strategies, community strategies and local transport plans. Wherever possible, spatial plans should be consistent with these other strategies (including any strategies for or relating to tourism) and be drawn up in collaboration with those responsible for them.

Development plans should have a clear vision about the pattern of development they are seeking to achieve in the area and clear objectives for achieving it.

These should reflect the needs and problems of the communities in that area. They should be concerned not just with what can be built where and in what circumstances but also how the range of social, economic and environmental objectives will be achieved through plan policies. The plans should focus on outcomes, with specified indicators so that the progress made by the policies in meeting these desired outcomes can be measured. Developing Tourism through Strategies and Plans

Regional Spatial Strategies (RSS)

At the regional level, regional planning bodies will need to decide how to deal with tourism in their RSS. Specifically they will have to decide whether:

- to treat tourism as an issue in itself;
- to subsume it within another issue such as economic development; or
- to deal with it as a consideration affecting a number of issues like the economy, the environment, regeneration and transport.

They should do this on the basis of the overall approach that they are taking in their RSS and in the light of the information they have gathered.

Whatever the chosen approach, the RSS should make clear:

- its vision and strategy for tourism in the region;
- how this contributes to broader regional objectives;
- what level of growth in tourism it is trying to achieve; and
- what the spatial characteristics of this will be.

Where the regional development agencies (RDAs) have produced Regional Tourism or Visitor Economy Strategies, the RSS should draw on these as well as providing a context when such strategies are reviewed. They provide greater detail than the

Regional Economic Strategies and may have specific spatial or locational dimensions. The West Midlands Visitor Economy Strategy contains the following vision for the future of tourism in the region, and an important context for RSS review.

The RSS should also make clear what the key tourism characteristics are and how these are expected to change during the period of the strategy. This should cover:

- what the scale and distribution of tourist activity within the area is and what it is likely to be. The strategy needs to be clear what degree of change it is seeking to oversee, what the nature of that change will be and where it will occur;
- likely future trends and change in volume, distribution and type of activity. There needs to be an understanding of what the underlying trends are and how the strategy intends to respond to the opportunities which they present;
- what the implications of those trends are for land-use, traffic flows, and the transport system. It should explain the extent to which these trends are (i) dependent upon improvements to the transport network and (ii) where they are likely to increase the need for such improvements;
- identification of areas within the region where there are, or are likely to be, any problems associated with growth or decline in tourism. For example, it might be necessary to reconcile demand for tourist accommodation with the need for affordable housing within an area;
- how increased demand for tourism might be best accommodated. It might be that the provision of accommodation and attractions should be increased in towns adjoining existing resorts in order to spread the benefits and to diffuse pressures;
- environmental impacts of tourism and, where these have adverse effects, how they can be tackled;
- the need to protect key tourism assets. In addition to features that already have statutory protection (eg national parks), there will be other features such as the wider environment, the quality of beaches, choice of accommodation, availability of sports and leisure facilities and the presence of 'night life' that are important in sustaining the attractiveness of the area; and

- ways in which tourism can contribute positively to other objectives eg economic development, regeneration, rural diversification, conservation, and environmental improvements.

Local Development Frameworks (LDFS)

LDFs should comprise a number of development plan documents including the core strategy, site specific allocations of land and area action plans. Any need for further development plan documents, or supplementary planning documents, should be identified in the local development scheme, the purpose of which is to inform the public of the planning authority's programme for the production of local development documents. In a similar way to regional planning bodies, those preparing LDFs will need to decide how to deal with tourism issues within the framework. Like RSS, the approach should seek to produce a plan which is integrated with other strategies that have been prepared for the area, including any that relate to the future of tourism.

In those locations where the future development of tourism is a key issue for the local authority, it will be appropriate for the core strategy to cover tourism issues together with any objectives relevant to tourism. In other local authorities it may be that the plan's broad approach to economic growth and regeneration sets the framework for the future development of tourism. In these cases this relationship should be acknowledged and taken into account in the development of the core strategy.

Those preparing LDFs should consider whether any policies for tourism are needed beyond what is set out in the core strategy. In determining the scope of the work required and what planning documents should be prepared, it will again be necessary first to decide whether tourism is to be addressed as a single issue or as part of a wider topic, such as economic growth.

Where site allocations for tourism are made, these should follow from the objectives set out in the core strategy. In some areas in which tourism and its growth are a key part of the spatial strategy, it may be appropriate to depict this in spatial terms in the core strategy such as in a key diagram. In specific locations where development for tourism is particularly crucial to meeting the plan's objectives, the core strategy could propose an area action plan to focus and programme the elements of that development.

In order to keep policies to a manageable number, authorities should aim to support the policies affecting tourism in the core strategy in the following ways:

- putting detail on matters such as mitigating the effects of development (e.g. by landscaping) into supplementary planning documents;
- putting good practice messages in other documents or in supporting text; and
- not repeating national or regional policies in LDFs, although LDFs should indicate how the objectives and any targets for tourism contribute to those set out in the RSS.

Where tourism is an important element of a LDF, the approach will need to be based upon a robust understanding of the characteristics of, and trends within, the tourism industry based on similar issues to those set out in RSS. Bournemouth offers an example of where such an analysis of trends has occurred. This has provided the basis for the planned approach of diversifying tourism facilities at an important tourism destination whilst at the same time retaining the essential tourist accommodation. Although this was done through its preparation of its Local Plan and Supplementary Planning Guidance under the previous system of development plans, the approach in terms of analysis and response would be equally applicable to a LDF approach.

Devising Good Tourism Policies

General Principles

The strategy for tourism in the emerging development plan will provide the context for producing any specific policies for tourism. Whilst policies need to be developed to suit the particular circumstances of an area, there will be certain common features of a good tourism policy. Where specific tourism policies are included in a plan, they should aim to:

- maximise the benefits of tourism, in particular ensuring that the development is able to reach its potential to contribute to tourism in the area and for local communities to enjoy those benefits;
- identify optimal locations, for example to maximise synergies with other tourist attractions and to promote opportunities for access by public transport;

- integrate development with its surroundings both in terms of design and layout and in the way that the service or facility is able to function; and
- avoid adverse impacts, for example by disturbance to activities on adjacent land.

Planners will need to understand and often reconcile a number of important factors when preparing such policies, in particular:

- market demand – sometimes market demand will exist in a very precise location. This might be to do with prominence or accessibility. In other cases the demand will be of approximately the same level throughout a wide area;
- environmental impact – this can have a large number of facets, such as visual and noise impact, impacts on an historic setting, impact upon.

Bournemouth Local Plan and Supplementary Planning Guidance

Bournemouth Local Plan, adopted 2002 and Supplementary Planning Guidance (SPG) on Tourism, adopted in 2004 both emphasise the need to diversify tourism facilities. This need manifested itself in particular through the continued loss of hotels despite planning policies aimed at retention. In its analysis, the Plan has noted that Bournemouth's popularity as a prime holiday destination has been offset by other markets opening up, such as short breaks, activity holidays and business and conference tourism.

The Local Plan has recognised the need to respond to this and for the seaside resort to serve a variety of functions and widen its economic base as a shopping and commercial centre. In response to this, the plan contains policies for the defined Town Centre Tourism Area and Tourism Core Areas as the hub of tourism facilities containing major tourism related facilities such as theatres, cinemas, night clubs, shops and restaurants, the Gardens, Pier and beach; Bournemouth International Centre; and hotels, guest houses and blocks of self catering accommodation.

Biodiversity and upon landscape quality. Impacts may be positive, negative or a mix of both;

- transport and accessibility – travel is an inherent element of tourism. Whilst recognising that it is a principle of the planning system to seek to promote more sustainable transport choices, improve accessibility and reduce the need to travel, this may be particularly difficult for some types of tourism projects or for areas that are poorly served by public transport;

- functional links – whilst some forms of tourism may, in commercial terms, be able to be directed to a variety of locations (e.g. a hotel) others will be much more specific in their land use requirements (e.g. a visitor centre for a cathedral);
- regeneration benefits – tourism developments have the potential to bring jobs to an area, to improve physical appearance and to support local businesses and services. Plans to bring tourism into an area will often be developed in order to realise some of these advantages; and
- labour supply – the amount and quality of the labour supply will vary from place to place. Planning will often seek to locate new development where the need for jobs exist or where the population might benefit from a wider range and quality of employment.

The importance of these factors may vary for different developments and over time.

Tourists visit different areas for different reasons and to enjoy different experiences. It follows that the built infrastructure required for tourism will therefore vary from area to area. Tourism is certainly not a 'one-size fits all' product. In particular, different approaches may be needed in urban areas from those in rural areas.

Tourism in Urban Areas

Tourism can bring benefits to urban areas and help to deliver development that is sustainable. Amongst the particular advantages that tourism can bring to towns and cities is to:

- be the focus of regeneration, or help to underpin it;
- help to increase urban vitality and support linked trips;
- be a key ingredient of mixed-use schemes;
- support important services and facilities; and
- facilitate improved access by sustainable modes of transport.

A Planning Framework for Tourism

There are many types of tourist and leisure activities that particularly lend themselves to urban locations and which exhibit these advantages. These include:

- hotel, guest house and bed & breakfast accommodation;
- cinemas, theatres and concert and bingo clubs;
- museums, galleries and conference facilities;
- restaurants, bars, pubs, casinos and night clubs; and
- indoor and ten-pin bowling and health & fitness centres.

Planning authorities need to ensure that they have assessed the need for these facilities and have allocated an appropriate range of sites which allow genuine choices to meet those needs. Similarly, it is for developers and operators to ensure that they have anticipated what their need for such sites is likely to be and that they undertake active discussions with local planning authorities about these requirements.

An example of how planning authorities have worked with the industry to assess and meet demand is provided by Portsmouth City Council. It has recently approached the issue of hotel provision by establishing the need for hotels and then identifying sites through the development plan that could help to meet those needs.

Tourism in Rural Areas

The provision of essential facilities for visitors is vital for the development of the tourism in rural areas. Tourism can:

- be a key element in rural and farm diversification;
- help to revitalise market towns and villages;
- support important rural services and facilities; and
- underwrite environmental schemes and improvements to the built and natural environment.

RSS and LDF policies should therefore engender a positive approach to rural tourism proposals, applying the following principles:

- Wherever possible, tourist and visitor facilities should be housed in existing or replacement buildings, particularly where they are located outside existing settlements.
- In statutorily designated areas they should seek to conserve and enhance the qualities and features that justified the designation.

- Large-scale tourist proposals must be assessed against the whole range of sustainable development objectives. This includes not only their transport implications but also other sustainability considerations such as how they assist rural regeneration and the well being of communities.

Planning Policy Statement 7 (PPS7) : Sustainable Development in Rural Areas sets out specific national planning policies on tourism and leisure in rural areas.

How to Plan for Tourism

To ensure that their development plans are effective for future development of tourism and thereby provide a framework to make sound planning decisions on tourism proposals, planning authorities should:

- develop and maintain a thorough dialogue with representatives of the tourism industry;
- ensure that this dialogue helps to support a sound data base on the characteristics and needs of tourism in the area; and
- use that data in applying effective techniques designed to ensure that those needs are met as fully as possible.

Involving Stakeholders

It is likely that a large number of groups and individuals will be affected by strategies and proposals for tourism in a particular area. Planners will need to ensure that they have:

- adequately canvassed and considered all of these views;
- in particular, received and understood the views of the community affected and those with a commercial interest in what is proposed; and
- done this at the earliest possible time, in accordance with the principle of 'front-loading' that is an element of the new development plan process.

8

Environmental Impacts of Tourism

The quality of the environment, both natural and man-made, is essential to tourism. However, tourism's relationship with the environment is complex. It involves many activities that can have adverse environmental effects. Many of these impacts are linked with the construction of general infrastructure such as roads and airports, and of tourism facilities, including resorts, hotels, restaurants, shops, golf courses and marinas. The negative impacts of tourism development can gradually destroy the environmental resources on which it depends.

On the other hand, tourism has the potential to create beneficial effects on the environment by contributing to environmental protection and conservation. It is a way to raise awareness of environmental values and it can serve as a tool to finance protection of natural areas and increase their economic importance.

Three main impact areas: natural resources, pollution, and physical impacts

Three Main Impact Areas: Natural Resources, Pollution, and Physical Impacts

Tourism's Three Main Impact Areas

Negative impacts from tourism occur when the level of visitor use is greater than the environment's ability to cope with this use within the acceptable limits of change. Uncontrolled conventional tourism poses potential threats to many natural areas around the world. It can put enormous pressure on an area and lead to impacts such as soil erosion, increased pollution, discharges into the sea, natural habitat loss, increased pressure on endangered species and heightened vulnerability to forest fires. It often puts a strain on water resources, and it can force local populations to compete for the use of critical resources.

Depletion of Natural Resources

Tourism development can put pressure on natural resources when it increases consumption in areas where resources are already scarce.

Water Resources

Water, and especially fresh water, is one of the most critical natural resources. The tourism industry generally overuses water resources for hotels, swimming pools, golf courses and personal use of water by tourists. This can result in water shortages and degradation of water supplies, as well as generating a greater volume of waste water.. In dryer regions like the Mediterranean, the issue of water scarcity is of particular concern. Because of the hot climate and the tendency of tourists to consume more water when on holiday than they do at home, the amount used can run up to 440 liters a day. This is almost double what the inhabitants of an average Spanish city use.

Golf course maintenance can also deplete fresh water resources. In recent years golf tourism has increased in popularity and the number of golf courses has grown rapidly. Golf courses require an enormous amount of water every day and, as with other causes of excessive extraction of water, this can result in water scarcity. If the water comes from wells, overpumping can cause saline intrusion into groundwater. Golf resorts are more and more often situated in or near protected areas or areas where resources are limited, exacerbating their impacts.

Local Resources

Tourism can create great pressure on local resources like energy, food, and other raw materials that may already be in short supply. Greater extraction and transport of these resources exacerbates the physical impacts associated with their exploitation. Because of the seasonal character of the industry, many destinations have ten times more inhabitants in the high season as in the low season. A high demand is placed upon these resources to meet the high expectations tourists often have (proper heating, hot water, etc.).

Land Degradation

Important land resources include minerals, fossil fuels, fertile soil, forests, wetland and wildlife. Increased construction of tourism and recreational facilities has increased the pressure on these resources and on scenic landscapes. Direct impact on natural resources, both renewable and nonrenewable, in the provision of tourist facilities can be caused by the use of land for accommodation and other infrastructure provision, and the use of building materials.

Forests often suffer negative impacts of tourism in the form of deforestation caused by fuel wood collection and land clearing. For example, one trekking tourist in Nepal-and area already suffering the effects of deforestation-can use four to five kilograms of wood a day.

Pollution

Tourism can cause the same forms of pollution as any other industry: air emissions, noise, solid waste and littering, releases of sewage, oil and chemicals, even architectural/visuaı pollution.

Air Pollution and Noise

Transport by air, road, and rail is continuously increasing in response to the rising numbe reported that the number of international air passengers worldwide rose from 88 million in 1972 to 344 million in 1994. One consequence of this increase in air transport is that tourism now accounts for more than 60% of air travel and is therefore responsible for an important share of air emissions. One study estimated that a single transatlantic return flight emits almost half the CO2 emissions produced by all other sources (lighting, heating, car use, etc.) consumed by an average person yearly.

Transport emissions and emissions from energy production and use are linked to acid rain, global warming and photochemical pollution. Air pollution from tourist transportation has impacts on the global level, especially from carbon dioxide (CO2) emissions related to transportation energy use. And it can contribute to severe local air pollution. Some of these impacts are quite specific to tourist activities. For example, especially in very hot or cold countries, tour buses often leave their motors running for hours while the tourists go out for an excursion because they want to return to a comfortably air-conditioned bus.

Noise pollution from airplanes, cars, and buses, as well as recreational vehicles such as snowmobiles and jet skis, is an ever-growing problem of modern life. In addition to causing annoyance, stress, and even hearing loss for it humans, it causes distress to wildlife, especially in sensitive areas. For instance, noise generated by snowmobiles can cause animals to alter their natural activity patterns.

Solid Waste and Littering

In areas with high concentrations of tourist activities and appealing natural attractions, waste disposal is a serious problem and improper disposal can be a major despoiler of the natural environment-rivers, scenic areas, and roadsides. For example, cruise ships in the Caribbean are estimated to produce more than 70,000 tons of waste each year. Today some cruise lines are actively working to reduce waste-related impacts. Solid waste and littering can degrade the physical appearance of the water and shoreline and cause the death of marine animals.

In mountain areas, trekking tourists generate a great deal of waste. Tourists on expedition leave behind their garbage, oxygen cylinders and even camping equipment. Such practices degrade the environment with all the detritus typical of the developed world, in remote areas that have few garbage collection or disposal facilities. Some trails in the Peruvian Andes and in Nepal frequently visited by tourists have been nicknamed "Coca-Cola trail" and "Toilet paper trail".

Sewage

Construction of hotels, recreation and other facilities often leads to increased sewage pollution. Wastewater has polluted seas and lakes surrounding tourist attractions, damaging the flora and fauna. Sewage runoff causes serious damage to coral reefs because it stimulates the growth of algae, which cover the filter-feeding corals, hindering their ability to survive. Changes in salinity and siltation can have wide-ranging impacts on coastal environments. And sewage pollution can threaten the health of humans and animals.

Aesthetic Pollution

Often tourism fails to integrate its structures with the natural features and indigenous architectural of the destination. Large, dominating resorts of disparate design can look out of place in any natural environment and may clash with the indigenous structural design.

A lack of land-use planning and building regulations in many destinations has facilitated sprawling developments along coastlines, valleys and scenic routes. The sprawl includes tourism facilities themselves and supporting infrastructure such as roads, employee housing, parking, service areas, and waste disposal.

Physical Impacts

Attractive landscape sites, such as sandy beaches, lakes, riversides, and mountain tops and slopes, are often transitional zones, characterized by species-rich ecosystems. Typical physical impacts include the degradation of such ecosystems.

An ecosystem is a geographic area including all the living organisms (people, plants, animals, and microorganisms), their physical surroundings (such as soil, water, and air), and the natural cycles that sustain them. The ecosystems most threatened with degradation are ecologically fragile areas such as alpine regions, rain forests, wetlands, mangroves, coral reefs and sea grass beds. The threats to and pressures on these ecosystems are often severe because such places are very attractive to both tourists and developers.

Physical impacts are caused not only by tourism-related land clearing and construction, but by continuing tourist activities and long-term changes in local economies and ecologies.

Physical Impacts of Tourism Development

Construction Activities and Infrastructure Development

The development of tourism facilities such as accommodation, water supplies, restaurants and recreation facilities can involve sand mining, beach and sand dune erosion, soil erosion and extensive paving. In addition, road and airport construction can lead to land degradation and loss of wildlife habitats and deterioration of scenery.

In Yosemite National Park (US), for instance, the number of roads and facilities have been increased to keep pace with the growing visitor numbers and to supply amenities, infrastructure and parking lots for all these tourists. These actions have caused habitat loss in the park and are accompanied by various forms of pollution including air pollution from automobile emissions; the

Sierra Club has reported "smog so thick that Yosemite Valley could not be seen from airplanes". This occasional smog is harmful to all species and vegetation inside the Park.

Deforestation and Intensified or Unsustainable Use of Land

Construction of ski resort accommodation and facilities frequently requires clearing forested land. Coastal wetlands are often drained and filled due to lack of more suitable sites for construction of tourism facilities and infrastructure. These activities can cause severe disturbance and erosion of the local ecosystem, even destruction in the long term.

Marina Development

Development of marinas and breakwaters can cause changes in currents and coastlines. Furthermore, extraction of building materials such as sand affects coral reefs, mangroves, and hinterland forests, leading to erosion and destruction of habitats. In the Philippines and the Maldives, dynamiting and mining of coral for resort building materials has damaged fragile coral reefs and depleted the fisheries that sustain local people and attract tourists.

Overbuilding and extensive paving of shorelines can result in destruction of habitats and disruption of land-sea connections (such as sea-turtle nesting spots).

Coral reefs are especially fragile marine ecosystems and are suffering worldwide from reef-based tourism developments. Evidence suggests a variety of impacts to coral result from shoreline development, increased sediments in the water, trampling by tourists and divers, ship groundings, pollution from sewage, overfishing, and fishing with poisons and explosives that destroy coral habitat.

Physical Impacts from Tourist Activities

Anchoring and other Marine Activities

In marine areas (around coastal waters, reefs, beach and shoreline, offshore waters, uplands and lagoons) many tourist activities occur in or around fragile ecosystems. Anchoring, snorkeling, sport fishing and scuba diving, yachting, and cruising are some of the activities that can cause direct degradation of marine ecosystems such as coral reefs, and subsequent impacts on coastal protection and fisheries.

Trampling

Tourists using the same trail over and over again trample the vegetation and soil, eventually causing damage that can lead to loss of biodiversity and other impacts. Such damage can be even more extensive when visitors frequently stray off established trails.

Trampling Impacts on Vegetation	*Trampling Impacts on Soil*
Breakage and bruising of stems	Loss of organic matter
Reduced plant vigor	Reduction in soil macro porosity
Reduced regeneration	Decrease in air and water permeability
Loss of ground cover	Increase in run off
Change in species composition	Accelerated erosion

Source: University of Idaho

Alteration of Ecosystems by Tourist Activities

Habitat can be degraded by tourism leisure activities. For example, wildlife viewing can bring about stress for the animals and alter their natural behavior when tourists come too close. Safaris and wildlife watching activities have a degrading effect on habitat as they often are accompanied by the noise and commotion created by tourists as they chase wild animals in their trucks and aircraft.

This puts high pressure on animal habits and behaviors and tends to bring about behavioral changes. In some cases, as in Kenya, it has led to animals becoming so disturbed that at times they neglect their young or fail to mate.

Environmental Impacts at the Global Level

Loss of Biological Diversity

Biological diversity is the term given to the variety of life on Earth and the natural patterns it forms.

The effects of loss of biodiversity:

- It threatens our food supplies, opportunities for recreation and tourism, and sources of wood, medicines and energy.
- It interferes with essential ecological functions such as species balance, soil formation, and greenhouse gas absorption.

- It reduces the productivity of ecosystems, thereby shrinking nature's basket of goods and services, from which we constantly draw.
- It destabilizes ecosystems and weakens their ability to deal with natural disasters such as floods, droughts, and hurricanes, and with human-caused stresses, such as pollution and climate change.

Tourism, especially nature tourism, is closely linked to biodiversity and the attractions created by a rich and varied environment. It can also cause loss of biodiversity when land and resources are strained by excessive use, and when impacts on vegetation, wildlife, mountain, marine and coastal environments and water resources exceed the carrying capacity. This loss of biodiversity in fact means loss of tourism potential.

Introduction of Exotic Species

Tourists and suppliers-often unwittingly-can bring in species (insects, wild and cultivated plants and diseases) that are not native to the local environment and that can cause enormous disruption and even destruction of ecosystems.

Depletion of the Ozone Layer

The ozone layer, which is situated in the upper atmosphere (or stratosphere) at an altitude of 12-50 kilometers, protects life on earth by absorbing the harmful wavelengths of the sun's ultraviolet (UV) radiation, which in high doses is dangerous to humans and animals. For instance, one of the reasons scientists have put forward for the global decrease of amphibian populations is increased exposure to UV radiation.

Ozone depleting substances (ODSs) such as CFCs (chlorofluorocarbon) and halons have contributed to the destruction of this layer. The tourism industry may be part of the problem; direct impacts start with the construction of new developments and continue during daily management and operations.

Refrigerators, air conditioners and propellants in aerosol spray cans, amongst others, contain ODSs and are widely used in the hotel and tourism industry. Emissions from jet aircraft are also a significant source of ODSs. According to Tourism Concern, scientists predict that by 2015 half of the annual destruction of the ozone layer will be caused by air travel.

UNEP's OzonAction Programme works with governments and industries, including the tourism industry, to phase out ODSs and find safer alternatives. UNEP has developed extensive information and guidance on how many types of businesses can eliminate ODSs and contribute to preservation of the ozone layer. For further reading see the publication How the Hotel and Tourism Industry can Protect the Ozone Layer.

Climate Change

Climate scientists now generally agree that the Earth's surface temperatures have risen steadily in recent years because of an increase in the so-called greenhouse gases in the atmosphere, which trap heat from the sun. One of the most significant of these gases is carbon dioxide (CO2), which is generated when fossil fuels, such as coal, oil and natural gas are burned (e.g. in industry, electricity generation, and automobiles) and when there are changes in land use, such as deforestation. In the long run, the accumulation of CO2 and other greenhouse gases in the atmosphere can cause global climate change-a process that may already be occurring.

Global tourism is closely linked to climate change. Tourism involves the movement of people from their homes to other destinations and accounts for about 50% of traffic movements; rapidly expanding air traffic contributes about 2.5% of the production of CO2. Tourism is thus a significant contributor to the increasing concentrations of greenhouse gases in the atmosphere.

Air travel itself is a major contributor to the greenhouse effect. Passenger jets are the fastest growing source of greenhouse gas emissions. The number of international travellers is expected to increase from 594 million in 1996 to 1.6 billion by 2020, adding greatly to the problem unless steps are taken to reduce emissions.

For more information on the relationship between energy and the environment, see UNEP's Energy Programme, which provides information and publications on energy efficiency and alternative energy sources to reduce the environmental impacts of energy use and of transportation.

How Global Environmental Impacts Affect Tourism

Natural Disasters

Catastrophes like floods, earthquakes, wildfires, volcanoes, avalanches, drought and diseases can have a serious effect on inbound and domestic tourism and thus on local tourism industries. The outbreak of the foot and mouth disease epidemic in England earlier this year (2001), for instance, has severely affected Great Britain's inbound tourism market. A BHA/Barclays Hospitality Business Trends Survey found that 75% of hotels in England, 81% in Scotland and 85% in Wales continued to be affected by the foot and mouth outbreak, and over 60% forecast a decline in business in the June-September 2001 period.

Climate Change

Tourism not only contributes to climate change, but is affected by it as well. Climate change is likely to increase the severity and frequency of storms and severe weather events, which can have disastrous effects on tourism in the affected regions. Some of the other impacts that the world risks as a result of global warming are drought, diseases and heat waves.

These negative impacts can keep tourists away from the holiday destinations. Global warming may cause:

- Less snowfall at ski resorts, meaning a shorter skiing seasons in the Alpine region. In already hot areas like Asia and the Mediterranean, tourists will stay away because of immense heat, and out of fear of diseases and water shortages.
- Harm to vulnerable ecosystems such as rainforests and coral reefs because of rising temperatures and less rainfall. A major risk to coral reefs is bleaching, which occurs when coral is stressed by temperature increases, high or low levels of salinity, lower water quality, and an increase in suspended sediments. These conditions cause the zooxanthallae (the single-celled algae which forms the colours within the coral) to leave the coral. Without the algae, the coral appears white, or "bleached"-and rapidly dies. The Great Barrier Reef, which supports a US$ 640 million tourism industry, has been experiencing coral bleaching events for the last 20 years.
- Rising sea levels, the result of melting glaciers and polar ice. Higher sea levels will threaten coastal and marine areas with widespread floods in low-lying countries and island states, increasing the loss of coastal land. Beaches and islands that are major tourism attractions may be the first areas to be affected.

- Increased events of extreme weather, such as tornadoes, hurricanes and typhoons. These are already becoming more prevalent in tourist areas in the Caribbean and South East Asia. Hurricane Mitch in 1998, for instance, heavily affected tourism in the Caribbean. Wind damage, storm waves, heavy rains and flooding caused major losses in the local tourism sector.

Effects of Other Industries on Tourism

Impacts from other industries often have a more dramatic effect on the environment and can seriously affect tourism.

- Oil spills, like the oil tanker disaster that occurred off the Galapagos Islands (Ecuador) in January 2001, can cause severe short-term damage to tourist attractions. In that case, a freight ship loaded with 160,000 gallons of diesel fuel and 80,000 gallons of other petroleum products ran aground on the coast of San Cristobal and spilled nearly all of its load. Unique local marine and land species and the tourism potential of the area were badly affected.
- Agricultural runoff or industrial discharges can cause water pollution and may cause algae blooms like those that occurred in the Adriatic Sea in the early 1990s. In spite of improved control of sewage from tourism developments, the Mediterranean sea floor is increasingly carpeted with these quick-growing invaders, many rising 30 inches or more above anchoring runners. They appear equally adept at colonizing rock, mud, and sand in a virtually continuous swath that can extend from the beach out to a depth of about 150 feet, smothering coral reefs, fish and other sea flora and fauna in the process.
- Destructive practices such as blast fishing, fishing with poisonous chemicals like cyanide, and muroami netting (pounding reefs with weighted bags to scare fish out of crevices) directly destroy corals. They can also destroy a major draw for tourists.

How Tourism can Contribute to Environmental Conservation

- Direct financial contributions: Tourism can contribute directly to the conservation of sensitive areas and habitat. Revenue from park-entrance fees and similar sources can be allocated specifically to pay for the protection and management of environmentally sensitive areas. Special fees for park operations or conservation activities can be collected from tourists or tour operators.

- Contributions to government revenues: Some governments collect money in more far-reaching and indirect ways that are not linked to specific parks or conservation areas. User fees, income taxes, taxes on sales or rental of recreation equipment, and license fees for activities such as hunting and fishing can provide governments with the funds needed to manage natural resources. Such funds can be used for overall conservation programs and activities, such as park ranger salaries and park maintenance.

For Costa Rica, for example, tourism represents 72% of national monetary reserves, generates 140,000 jobs and produces 8.4% of the gross domestic product. The country has 25% of its territory classified under some category of conservation management. In 1999, protected areas welcomed 866,083 national and foreign tourists, who generated about US$ 2.5 million in admission fees and payment of services.

Improved Environmental Management and Planning

Sound environmental management of tourism facilities and especially hotels can increase the benefits to natural areas. But this requires careful planning for controlled development, based on analysis of the environmental resources of the area. Planning helps to make choices between conflicting uses, or to find ways to make them compatible. By planning early for tourism development, damaging and expensive mistakes can be prevented, avoiding the gradual deterioration of environmental assets significant to tourism.

Cleaner production techniques can be important tools for planning and operating tourism facilities in a way that minimizes their environmental impacts.

For example, green building (using energy-efficient and non-polluting construction materials, sewage systems and energy sources) is an increasingly important way for the tourism industry to decrease its impact on the environment. And because waste treatment and disposal are often major, long-term environmental problems in the tourism industry, pollution prevention and waste minimization techniques are especially important for the tourism industry. A guide to sources of information on cleaner production (free) is available here.

Environmental Awareness Raising

Tourism has the potential to increase public appreciation of the environment and to spread awareness of environmental problems when it brings people into closer contact with nature and the environment. This confrontation may heighten awareness of the value of nature and lead to environmentally conscious behavior and activities to preserve the environment. For instance, Honduran schoolchildren from the capital city of Tegucigalpa are routinely taken to visit La Tigra cloud forest visitor centre, funded in part by eco-tourist dollars, to learn about the intricacies of the rainforest.

If it is to be sustainable in the long run, tourism must incorporate the principles and practices of sustainable consumption. Sustainable consumption includes building consumer demand for products that have been made using cleaner production techniques, and for services-including tourism services-that are provided in a way that minimizes environmental impacts. The tourism industry can play a key role in providing environmental information and raising awareness among tourists of the environmental consequences of their actions. Tourists and tourism-related businesses consume an enormous quantity of goods and services; moving them toward using those that are produced and provided in an environmentally sustainable way, from cradle to grave, could have an enormous positive impact on the planet's environment.

Protection and Preservation

Tourism can significantly contribute to environmental protection, conservation and restoration of biological diversity and sustainable use of natural resources. Because of their attractiveness, pristine sites and natural areas are identified as valuable and the need to keep the attraction alive can lead to creation of national parks and wildlife parks.

In Hawaii, new laws and regulations have been enacted to preserve the Hawaiian rainforest and to protect native species. The coral reefs around the islands and the marine life that depend on them for survival are also protected. Hawaii now has become an international centre for research on ecological systems-and the promotion and preservation of the islands' tourism industry was the main motivation for these actions.

Grupo Punta Cana, a resort in the Dominican Republic, offers an example of how luxury tourism development and conservation can be combined. The high-end resort was established with the goal of catering to luxury-class tourists while respecting the natural habitat of Punta Cana. The developers have set aside 10,000 hectares (24,700 acres) of land as a nature reserve and native fruit tree garden. The Punta Cana Nature Reserve includes 11 fresh water springs surrounded by a subtropical forest where many species of unusual Caribbean flora and fauna live in their natural state. Guests can explore a "nature path" leading from the beach through mangroves, lagoons of fresh water springs and dozens of species of Caribbean bird and plant life. The Punta Cana Ecological Foundation has begun reforesting some parts of the reserve that had been stripped of their native mahogany and other trees in the past. Other environmentally protective policies have been put into effect at the resort, such as programs to protect the offshore barrier reefs and the recycling of wastewater for use in irrigating the grounds. The fairways of the resort's new golf course were planted with a hybrid grass that can be irrigated with sea water The grass also requires less than half the usual amounts of fertilizer and pesticides. The resort has also established a biodiversity laboratory run by Cornell University.

Tourism has had a positive effect on wildlife preservation and protection efforts, notably in Africa but also in South America, Asia, Australia, and the South Pacific. Numerous animal and plant species have already become extinct or may become extinct soon. Many countries have therefore established wildlife reserves and enacted strict laws protecting the animals that draw nature-loving tourists. As a result of these measures, several endangered species have begun to thrive again.

9

Tourism Research, Education and Training

Tourism and Hospitality SME Training needs and Provision: A Sub-Regional Analysis

There is now a significant and growing body of knowledge concerning small business and entrepreneurship in tourism and hospitality. It is often emphasised that this focus is justified by the fact that, in many areas, particularly resort and rural or peripheral areas, small, often family owned and operated firms, provide most of the services and attractions and are the foundation of destination competitiveness (Getz *et al.*, 2004).

The requirement for tourism destinations to deliver high-quality service and products, coupled with the labour intensive nature of the industry, results in a need for the tourism sector to recruit and retain well-educated and well-trained professionals. Indeed, as Government's have increasingly come to recognise the economic significance of tourism and hospitality there has emerged a growing emphasis on the need for workforce development and the provision of business support services (Thomas *et al.*, 2000). Within the UK, the Department for Culture Media and Sport (DCMS, 2004: 22) has stated thatIf the [tourism] industry is to deliver a truly high quality product, it must become the career of choice for more of our brightest and most ambitious people. If that is to happen, high quality training and development strategies are needed, covering the entire range of activities from 'hands on' skills to management, and addressing the needs of both the industry and individuals.

Yet in spite of the strategic priority being afforded to training and development initiatives, as manifested in the activities of agencies such as People 1st, Learndirect and Business Link, there has been little direct research into the precise nature of the skills development and workforce training needs of SMEs operating in the different subsectors of the visitor economy. The work that does exist, has only rarely considered the skills and training issues associated with SMEs operating in particular sub-regions or within specific localities. This represents a potential difficulty for those seeking to provide small business support services as an insight into the influence of such factors as geographic location and local economic conditions, business size and ownership profiles is likely to be crucial if local and regional development agencies are to intervene effectively to support the development of the industry.

This paper utilises some of the findings gathered for a research project that was completed in 2002 for the Telford and Shropshire Marketing Partnership (TSMP). The purpose of the research was to identify the recruitment, training and skills issues pertinent to Shropshire's tourism industry in order that this insight could then be used to inform training policy in the county. As such, the research was not intentionally small firm specific but, in common with many predominantly rural destinations, Shropshire's tourism industry is dominated by small firms and 95 percent of the final sample was comprised of small (20 percent) or micro (75 percent) firms as defined by the European Union (European Commission, 1996). The data gathered for the research is used in this paper to provide a case study insight into a range of small firm attitudes to training and training supply in the sub-region. First, a review of the literature that informed the empirical study is presented.

Training Needs and Provision: A Literature Review

Industry-specific analyses have concluded that recruitment difficulties and skills shortages are affecting the UK tourism and hospitality industry to a greater extent than in other industrial sectors (Hospitality Training Foundation. Some attribute the industry's skills shortages to recruitment difficulties associated with the industry's poor reputation as an employer. There is also evidence that the reported link between a lack of skills/experience and recruitment difficulties is specific to certain sectors of the industry, in particular to hotels, restaurants and travel agents and to certain operative level occupations, in particular chefs/cooks and waiters/waitresses. Regional imbalances are also apparent with Thomas *et al.* (2000) and more recently Impact Research (2003), highlighting the West Midlands as a region reporting significant skills shortages.

The size of an organisation is also likely to play a part in determining an employer's perception of skills shortages and recruitment difficulties. Small tourism and hospitality firms in particular have been found to be less likely to perceive recruitment difficulties than larger firms (Thomas and Long, 2001) and this has been linked to a lower perceived level of need for skilled staff and to the lower level of labour turnover in such firms. It is more likely that in small firms, skill needs will be firm specific and multi-skilled employees will be in higher demand (Curran *et al.*, 1997).

It is important at this juncture to explore what is meant by 'skills'. First, there are a number of broad skills categories. These are generally accepted to include generic transferable skills, vocational/sector transferable skills and organisation/job-specific skills. Generic skills are widely recognised as those that can be used across all occupations, for example, communication, problem solving, IT skills, numeracy, team working and work planning, as well as personal values and attitudes. Vocational skills in contrast are those needed in specific occupations, such as those described in national Occupational Standards. Some of them are transferable from job to job, for example language skills, while others are job specific.

Research in the hospitality industry suggests that the most valued skills are generic, such as the ability to follow instructions, the willingness to learn, the ability to be flexible and adaptive and show initiative, as well as personal presentation and appearance. This is closely followed by a need for vocational/sector transferable skills such as customer care skills. This research also suggests that the importance of these skills is likely to increase in the future. This confirms the importance of personal, 'softer' skills that have been identified as important to UK industry in general across other research projects. Other authors identify a wide range of desirable skills including diversity management, managing skills shortages, negotiation, political and commercial awareness. Interestingly, contemporary skills, such as IT skills, are least likely to be considered important by employers, in both general studies and tourism sector-specific studies (HtF, 2001a, 2001b). Also less important, according to surveys of hospitality employers, are a need for skills in people management, literacy and numeracy (HtF, 1999a).

Evidence is conflicting as to which skills are considered by employers to be deficient among their workforce and the extent to which this is considered problematic. The HtF (1995) has condemned the hospitality industry as 'one of the most under qualified in the UK' and numerous surveys have indicated that large percentages of small tourism and hospitality firm employers believe that their employees could improve their skills. A more detailed analysis of these findings reveals that the percentage of businesses reporting skills deficiencies varies by subsector, with Thomas *et al.* (2000) noting that tour operators and hotels were the most likely to identify skills gaps.

Hospitality employers' surveys have found that the top five skills that employers perceived employees to lack were communication skills, job-specific skills, initiative, customer service and willingness to learn. This, the HtF (2001a, 2001b) argue, highlights a paradox in expectation: organisations want people who are good at following instructions while also being capable of exercising their initiative. Surveys of the tourism and leisure sectors have also found skills gaps in customer care to be a key area of concern. These surveys, however, also identified IT/ computing as a key area of concern. This points to an interesting difference between the skills felt to be most important and those that are considered deficient. It would seem that while customer service and IT skills are considered less important than some other softer skills, their lack is felt when they are not evident.

It is at this point that the findings of different surveys conflict. Keep and Mayhew (1999) found additional skills gaps in entrepeneurial and management skills, and in the training of volunteers, while employers surveyed by Thomas *et al.* (2000) identified commercial awareness as a further area of concern. Beaver and Lashley (1998) have suggested the existence of a number of perceived managerial skill deficiencies across hospitality SMEs. These include financial, market, communications, people management, legal responsibility, quality, computer skills, maintenance and general management. Once again, sectoral differences and firm size issues are also apparent. The CBI (1995) and Thomas *et al.* (2000) found that language skills are seen as the most significant skills gap by tourism firms, in particular tour operators, while higher proportions of hotels, public houses and restaurants noted a deficiency of customer care skills. Meanwhile, research undertaken for a recent DCMS (2005) report suggests that smaller businesses in hospitality, leisure and tourism are less likely to perceive skills gaps.

Training in Tourism: A Demand Side Perspective

Where skills gaps are identified, the main remedy is still training. While there are a variety of perspectives on the relative value of different forms of training intervention, it is widely accepted that training is beneficial to business performance. Despite this, the tourism industry has a reputation as being a poor trainer. Indeed, Keep and Mayhew (1999) argue that much of the training that does take place is driven by legislative requirement. Surveys of the industry have revealed that up to 75 percent of employees have received no job-related training since leaving full-time education (DNH, 1996a), although, again, survey findings vary. For example, Thomas *et al.* (2000) found that just under 50 percent of the small firms surveyed were engaging in training (Thomas *et al.*, 2000), while the HtF (1999b) found that 85 percent of hospitality employers surveyed provided some training for some employees. It is likely that these headline figures vary so dramatically because they conceal a wide and complex variety of practice and attitudes to training (Lynch, 1994).

Once again, sectoral variations can be considered but survey findings are not consistent. The HtF (1999b) identified that restaurants and hotels provided lower levels of post-induction training than other sectors, while Thomas *et al.* (2000) found that this was the case for B&B/guesthouses and self-catering operators. When the formality of training provision was considered, travel agents and visitor attractions were, however, most likely to make use of external training provision. This distinction between formal and informal training provision is an important one, especially when considered alongside the size of the organisation. As Kitching and Blackburn (2002: viii) note,' there is considerable evidence that small employers provide less formal training than larger companies and are less likely to participate in government training schemes'.

Evidence from the tourism and hospitality industry appears to confirm this conclusion. The HtF (1999b) noted that training activity among smaller employers was significantly lower than among medium and large employers, while Thomas *et al.* (2000) found that the use of external training provision increases with firm size and identified a particularly low participation of tourism employers in accredited training schemes, such as S/NVQs and Modern Apprenticeships. There is evidence that SMEs are 'unconvinced of the value of outside assistance' in skills development (Smith *et al.*, 2002: 4) and that they are constrained by the higher average cost of training provision (Lange *et al.*, 2000). It would seem that the majority of training that does occur in tourism firms is informal and undertaken on the job.

This, in itself, is not necessarily negative. As Kitching and Blackburn (2002) note, in-house training can be perceived as relevant and convenient and also brings the benefit of being low cost, advantages that are likely to be particularly attractive to small firms. The nature and quality of this kind of training may, however, vary significantly. As Westwood (2001) argues 'sitting next to Nellie' is neither cost effective, creative, nor taken seriously by staff.

Kitching and Blackburn (2002) suggest that 15 percent of small firms are 'low trainers' training as a last resort, if at all. Fifty-five percent are 'tactical trainers' training as and when necessary, 30 percent are 'strategic trainers', with a positive and systematic approach. Their research suggests that small firms are more likely to be strategic trainers if they are larger, younger, innovative and exhibiting fast growth. The propensity to hire other managers/professionals also has an impact here. They go on to suggest a focus on initial training as the only training especially in small hotel and catering firms (Kitching and Blackburn, 2002). This seems disturbing, although research by the HtF shows an increasingly positive picture. For instance, the incidence of post-induction training in small firms increased from 40 percent in 1995 to 53 percent in 1999.

The concept of training is taken on board by most managers, but often does not become a reality (Wilson *et al.*, 1998). Kitching and Blackburns survey (2002) suggests that, despite identifying a lack of skills, and with 77 percent of respondents agreeing that training leads to better business performance, 52 percent of small firms feel that there is no need to provide more training while the other 48 percent suggest genuine supply-side reasons for not training further. Lange *et al.* (2000) categorise these barriers as being cultural, financial, access/provision and awareness related. The HtF (2001b) suggests that barriers to training tend to come from the employer rather than the employee side, and many authors concur that these barriers include lack of time, cost, lack of staff, difficulty in providing cover, staff not staying long enough to be trained and the perceived unsuitability of training courses.

The explicit impact on the 'bottom line' is considered by Clements and Josiam (1995) who state that 'while the costs of training are up front and obvious, the benefits are frequently unmeasurable'. Others suggest that previous negative experiences of training can act as a barrier. While Boella (1996), for example, argues that 'many proprietors and managers have no formal training themselves and are unaware of the benefits of training', adding that 'many employers are concerned with immediate operational problems and, as such, do not have time to plan ahead'. Others may worry that training staff makes them more attractive to competitors and thus, in a high turnover industry, represents a waste of time and money (HtF, 2001b). Wilson *et al.* (1998) add that employers feel that potential employees should already be skilled, and that it is 'the responsibility of others, such as colleges, to provide them with trained staff'.

Given this context, it is not surprising to note that research has found that few tourism and hospitality organisations make financial provision for training. HtF research (1996) suggested that only 19 percent of hospitality firms had a training budget, while Jameson (2000) suggests that as little as 12 percent of small tourism and hospitality firms have training budgets. Yet, while these figures are disappointingly low, they are in line with data for SMEs in other industries.

There is a general consensus that this lack of an emphasis on training reflects a general 'unsophisticated' style of management, which is also frequently reflected in informal methods of recruitment. Szivas and Riley (1999) and the HtF (2001a, 2001b) argue that the core of the issue is the extent to which tourism is a professional career. Szivas and Riley (1999: 770) state that:' The reality in many countries is, for better or worse, a persistently 'contingent' workforce, employed under very flexible conditions, on non-standard terms and on a part-time and seasonal basis.... a refuge when job opportunities in other sectors are scarce.'

Training in Tourism: A Supply-side Perspective

There is a widespread lack of knowledge and confusion about the nature of training provision in the industry (Thomas *et al.* 2000). While government initiatives receive some research attention, there is less written about the effectiveness of existing programmes. National Vocational Qualifications (NVQs), Modern Apprenticeships and other qualifications have both their champions and their detractors. Experience suggests that the most popular programmes are those that are short, inexpensive, easily applied and with visible personal and business benefits. Perhaps the best example of this is the Welcome family of qualifications, with Welcome Host being completed by 115,000 people between 1992 and 1999.

It is, however, not just the relevance and accessibility of programmes that is of concern. Beeton and Graetz (2001), writing from an Australian perspective argue that the scattered urban/ rural, small firm-dominated nature of the industry makes it difficult for training providers to assess the industry and provide specific training.

What emerges from the literature is that larger providers are more visible and more active than independent providers. Thomas *et al.* (2000) found that most tourism firms surveyed approach Tourist Boards, Trade Associations and colleges for training provision.

Sector-specific training-related organisations such as the Training and Enterprise Councils (TECs) seem to have been ineffective in establishing themselves as intermediary agencies for skills development among small tourism and hospitality firms. This is a key issue for their successors, the Learning and Skills Councils (LSCs) and for the Sector Skills Councils (SSCs) who seek to promote education and training and ensure investment in skills and innovation (HTF, 2002).

The literature presents a complex picture of skills and training in the UK tourism and hospitality industry. Despite variations in perceptions of skills deficiencies across sectors and regions and by organisational size, there do, however, appear to be some common issues. Generic skills are perceived to be lacking, with an emphasis on softer skills and customer service. The general response to skills issues is still training, but training is often patchy, informal and reactive rather than proactive.

The issue of regional complexity is reflected by Thomas and Long (2001: 231), who contest that the industry as a whole has to want to train 'from a local policy making perspective'. They argue that 'a key challenge is to understand the extent to which organisations within particular localities demand and utilise appropriate skills and the extent to which the local skills infrastructure is geared to their provision'. Small businesses, particularly, need easily accessible training provision that understands their particular needs. In addition, regional and sub-regional differences in tourism consumption mean that different skills are required. This leads us into a consideration of the findings of this sub-regional research.

Methodological Approach

The primary research investigation on which this paper is based was carried out between March and July 2002 and comprised a business questionnaire survey and a telephone survey of training providers. The business questionnaire survey sought to establish tourism organisations' perceptions of their own skills, training and recruitment needs and to identify reasons for participation and non-participation in training. The survey comprised of 30 closed format questions, developed to mirror the themes that had emerged from the secondary research.

A sample of 1,319 Telford and Shropshire-based businesses was identified, which collectively reflected the sub-region's broad range of tourism and hospitality business activities. The business questionnaire was mailed out and responses encouraged with covering letters from key local industry organisations likely to be familiar to most respondents. Despite this, the response was still disappointing even for a mail survey with a final response rate of 10.5 percent (141 usable responses). It should be noted, however, that this was, at the time, the second biggest survey of this type administered in the UK.

The training providers' survey sought to identify the nature of the training available, the training providers' level of involvement in the tourism industry, together with the providers' understanding of the tourism industry's view on training. Thirty-seven training providers were identified within the Shropshire survey area and 21 (57 percent) completed a telephone interview. The quantitative data generated from both surveys were analysed using the SPSS package to detect associations and patterns between the variables, while the more limited qualitative data were analysed thematically.

The Field Area

Shropshire, together with Telford and Wrekin, is defined as a rural area by the regional tourist board and is situated in the west of the West Midlands bordering Cheshire to the north, Staffordshire to the east, Herefordshire and Worcestershire to the south and Wales in the west. Together Telford and Shropshire have a population of 435,900 (Shropshire County Council (SCC), 2002), of which 45 percent live in Shrewsbury and Telford (SCC, 2002).

The county is visited by around 9 million visitors per annum, spending a total of around £254m (Heart of England Tourist Board (HETB), 2002). Approximately 60 percent of these visitors come on a holiday or irregular long leisure trips away from home and around 1 million of the total stay overnight. Around 14 percent are overseas visitors and although figures for the county do not show the country of origin of these visitors, for the tourist board region as a whole the key markets are USA (15 percent), Germany (12 percent) and France (12 percent).

The tourism industry directly supports approximately 6,630 jobs and an additional 2,120 non-tourism jobs in the area (HETB, 2002). Of the directly supported jobs, around 22 percent are in the accommodation sector, 35 percent in catering, 25 percent in retailing, 14 percent in leisure/attractions/entertainment and 4 percent in transport services (HETB, 2002). The importance of the tourism industry and the need for investment have been acknowledged in the Shropshire and Telford and Wrekin Joint Structure Plan 1996–2011 (SCC, 2000). Furthermore, the latest strategic review of tourism in Shropshire (Stevens and Associates, 2004) recognises the need for a robust framework for business development if the area is to achieve its potential as a visitor destination.

Although little information about the nature of firms in the area is available, the picture in Shropshire suggests a widely dispersed industry with some dependence on tourism, which supports approximately 4 percent of the economically active workforce. Unemployment in the area is broadly commensurate with national figures, although geographic and economic factors could make it difficult to match vacancies to potential recruits.

Findings

The Tourism Business Survey

The tourism industry in Shropshire was, as expected, predominantly made up of well-established, independent, rural micro-businesses. The survey included representation across most tourism subsectors, with the majority being accommodation or food and beverage providers. The vast majority of respondents recognised themselves to be either the owner or owner-manager of their business, with over half stating that they had worked in the same capacity for more than five years. Few had seen their performance decrease over the past 12 months and most were optimistic about future business levels.

There was evidence of labour turnover in the region, although there were some sector variations here. The problem was, unsurprisingly, less pronounced in micro-businesses, many of which employed few or no staff. Recruitment problems were broadly in line with national findings and the main reason was cited as a failure to attract applicants, although the reasons for this varied across sectors. Rural firms were the most likely to have unfilled vacancies, and operative staff were identified as the hardest to find. Larger firms were more likely to have difficulties filling vacancies and tended to look for more qualified/experienced staff than smaller firms. Local channels, especially word of mouth, were the most popular method of trying to fill vacancies.

The majority of employers stated that they were convinced about the benefits of training, especially its impact on customer satisfaction. Despite this awareness and despite seeing skills gaps in their workforce, most were, however, happy with the level of training they provided. Their analysis of needs reflected their generally informal approach, emerging predominantly from observation and employee feedback. Furthermore, while employers were concerned about some skills among employees, they did not appear concerned about their own development. Some suggested that, as small businesses, they did not need training and that they knew their business better than anyone else. Others recognised very specific gaps in their own knowledge (for example, general maintenance, web design, advertising). On the whole, though, the perception was that skills gaps rest with their employees, rather than with themselves. The literature bears this out to an extent. While some authors see definite gaps in management skills and business awareness, the generally *ad hoc* approach to management and the lifestyle nature of many of these organisations often means that self-development is undervalued.

Training levels, at first glance, appeared to be higher than the national picture but much of this training was informal, on-the-job training. The key barriers to further engagement in formal training were time and cost related, with low levels of agreement concerning willingness to fund skills development. In fact, the only training that employers agreed they would fund was customer care/service. Where formal training did take place, there was a propensity to access programmes provided by tourist boards and trade association/industry bodies. To be acceptable to employers, respondents agreed that training needed to be short, inexpensive, convenient (location/time) and relevant.

The Training Providers' Survey

The profile of the training providers was very similar to that of the tourism organisations surveyed, being predominantly independent organisations (86 percent) and micro-businesses (95 percent). Most had a bank of freelance trainers available, or worked closely with associates in order to widen their provision as necessary. Providers offered training across a range of enterprises in a variety of industries but this was not often accessed by tourism organisations. Many of the smaller training providers surveyed were passionate about their services and showed a degree of insight into the tourism industry. They were often willing to tailor their programmes and delivery to clients' specific needs and work closely with them to analyse their training needs. Most were keen to provide training for tourism-related organisations, but had found demand for their services was low. The predominant method of attracting new business was word of mouth referral, yet many of the providers were simply not coming into contact with tourism networks. In short, the region has a valuable source of both industry specific and generic expertise available to tourism organisations but this was largely untapped.

Conclusion

The sub-regional picture of small tourism and hospitality firm attitudes to training and training provision that is presented in this paper, in many ways mirrors what is known at a national level. In terms of training supply, a wide range of generally appropriate provision is available but this is often poorly understood and rarely accessed by employers. Trade organisations and bodies, especially the RTBs, are most likely to be perceived as the most suitable source of training provision by small firms. Essentially, there is evidence of a great deal of untapped potential among Shropshire training providers, both the larger public organisations and the smaller independents. Often this is down to a lack of awareness of the available products, especially the opportunities for flexible, tailored programmes. This leads directly to the first recommendation that work needs to be undertaken not only into the content of training programmes, but also the format, modes of delivery and the associated logistics, in order to establish what offering is likely to prove most attractive to small business operators. Of course, the ideal programme of training provision is likely to vary from business to business, but this should not detract from an investigation into which approaches to training are likely to prove most successful in engaging specific sub-categories of small firm.

The key finding of this paper is, however, not related to training provision, but rather the fact that it is on the demand side that most workforce development problems exist. This in itself should not be surprising. It has now been repeatedly demonstrated that tourism and hospitality attracts many business owners for reasons that may collectively be termed as 'lifestyle oriented' (Dewhurst and Horobin, 1998). Such orientations tend to emphasise a focus on personal and social goals with fewer focusing exclusively upon the more commercially oriented goals such as business growth that are more commonly associated with classical interpretations of entrepreneurship. The extent to which such businesses are likely to engage in business development measures such as training will perhaps always be questionable.

There is therefore a need to focus on developing and shaping the demand for training from a lifestyle-dominated industry. As we (Dewhurst and Horobin, 1998) and others (eg Brownlie, 1994) have previously argued this will require a better understanding of the owner-managers' goals for success and associated business strategies and a tailoring of training provision to match such priorities. This is, however, not in itself enough, as there is also a need to work with small firms to achieve a broader realisation among small business owner-managers that a better business organisation can also assist in the attainment of lifestyle-oriented goals (Wanhill, 2004). Subsequent to the primary research investigation profiled in this paper, funding was secured for a two-year training project aimed specifically at small firms in Shropshire. This sought to engage firms over the period, to reduce or eliminate some of the key identified barriers to training — cost, location and time — and work with the recognised public sector organisations to deliver a suite of tailored training programmes. It will be the focus of a future paper to report the findings of this project and to reflect upon the extent to which the perceived barriers to engagement in training identified in this paper, are more or less real than those created by a focus on lifestyle-oriented goals.

Sustainable Development of Tourism, CSR and Innovation

The concept of sustainable development was introduced in 1987 by the World Conference on Environment and Development (known as the 'Brundtland Commission', whose report defined sustainable development as development meeting the needs of the present without compromising the ability of future generations to meet their own needs; (WCED, 1987). Tourism was not specifically addressed either by the Brundtland report or by the 'Agenda 21', the outcome action programme that emerged from the 'Earth Summit' held in Rio de Janeiro in 1992 (UNCED, 2000). Only in 1997 did the travel and tourism sector issue its first programmatic affirmation to the sustainable development principles in the document *Agenda 21 for the Travel and Tourism Industry,* jointly elaborated by the World Tourism Organization, the World Travel and Tourism Council and the Earth Council.

Some of the reasons for the difficulties on sustainability research in tourism refer to the multidisciplinary nature of the sector (WTO, 2001) and a general conceptual 'fuzziness' of the area.

For a long period, the sustainable tourism investigations have been focusing on identifying and documenting social, ecological, cultural and economic impacts of tourism, etc. In recent years, however, concerns related to tourism development expanded beyond the issue of impacts, and are increasingly explored in the context of globalization. Implementation of neo-liberal development policies also raised the issue of responsibility of the business sector for promoting sustainable development, leading to the emergence of CSR and business ethics as new business studies areas.

In its generic use, the term CSR is understood as the explicit adoption and implementation of environmentally conscious, ethical and socially responsible standards of conduct in and by the business, on a voluntary basis and going beyond the minimum legal requirements. In recent years, the concept has been institutionalised politically in the international context both by the European Union and by the UN. Under the definition of the European Commission (2001), CSR is 'a concept whereby companies integrate social and environmental concerns in their business operations and in their interaction with their stakeholders on a voluntary basis' (European Commission, 2001).

The Commission further emphasises four relevant aspects: first, that CSR covers *both* social and environmental issues, in spite of the English term CSR; secondly, that CSR is not or should not be separate from business strategy and operations; thirdly, that CSR is voluntary; and fourthly, that interaction with internal and external stakeholders is an important aspect of CSR. The United Nations is also playing an important role in promoting the CSR agenda through the Global Compact (UN Global Compact, 2007), a framework for businesses to align their operations and strategies within ten universally accepted principles of human rights, labour, environment and anti-corruption.

Tourism adoption of CSR practices is still in its infancy. Of all the industrial sectors that the World Bank Group CSR Practice reviewed in 2003, tourism was the 'least developed' in terms of codes of conduct and CSR initiatives. With regards to the content of existing initiatives, Epler-Wood and Leray (2005) point out that existing voluntary schemes, guidelines and codes of conduct have predominantly addressed questions of environmental management, with little or no focus on issues of human rights and labour.

In his *Tourism Ethics*, Fennell (2006) sees the research concentration on tourism environmental impacts as excessive and limiting for the field, noting the 'absence of an underlying ethical basis for critical thought in tourism'. Fennell argues that it may be the recognition of the 'immense void in ethics' that determined tourism being pulled behind other disciplines that progressed both conceptually and theoretically. Fennel further suggests that tourism ethics 'has the potential to emerge as the next main research platform' (2006: 358) in this field.

Ethics and CSR are also promising operating frameworks for the private sector. Among the first industry publications specifically addressing CSR was a World Travel and Tourism Council report from 2002, which reviews selected examples of social leadership by top companies of the sector (WTTC, 2002). In WTTC's view, the business case for CSR by tourism companies results from: favouring of responsible companies by governments and communities prioritising sustainability; building brand value and the market share of socially conscious travellers; attracting socially conscious investors; enhancing businesses' ability for recruitment of highly skilled workforce; improved risk assessment and response capacity.

Despite the reasons given by the industry, a study by Dodds and Joppe (2005) found that there is little overt demand for sustainable tourism, and both the consumer and the industry are still overwhelmingly driven by price. The same was noted when the Organization for Economic Co-operation and Development (OECD) organised an 'Innovation and Growth in Tourism' conference in 2003. In this context, private sector representatives noted that 'price competition and its consequences of productivity improvement, and not product innovation, has occupied the minds of senior managers in this [tourism] sector over the past ten years' (Brackenbury, 2003). Weiermair (2005) also points out that innovation is undertaken in the tourism value chain only in the areas where there is sufficiently high information dividend paying for the added cost and risk.

Price-driven improvements have been well studied in other industries. The discourse in the field of industrial innovation, however, rarely addresses the service sectors and is particularly silent in what concerns tourism. The research focusing on tourism innovation is limited, and as a field still sparse and fragmented. Hjalager (2002) builds on the model of Abernathy and Clark (1985), who describe the tourism innovation process in terms of: production, process, management, logistics and institutional improvements.

In further work, Hjalager connects the low occurrence of innovation with deficiencies of knowledge transfer, suggesting that in tourism, the central elements of innovativeness are generally human resources, competence, knowledge and access to networks.

While most traditional views of innovation in tourism, starting with Schumpeter's work (1934), concern technical and resource exploitation processes, researchers increasingly point to the need of a behavioural interpretation of innovation incorporating the social capital within the scope of innovations. In this direction, Macbeth *et al.* (2004) use the concept of social, political and cultural capital, arguing that The use of the concepts of SPCC in regional tourism development needs to have a broader agenda than pointing the finger at communities and telling them to take responsibility. There is also a need for corporations and government to accept the need to contribute to building social capital, and to do so equitably across gender, age, ethnicity and socio-economic level. [...] if tourism development is to be sustainable, it must ensure its development efforts accept corporate civic responsibility.

These comments point to a link between CSR and innovation, calling for tourism managers to see themselves and also to act as social entrepreneurs. On a more general basis, it appears that there is a need for innovation to be understood in a broader sense, as having a relationship with CSR in supporting the fulfilment of the 'social contract' of tourism.

Trafficking and Child Sex Tourism

Easily negotiated international borders and increased demand for cheap labour sustain a global slave industry worth approximately $9bn in annual profits, for which 600,000–800,000 immigrants are trafficked across international borders every year (Glover, 2006). The main premise of human trafficking is that increased poverty leads hopeless immigrants to seek opportunities beyond the borders of their homelands (Coonan and Thompson, 2005).

Trafficking and child sex tourism are among what Payne and Dimanche (1996) consider the myriad of issues and problems in the tourism industry tied to ethics, or lack of thereof. While sex tourism is better known in the tourism academic research circles, trafficking has been only recently associated to tourism. Child Sex Tourism (CST) is a narrow topic within the wider issue of sex tourism, which was developed as a legitimate area of tourism studies from the 1970s. Tourism researchers have reported extensively on sex tourism over the last two decades, significant exploratory work being carried out by Carter and Clift (2000), Garrick (2005), Hall (1996), Jeffreys (1999), O'Connell Davidson (2000), Oppermann (1999), Rao (1999), Ryan and Hall (2001), Seabrook (2000), Truong (1990), Ryan and Kinder (1996), and others.

Important field research was carried out in the 1990s in Thailand, Goa, Venezuela, Dominican Republic, South Africa, Cuba, and Costa Rica, by O'Connell Davidson and Sanchez Taylor (1995).

Their reports were commissioned by ECPAT International and used in preparation for the 1996 1st World Congress against the Commercial Sexual Exploitation of Children (reports available from ECPAT International (End Child Prostitution, Child Pornography and Trafficking of Children for Sexual Purposes) website www.ecpat.net). Moving beyond merely observing CST as a component of tourism and sexuality, recent works progressed toward more sophisticated aspects of CST, such as those including commonalities with sex tourism in general (O'Connell Davidson, 2004), tourists' rationalisations (Garrick, 2005), sex tourism and citizenship (Cabezas, 2004).

CST is distinguished from the wider topic of sex tourism studies by its classification as a national or international crime. As adult prostitution is legal in some countries, adult sex tourism, while controversial, is not a crime under certain national jurisdictions. Tourism, however, for the purpose of sexual relation with a minor is a crime and a clear and unambiguous violation of human rights (UNWTO, 2004) under the international legislation. A tourist who engages in sex with a minor commits a violation of the UN Convention of the Rights of the Child, and of the Optional Protocol on the Sale of Children, Child Prostitution and Child Pornography. Children's fundamental right to be protected against commercial sexual exploitation is addressed in the UN Convention on the Rights of the Child (CRC), whose Article 34 recognises the cross-border aspects that are typical of the phenomenon.

More recently, new information increasingly links CST with trafficking in human beings, a phenomenon considered by the UN Office on Drugs and Crime to be the 21st century form of the old worldwide slave trade (UNODC, 2006). UNODC defines trafficking in the context of the UN Convention against Transnational Organized Crime, and of two of its supplementing protocols: the Protocol to Prevent, Suppress and Punish Trafficking in Persons, Especially Women and Children, and the Protocol against the Smuggling of Migrants by Land, Sea and Air, both adopted by the UN General Assembly in 2000. Trafficking is defined as the recruitment, transportation, transfer, harbouring or receipt of persons, by means of the threat or use of force or tougher forms of coercion, of abduction, of fraud, or deception, or the abuse of power or of a position of vulnerability or of the giving or receiving of payments or benefits to achieve the consent of a person having control over another person, for the purpose of exploitation. Exploitation includes, at a minimum, the exploitation of the prostitution of others or other forms of sexual exploitation, forced labour or services, slavery or practices similar to slavery, servitude or the removal of organs. (UNODC, 2006: 7)

The links between trafficking and child sex tourism are also noted by the US Department of State Office to Monitor and Combat Trafficking in Persons (TIP Office), which issues an annual Trafficking in Persons Report (TIP Report). The Protection Project at John Hopkins University (Protection Project, 2007) reviewed the 2006 edition of the TIP report, finding that 29 countries were referenced as either origin or destination countries. These references point out the fact that the TIP Office lists other governments' efforts to combat CST among the measures to eliminate trafficking in persons. The aspects of 'transportation, transfer, harbouring or receipt of persons' in the trafficking definition make it possible for tourism businesses to be used, voluntarily or involuntarily, in relation to the trafficking phenomenon. In what concerns adult victims, there is often confusion between trafficking and smuggling of migrants. The differentiating aspects concern the nature of consent (coercive, deceptive or abusive in the case of trafficking), and the aspect of continuous exploitation and coercion for illegal profits which characterise trafficking. Also, unlike smuggling, which is always transnational, trafficking can be both internal and trans-boundary (UNODC, 2007).

In regard to minor victims of CST and trafficking, the legal determination is clear. According to the existing international legal framework, children under 18 cannot give valid consent, and any recruitment, transportation, transfer, harbouring or receipt of children for the purpose of exploitation is a form of trafficking regardless of the means used (UNODC, 2007). A common misconception is that sex tourists are primarily paedophiles. According to Glover (2006), however, the majority of perpetrators are primarily prostitute users in general. UNICEF quotes surveys indicating that 30–35 percent of all sex workers in the Mekong sub-region of south-east Asia are between 12 and 17 years of age (UNICEF, 2007a), 2 million children are believed to be exploited through prostitution and pornography, and 1.2 million children are trafficked every year (UNICEF, 2007b). While child sex tourism is booming worldwide, according to Glover (2006) Asia is at the centre of child prostitution, with 60,000 child prostitutes in the Philippines, 400,000 in India, 800,000 in Thailand. Most of them are girls under the age of 16, or boys in the case of Sri Lanka's 20,000 child prostitutes. Child prostitution and sex tourism, however, cannot be blamed on tourists alone, as they seem to be thriving in places where a culture of prostitution is connected to the local customs or historical circumstances. In Sachs (1994), Hnin Hnin Pyne estimates that 75 percent of Thai men have had sex with a prostitute. With such a demand, children are sought in the most impoverished areas to be brought to developed entertainment destinations, often tourism destinations, to serve the red light districts.

Models of Tourism Innovations Preventing Trafficking and Sex Tourism

The existing body of knowledge on child sex tourism and trafficking in the context of sustainability and CSR is thin. Furthermore, the theoretical contextualisation on CST and trafficking phenomena turns obsolete quickly, due to the volatile dynamics of these phenomena and the rapid changes of the tourism industry. Yet, some empirical developments have been recently taking place. Models of responsible practice to prevent and counteract trafficking and sex tourism have emerged in the last decade from a variety of tourism stakeholders, including nongovernmental organisations, international governmental organisations, industry and national tourism authorities. They come to complement national laws, including extra-territorial legislation created by many governments to prevent trafficking and sex tourism.

The general aims of tourism industry innovations were, first, to create awareness within the industry regarding its potential preventative role, and, secondly, to equip tourism businesses with the tools to exercise it. Other measures looked into creating alternative opportunities for development for the children at risk, facilitating public awareness, and creating incentives to report sex tourism and trafficking. Several such examples are briefly described in this section, clustered according to the type of stakeholders driving them.

Models of Innovation by Nongovernmental Organisations

The youth Career Initiative Programme of the International Business Leaders' Foundation

The youth career initiative (YCI) is a programme run by the London-based international business leaders' foundation (IBLF) through their International Tourism Partnership, seeking to increase youth employability in the hotel sector, and by doing so helping to end the cycle of poverty and social exclusion (IBLF, 2007). The programme engages international hotels (Marriott, Sheraton, Pan Pacific, Sol Melia, Starwood, Orient Express, Intercontinental, etc.) to provide five to six months education on the hotel premises for high-school graduates from disadvantaged backgrounds. It includes both theory and practical instruction by hotel staff, in finance, IT, interpersonal skills and personal health and wellbeing. Upon completing the programme, the participants are helped to make further career and education choices. Over 1,300 youth have graduated the programme since its inception in 1995 and with the initial support of UNICEF and the Pan Pacific Hotel in Bangkok. Currently YCI runs in eight countries: Brazil, Ethiopia, Thailand, Philippines, Indonesia, Australia, Romania and Poland (IBLF, 2007). Although the content of the YCI programme is not directly targeting CST or trafficking, it provides a useful example of innovative engagement by the hospitality industry with youth at risk in developing countries. Through the vocational and career skills it instils, YCI is likely to provide an opportunity for youth to start onto a path of healthy development.

'Travel with Care' and 'Child wise Tourism' Programmes of Child Wise™ Australia

The nongovernmental organisation Child Wise is focusing on work in destinations where Australians travel. Child Wise is the Australian representative of the ECPAT International, a network of organisations and individuals working to eliminate the commercial sexual exploitation of children. ECPAT started in 1996 in Thailand, is currently represented in another 62 countries, and has been one of the first organisations to begin campaigning against child prostitution in Asian tourism (ECPAT International, 2007). The approach of Child Wise to protect children builds on the observation that CST involving Australians tends to occur outside the work of the mainstream tourism industry (Hecht, 2001). Consequently, mainstream tourism industry codes of conduct would probably have a limited effect in deterring Australian child sex tourists.

Developed since 1999, 'Child Wise Tourism' is a training and network development programme running throughout the ASEAN region, including training modules and education materials for travel and tourism students, educators and the tourism industry. The programme builds skills for the tourism staff so they become capable of identifying and responding to situations where children may be at risk of sexual exploitation. The programme conducts community-based training sessions in the seven ASEAN countries: Thailand, Indonesia, Cambodia, Philippines, Lao PDR, Vietnam and Myanmar (Child Wise, 2007). Another Child Wise programme, 'Travel with Care', is an intensive travel and tourism industry education module, aimed at increasing awareness of the Australia Child Sex Tourism law. Since December 2003, an awareness raising campaign has been launched with the slogan 'Don't let child abuse travel!' involving distribution of posters, postcards, as well as TV and radio messages.

World Vision 'Child Sex Tourism Prevention Project' and Campaign Targeting US Travellers

World Vision, a Christian humanitarian organisation operating in nearly 100 countries, developed since 2004 through its US branch is a campaign aimed at deterring foreign sex tourists and raising awareness on the extra-territorial legislation against CST. The World Vision campaign slogan 'Abuse a child in this country, go to jail in yours' was used in Cambodia, Thailand, Costa Rica, Mexico and Brazil, targeting mainly American tourists. The campaign also included deterrent messages posted in the US airports, airline in-flight videos, billboards and street signs overseas (World Vision, 2007). ECPAT-USA Inc., a group working since 1996 against CST in the US, estimates that American citizens account for 25 percent of child sex tourists worldwide.

Multi-Stakeholder Models of Innovation

The Code of Conduct for the Protection of Children from Sexual Exploitation in Travel and Tourism (the Code) is an industry-driven multi-stakeholder initiative that seeks to increase protection of children from sex tourism. The companies — tour operators and their umbrella organisations, hotels, travel agents, airlines, etc. — that endorse the Code, commit themselves to implement six measures. These are elaborating corporate policies against CST; training company staff on how to prevent CST; providing information to the travellers in relation to CST; inserting clauses in contracts with suppliers jointly repudiating CST; working together with 'key persons' in destinations to prevent CST; and finally, reporting annually on the implementation of these measures.

The Code was initiated in 1998 by ECPAT Sweden (member of the ECPAT network) in cooperation with Scandinavian tour operators and the UN World Tourism Organization (UNWTO). Funding was provided by the European Commission for the Code's implementation in six European countries, between 2000 and 2004: Austria, Germany, Sweden, UK, the Netherlands and Italy. Following the launch of the Code in North America in April 2004, UNICEF became a supporting partner and a cofunding body of the Code organisation. Signed by over 600 tour operators, hotels, travel agents and their associations, tourism workers' unions from 23 countries in Europe, Asia, North America, Central and Latin America (Tepelus, 2004), the Code is internationally recognised by UNICEF and the UNWTO as one of the most advanced private sector tools for the prevention and combating of CST.

The Code process, however, has a number of shortcomings. Criticisms concern the lack of enforcement mechanisms once a company signs up, and insufficient monitoring of the implementation in destinations. As the structure of the Code is that of a multi-stakeholder process based on support from national partners (ECPAT groups, governments, UNICEF offices, etc.), the rigorousness of implementation varies greatly from country to country. Furthermore, since the Code marketing and promotion proceeded in parallel with attempts to strengthen its own internal organisation, the Code as an industry-driven, self-sustained organisation, independent of the ECPAT network, is still a work in progress.

Innovation through Government-Led Campaigns: Brazil

The Government of Brazil was among the first governments taking a clear and official stand against the phenomenon of CST, launching since 1997 a 'no child sex tourism' campaign. Brazil was the first country to design a logo for the tourism campaign against exploitation of children, logo adopted later by the UNWTO for the global campaign. National awareness started in Brazil since

2001 with the support of EMBRATUR and of the federation of hotels and conventions. More recently, under the presidency of Luiz Inacio Lula da Silva starting in 2002, a Ministry of Tourism was created and a 'Sustainable Tourism and Childhood Thematic Chamber' was institutionalised within the structure of the National Tourism Chamber. The principal objectives of the 'Sustainable Tourism and Childhood' programme are to assist the creation of public policies on the protection of children in relation to tourism, and to promote good practices of the private sector, including the introduction of codes of conduct. The Brazil Ministry of Tourism also spearheaded a regional South American 'Sustainable Tourism and Childhood' programme, by convening annually between 2004 and 2007 a World Tourism Forum for Peace and Sustainable Development. In the context of the Forum, national tourism authorities and tourism ministries from all South American countries came together and issued the 1st Declaration against CST on 26th October, 2005 in Rio de Janeiro. The declaration was followed by plans for a joint South American campaign against CST designed to be running in 12 countries starting in 2007. In its efforts to protect children and teenagers from sexual exploitation in tourism, the Brazilian Federal Government worked together with nongovernmental partners including Save the Children Sweden, World Childhood Foundation Brazil and others.

Engagement of Inter-Governmental Organisations: UNWTO, UNICEF, OSCE, ILO, etc.

Several inter-governmental organisations facilitated tourism innovation against trafficking and CST, mostly by acting as convening bodies for international meetings and by supporting dialogue and information exchange platforms.

UN World Tourism Organization (UNWTO/OMT)

UNWTO has been concerned on the issue of protection of children from sex tourism, providing inputs in the proceedings of the 1st and 2nd Congresses against Commercial Exploitation of Children held in Stockholm in 1996, and in Yokohama in 2001. Following the Stockholm Congress 'Declaration and Agenda for Action', UNWTO established in 1997 a Task Force to Protect Children from Sexual Exploitation in Tourism, a global multi-stakeholder action platform aiming to prevent, uncover, isolate and eradicate the sexual exploitation of children in tourism

(UNWTO, 2007a). The Task Force meets bi-annually at the largest international tourism fairs, ITB held in March in Berlin and WTM held in November in London. The framework for the UNWTO position on CST is provided by the Article 2, point 3 of the Global Code of Ethics for Tourism (GCTE), which reads: The exploitation of human beings in any form, particularly sexual, especially when applied to children, conflicts with the fundamental aims of tourism and is the negation of tourism; as such, in accordance with international law, it should be energetically combated with the cooperation of all the States concerned and penalized without concession by the national legislation of both the countries visited and the countries of the perpetrators of these acts, even when they are carried out abroad.

The GCTE is a set of ten principles aiming to guide stakeholders in tourism development, and was recognised by the UN General Assembly in 2001 through the resolution A/RES/56/212. While the GCTE is not a legally binding document, the UNWTO drafted policies and guidelines governing a voluntary implementation mechanism, whereby a World Committee on Tourism Ethics (WCTE) may intervene in the settlement of disputes. Another important contribution of UNWTO is the incorporation of sustainability indicators within the tourism sustainability framework, to better quantify and monitor the increasing CST phenomenon (UNWTO, 2004).

The United Nations Children's Fund (UNICEF)

UNICEF is the UN agency advocating for the protection of children's rights in relation to the provisions and principles of the CRC. The CST and child trafficking issues fall under the 'child protection' focus area of UNICEF's activity. Upon hosting the launch of the tourism industry Code of Conduct in North America in April 2004, UNICEF became a supporting agency of the Code in a tripartite partnership of ECPAT, UNICEF, UNWTO (UNICEF, 2004). In addition to awareness campaigns against CST in various countries including Dominican Republic (2001), Spain (2003), Sri Lanka (2006), Kenya (2006), Gambia (2004), UNICEF has also been actively advocating for the revision of penal codes in countries in Central America and the Caribbean area. The UNICEF Latin America and Caribbean Regional Office organised in 2005 and 2007 training and education courses for officials from national tourism administrations and ministries of tourism from the area.

The Organization for Security and Cooperation in Europe (OSCE)

The Organization for Security and Cooperation in Europe (OSCE) forms the largest regional security organisation in the world, with 56 participating states from Europe, Central Asia and North America, acting for early warning, conflict prevention, crisis management and post-conflict rehabilitation. In 2003, the Office of the Co-ordinator of OSCE Economic and Environmental Activities (OSCE-OCEEA) received a mandate to mobilise and strengthen the private sector's efforts to combat trafficking in human beings by raising awareness and by identifying and disseminating best practices, such as self-regulation, policy guidelines and codes of conduct (OSCE, 2007a).

The OSCE-OCEEA considers that hospitality and tourism, as one of the world's fastest growing sectors, can play an instrumental role in raising the awareness of tourists and business travellers of trafficking, and can help create an environment that does not accept trafficking in human beings and, in particular, the sexual exploitation of minors. OSCE used voluntary instruments such as the Code as 'valuable preventive and awareness raising tools' (OSCE, 2007b) and has supported the extension of the Code to tourism companies operating in south-eastern Europe. OSCE provided as well institutional support for gaining the commitment of the industry and of governments in the prevention and combat of trafficking in human beings and child sex tourism. These measures, as well as training and educational efforts have been undertaken with the support of other local partners since 2004 in Bulgaria, Romania, and as of 2005 also in Albania and Montenegro.

Other UN Agencies: International Labour Organization, UN Office on Drugs and Crimes, International Organization on Migration

Other UN agencies that carried out research to uncover the context of CST include the International Labour Organization(ILO), the UN Office of Drugs and Crimes (UNODC) and the International Organization on Migration (IOM). ILO explored CST in the context of eliminating one of the worst forms of child labour specified under the ILO Convention No. 182 (Black, 1995; Lean, 1998), through its International Program on the Elimination of Child Labour (IPEC). UNODC and IOM have also elaborated guidelines and training materials on the prevention and combat of trafficking in human beings. Although their work is not directly relevant to tourism, it is very informative in the context of smuggling migrants, trafficking and illegal labour, all topics recently connected to tourism (Stipanuk, 2006).

Discussion

The number of child victims of trafficking and CST calls for the mobilisation of tourism stakeholders — academia, private sector and policy-making bodies — to explore these issues more fully. Continuing the innovation on preventive practices is not an easy task, given the complexity of the phenomena and the still predominant perception that tourism is only marginally concerned with these occurrences. Furthermore, the debate is burdened by the confusion, persistent even in academic circles, with other related themes, including smuggling, illegal immigration, illegal labour, adult prostitution, etc. A 'first-generation' of innovations on the prevention of child sex tourism and trafficking, however, emerged in the early 2000s. They were, and some still are, in the process of being pilot tested in various mass tourism destinations While making an elaborate analysis of the advantages, disadvantages, similarities, differences or interrelationships of each of the models was not the main focus of the paper, the initiatives presented share several key elements relevant from an innovation perspective. What existing models against trafficking and CST seem to have in common irrespective of their location, and who created them, are elements of awareness raising, education and the need for professional training of staff.

A second feature of the examples presented concerns their origin, most of which result from lobbying efforts by civil rights activists and by nongovernmental organisations. The main driver of innovation creation was a reaction, mostly by media and NGOs, but also by inter-governmental bodies, to flagrant and visible violations of children's rights in tourism destinations. The media reports have led to significant damage to the reputation of several destinations whose names remained, for the general public, associated with CST and trafficking. Owing to these negative media reports, the industry was initially forced into a defensive position that mandated immediate reaction. Yet, this external pressure makes it difficult to facilitate innovation beyond the current status quo. Instead, given the sensitive nature of the topic for mainstream tourists, the publicity has arguably not encouraged the private sector to take proactive steps. Current CST and trafficking initiatives, represent innovations of a behavioural nature, and mostly of a voluntary character (guidelines, training kits, codes of conduct, etc.). All these models are still in their initial stages of development. They evolved on an *ad hoc* basis and as continuous trial and error processes. In many circumstances innovation emerged as a result of challenges encountered, rather than being induced by favouring factors. Such challenges included reluctance of governments to acknowledge the existence of the problems, lack or insufficient numbers of skilled trainers, low capacity of local law enforcement, corruption and weak legal systems in tourism destinations particularly in developing countries.

With all their gaps, limitations and even inconsistencies however, innovations so far developed contain valuable knowledge to be applied towards a 'second generation' of prevention programmes. These should ideally evolve beyond voluntary, behavioural measures, and shift in the direction of policies and incentives for responsible behaviour. Based on reviewing the content and extent of currently available innovation models, it is argued here that existing innovation against CST and trafficking needs to increasingly morph towards policy making.

From a destination perspective, policies deterring any type of social risk, especially those that potentially tarnish the reputation of destinations, are very desirable. They support destinations to be more competitive in the national and international marketplaces, and intervene to extend the destination's lifecycle. This is also supported by Keller (2003), who notes that, 'the future of traditional destinations will depend on a more innovation-oriented tourism policy'. The need for policy makers not to replace, but to complement CSR measures is also acknowledged by politicians. The head of the Tourism Policy Division of the German Federal Ministry of Economics and Labour, Helmut Kruger, stated, 'in Germany, tourism policy does not intervene in areas where solutions could be found by the industry itself. The industry has the know-how and the necessary momentum needed for innovation,' however, 'the federal government must react to the big challenges and trends of our time'. Hjalager's observations on the role of policy instruments on environmental innovation may also shed some light on the role of policies for tourism social innovations.

Tourism Innovation on Preventing Trafficking and CST

A number of contextual factors may intervene in the morphing from *ad hoc,* pressure-driven innovation, towards innovation-oriented tourism policies. For this to happen, further academic research on tourism CSR needs to incorporate CST and trafficking in the ethical framework for tourism. Academic study of the CST phenomenon focused mostly on definitional aspects, sexuality interferences and representations in rapport to tourism. The academia feedback to the existing actions against CST and trafficking has been extremely limited, although O'Connell (2004) initiates this discussion. There is still insufficient awareness in the tourism academic environment to the global dimensions of CST and trafficking. Emerging CSR research should include these topics in relation to social issues in tourism destinations and along with environmental concerns.

Linkages from the research published in law, social sciences and criminology need to be drawn and incorporated in the research on social impacts and globalization in tourism. As CST and trafficking have been mostly studied in social sciences, legal and law enforcement circles, the body of work currently available may be insufficiently scrutinised by the tourism researchers. Incipient research (Stipanuk, 2006) points to possible implications of illegal labour in US tourism, and calls for the further development of solutions to social impacts of tourism.

Governments and authorities need to create incentives and acknowledge the leaders of socially responsible tourism. Andrews (2004) reported that in 1996, over 25 companies in the US were known to offer <sex tour> package deals to either south-west Asia or other developing countries. While the public promotion of sex tourism has largely stopped in recent years, mostly thanks to the advances in law enforcement, a follow-up step needs to be taken in acknowledging and creating incentives for tourism companies to actively engage in the prevention of CST and trafficking.

Coordination between the relevant UN bodies, tourism policy makers and the civil society has to be improved. As the phenomena of CST and trafficking are closely related to illegal migration, smuggling, international crime and security, there is a strong need for improved interaction and more effective coordination between UN agencies that have the resources to address these issues at a global scale. Some of the concerned agencies include UNWTO,

UNICEF, OSCE, ILO, IOM, Interpol, etc. A particularly important role remains for the UNWTO Task Force for the Protection of Children, and the UNWTO WCTE, which are called to support and facilitate exchange of information and to identify emerging international trends. As agendas of different organisations focus on different aspects, the discourse on CST and trafficking risks to become highly politicised, or vulnerable to pressures from the private sector. In order to bring the debate forward, focusing on elements of commonality would prevent territoriality and competition among the agencies concerned.

Hospitality Travel and Tourism Education

In today's rapidly changing business environment, Hospitality Management has come up as a fast growth career for young men and women who possess a pleasant personality, the capacity for hard work and a flair for creativity. Emerging trends for the growth of tourism and expansion of the accommodation sector has necessitated a substantial increase in the additional requirement of trained manpower.

If you have a natural gift for meeting people with a sense and spirit creative hospitality, a healthy dignity of labour, capacity and stamina to ramain cool in ticklish situations.

Hoteliering offers you a very fast-track career. It is the right place for the people who like people.

A career in hospitality management offers glamour, excitement, challenge a fast-track growth and elevated life style. It is in fact a unique and specialised discipline as Engineering, Finance, Medicine, MBA and/or civil services.

10

New Dimension of Tourism

Medical Tourism

When there is a significant price difference between countries for a given medical procedure, particularly in Southeast Asia, India, Eastern Europe and where there are different regulatory regimes, in relation to particular medical procedures (e.g. dentistry), travelling to take advantage of the price or regulatory differences is often referred to as "medical tourism". With soaring health care costs and long waits for medical procedures, it is becoming increasingly difficult to find quality, affordable treatment. Whether you want cosmetic surgery or life-saving procedures, you might have to dig deep into your wallet or wait several months before receiving the medical or dental care that you require.

Or you could try medical tourism and receive quality care for a fraction of the price and without the long wait!

According to the National Coalition on Health Care, more than 500,000 Americans traveled abroad to receive medical and dental work in 2006. And this is not an isolated trend. Every year, millions of patients from around the globe flock to some of the hottest medical tourism destinations in order to receive five-star treatment at unbelievable prices. Experts predict that by 2012, medical tourism will grow to be a $100 billion business with more than 780,000,000 patients travelling abroad to receive care from foreign doctors, dentists, and hospitals. These impressive figures don't necessarily include the growing alternative healing sector either. With wellness spas and Ayurvedic healing on the rise, medical tourism is clearly a global phenomenon that deserves greater attention.

Medical Tourism' Industry Grows Rapidly

In a global economy characterized by better access to information and lower transportation costs, North American consumers are discovering that they can get high-quality health care more cheaply and more quickly in some developing countries. However, such "medical tourism" may only have a marginal effect on health costs in North America.

Rising health care costs in the United States and longer waiting times in Canada are inducing patients to seek treatment overseas. The appeal of this phenomenon is driven by cost savings as high as 90%, depending on the procedure and the country in which it is performed, and virtually no wait times.

There are more than 45 million U.S. citizens without health insurance, and even more with health coverage that they consider inadequate. While U.S. consumers are concerned mainly with the exorbitant cost of care, Canadians are more troubled by wait times for certain treatments. Indeed, approximately 1 million Canadians claim to be experiencing difficulties in access to care.

Official statistics on medical tourism have not been collected, but an estimated 150,000 foreigners sought care in 2004 in India alone—and this number is growing at a rate of about 15% annually. Most of these patients are from the Middle East or Asia, but the proportion of U.S. citizens and Canadians is rising. Although providers offer a diverse range of services, the most common procedures are elective.

The benefits go beyond cost:

- Consumers gain from cost savings, but may also receive excellent care from highly qualified doctors.
- Many providers offer more personalized care—i.e., a higher physician-to-patient ratio—than is commonly available in the United States or Canada.
- Some services that are not yet approved by the U.S. Food and Drug Administration, such as certain hip replacement surgery techniques, are available overseas.

However, consumers also face risks when undergoing treatment in a foreign country:

- Follow-up is difficult when the patient returns home, and expensive care may be required if complications occur.

- Quality assessment is problematic, and the language barrier can complicate matters.
- Malpractice laws in other countries are different.

Foreign providers stand to gain from the looming demand and are eager to increase supply. Nevertheless, competition is fierce, leading to consumer-directed advertising campaigns. This burgeoning international market for medical care may also drive U.S. providers to respond to the increase in competition:

- Overseas impact. Hospitals, physicians and medical staff are benefiting from higher revenues. For example, medical tourism in India is forecast to generate over $2 billion in revenue by 2012, according to a study by McKinsey and the Confederation of Indian Industry.
- Domestic changes. U.S. hospitals make most of their money on high-margin elective surgeries not typically covered by insurance plans. They may need to become more efficient and affordable to avoid losing business overseas.

Some U.S. employers, concerned about rising health care costs, are using financial incentives to encourage employees to experiment with medical tourism. This is an especially common practice at large firms that self-insure and pay directly for their employees' medical expenses. Opponents, including unions, argue that it exposes employees to greater uncertainty and risk.

Medical tourism will continue to expand rapidly. However, its long-term growth rate depends on several factors:

- Insurance market. While companies specializing in arranging trips for medical tourists are flourishing, insurers have been slow to adapt to this new market.
- Legislation. North American governments may consider facilitating this assimilation of foreign care into domestic insurance plans—both private and public—through legislative action. Such legislation will face stiff opposition from unions and domestic medical groups.
- Image problem. Rich world consumers will have to overcome stereotypes of developing world poverty, lack of education and hygienic problems in order for the industry to thrive. Positive outcomes for those patients who do venture overseas may help to quell these fears.

- Inelastic demand. Uninsured U.S. citizens represent the largest group of prospective medical tourists. However, research shows patient demand tends to be relatively price inelastic for procedures that cost under $1,000 dollars. As median annual health care expenditures per capita for the uninsured are well under this level, more than half may have no interest in medical tourism.

The knowledge that the same care is available elsewhere at a much lower cost may encourage consumers to be more price-sensitive about certain medical procedures, increasing transparency, lowering costs and improving quality. However, this is unlikely to benefit most consumers—particularly the poor and uninsured.

Medical Tourism Statistics

Every statistic available testifies to the popularity and exponential growth rates of medical tourism. Although the practice of travelling abroad to have a special surgery performed is an ancient concept, today the industry is more about saving money and time than seeking out the world's best practitioner.

There are currently 28 countries catering to medical tourists, providing care to more than two million foreign patients annually. Many governments in developing countries see medical tourism as an excellent way to boost the local economy while improving their own health-care systems. The costs of a surgery in another country can be as much as 50 percent less than at home. The savings can be so significant that they are literally 'life saving'.

The global medical tourism industry is estimated to generate around US$20 billion of dollars per year, and by 2010 it is expected to more than double this amount of revenue. Americans, Canadians and Europeans compose the bulk of all medical tourists, likely due to the costs of surgery in these countries. Hundreds of thousands of Americans travel abroad each year for medical procedures. In Asia, most medical tourists come from Japan and the Middle East. The main destinations for Americans are India, Mexico, Thailand, Singapore and Costa Rica. An estimated 85 million Americans are uninsured or underinsured, a major factor for seeking medical treatment abroad. Savings can range from 25 percent up to 75 percent of the cost to have the procedure done in the US. Over the past five years around 100 hospitals around the world have become JCI accredited, a US-based standard for quality.

Thailand

In 2007, 600,000 foreigners sought medical treatment in Thailand. Bumrungrad Hospital is the world's largest private hospital complex. Bumrungrad treated more than 440,000 foreigners in 2007 alone. There are four JCI accredited hospitals in Thailand.

Singapore

More than 410,000 foreign patients visited in 2006. The government plans to service one million medical tourists by 2012. There are 13 JCI accredited hospitals in Singapore.

Brazil

Brazil has 4,500 licensed cosmetic surgeons, the highest per capita in the world.

India

More than 450,000 foreign patients sought treatment in 2007. There are 10 JCI accredited hospitals in India.

Malaysia

In 2007, more than 350,000 patients sought medical care. One in five hospitals in Malaysia cater to foreigners.

Medical Tourism in India

Medical tourism in India has emerged as the fastest growing segment of tourism industry despite the global economic downturn. High cost of treatments in the developed countries, particularly the USA and UK, has been forcing patients from such regions to look for alternative and cost-effective destinations to get their treatments done. The Indian medical tourism industry is presently at a nascent stage, but has an enormous potential for future growth and development.

As per our new market research report "Booming Medical Tourism in India", India's share in the global medical tourism industry will climb to around 2.4% by the end of 2012.

Moreover, the medical tourism is expected to generate revenue of US$ 2.4 Billion by 2012, growing at a CAGR of over 27% during 2009–2012. The number of medical tourists is anticipated to grow at a CAGR of over 19% in the forecast period to reach 1.1 Million by 2012.

Medical Tourism industry according to CII is expected to be worth US$ 4billion by 2017. India has a potential to attract 1 million health tourists per annum which will contribute US$ 5 billion to the economy. Patients from various countries are becoming medical tourists to India for low cost and health restorative alternative treatments.

The Medical Tourists undergo health restorative treatments of a combination of Ayurveda, Yoga, acupuncture, herbal oil massage, nature therapies, and some ancient Indian healthcare methods – such as Vedic care, an alternate healthcare service. Cost Advantage is the attractive aspect of Indian modern medicine which is 10-15 times lower than anywhere in the world.

The CII-McKinsey report suggests that medical tourism could fetch as much as $2 billion by 2012, compared to an estimated $ 333 million in 2006-07.

Medical Tourism in Kerala

Kerala has established itself as a prominent Destination of world leisure tourism for its natural beauty and cultural assets. The growth of Tourism in Kerala has been induced by the buyer driven factors.

The collective marketing effort through the tourism department has been limited. The scenario of Medical Tourism is also not much different from leisure tourism.

Medical tourism in Kerala grew without much wilful collective effort. It was recognized as an opportunity by some sectors, particularly the Ayurveda sector who took some collective effort to convert Kerala as source for Ayurveda treatment. Then came Dentistry and Modern Medicine. A combination of many

factors has led to the increase in popularity of medical tourism in Kerala:

- Traditional systems of medicine like Ayurveda and Siddha are widely popular in the state, and draws increasing numbers of tourists
- High costs of healthcare in industrialised nations
- Ease and affordability of international travel
- Improving technology and standards of care.

The major specialties of Medical Tourism in Kerala are the following:

Presentation and Analysis

General Categories of Respondents

Out of the 36 respondents, 17 (47%) are from the Modern Medicine and 19 (53%) from the Alternate Medicine sector. The sample units belong to almost all the major cities in the state and cover 9 districts.

The Country-wise Distribution of Health Tourists

An attempt was made to analyze the country-wise distribution of Health Tourists. But due to the insufficiency of data it was not possible to arrive at an accurate distribution pattern. Also there is no secondary data available with the Tourism Department regarding Medical Tourism. Subject to this caveat, we present here the findings of our study. In the absence of more reliable data it may be taken as indicative.

- 52.63% in Alternate Medicine and 70.59% in Modern Medicine responded that 'better medical facility' was a highly significant factor in patients visiting their hospitals. This is a reflection of the quality of the medical service offered by the service providers in the Medical Tourism Industry in the state.
- 82.35% in Modern Medicine responded for 'Higher expense in their country' as having high significance which reflects the cost advantage of the state's medical facilities.
- 68.42% from Alternate Medicine stressed on 'More confidence'. It underlines the pride of place Kerala enjoys in Ayurveda and Alternate Medicine.
- For the reason, 'Opportunity to club health and tourism' only 26.32% from Alternate Medicine and 29.41% from Modern medicine voted 'High' and 52.63% and 47.06% respectively has voted 'low'.

This shows the lack of confidence and commitment to convert their facilities and capabilities for the growth of Medical Tourism.

Chi-Squire test was conducted for the above data and found that at 95% confidence level;

- Only 'More Confidence' is statistically significant for Alternate Medicine
- Only 'Better Medical Facility' and 'High Expense in their country' are statistically significant for Modern Medicine.

How the Foreign Patients get information about your facilities;

Method	*Alternative Medicine*	*Modern Medicine*
Word of mouth from old patients	19 (100%)	15 (88.24%)
Own Website	14 (73.68%)	10 (58.82%)
Website of Tourism Department	5 (26.32%)	3 (17.65%)
Tie ups	1 (5.26%)	2 (11.76%)
Advertising	1 (5.26%)	1 (5.88%)
Direct Marketing	1 (5.26%)	1 (5.88%)
Fairs	1 (5.26%)	0

Initiatives for Marketing Medical Tourism

To a sub question, 'Do you participate in any collective effort taken by the Hospitals involved in marketing.

Medical Tourism', only 5 (26.32%) from Alternate Medicine and 6 (32.59%) from Modern Medicine respondents answered that they do. This shows the absence of any serious collective effort in Kerala for Medical Tourism. But on asked whether they take any initiative for marketing their service among foreign countries, 11 (57.89%) from Alternate Medicine and 12 (70.59%) from Modern Medicine sector answered that they do. This is an indication that the majority of them have realised the need for marketing Medical Tourism.

Table Initiative for marketing Medical Tourism in foreign countries;

Method	*Alternate Medicine*	*Modern Medicine*
Tie Ups	4 (21.05%)	1 (5.88%)
Maintenance Of Branch/Reps	1 (5.26%)	2 (11.76%)
Promotion	0	1 (5.88%)
Participation In Fairs	2 (10.52%)	0
Total Active Participation	7 (36.84%)	5 (23.53%)

When it comes to serious marketing efforts, Alternate Medicine is much ahead of Modern Medicine. When 37% of Alternate

Medicine sector takes some serious efforts, only 24% of Modern Medicine sector does something about it. It also showed that 63% from Alternate Medicine and 76% from Modern medicine are indifferent to serious marketing efforts.

All that they do basically is limited to some tie ups or having some representatives abroad.

Clubbing of Medical Treatment and Tourism

Table. Patients visit to other parts of Kerala

Level of Visits	Alternate Medicine	Modern Medicine
Many	9 (47.37%)	5 (29.41%)
A few	9 (47.37%)	8 (47.06%)
Not Known	1 (5.26%)	4 (23.53%)

For the sub question, 'Do you provide any assistance for the patients to club treatment with tour' 12 (63.16%) from Alternate Medicine and 5 (29.41%) from Modern Medicine answered that they provide assistance.

Table. Hospitals initiative for Patients Tour

Method	Alternate Medicine	Modern Medicine
Arrange through travel agents	6 (31.58%)	4 (23.53%)
Provide information, guidance	3 (15.79%)	0
Make travel Arrangements	2 (110.53%)	1 (5.88%)
Provide own resorts	1 (5.26%)	0

Examining Tables, we can understand that the Alternate Medicine sector sees the Tourism part of Medical Tourism and takes efforts for its promotion.

However, Modern Medicine sector gives very little stress to this area. The main assistance offered is through travel agents and that too by a segment only.

Government Effort for the Promotion of Medical Tourism

For the question, 'Is there any Government effort taken for the promotion of Medical Tourism?' only 8 (47.06%) from Alternate Medicine and 8 (42.11%) from Modern Medicine Sector respondents answered in the affirmative.

Table. Evaluation of the role of Government in the promotion of Medical Tourism

Level of Success	*Alternate Medicine*	*Modern Medicine*
Successful	3 (15.79%)	0
Satisfactory	5 (26.32%)	5 (29.41%)
Failure	11 (57.89%)	12 (70.59%)

While 15.79% of the Alternate Medicine sector says that the Government efforts are successful, nobody in the Modern Medicine feels that the Government efforts are successful. While 57.89% from Alternate Medicine feel that Government efforts are a failure, a much larger segment (70.59%) from Modern Medicine shared this view.

Accreditation of Hospitals

The above Table shows the reluctance of the players in Medical Tourism to achieve accreditations for Quality certification. Only 15.79% from Alternate Medicine and 41.18% from Modern Medicine have got ISO Certification. in the Ayurveda segment only 17.65% has Green Leaf and another 11.76% has Olive Leaf accreditation. Modern Medicine sector is more keen (82.35%) about acquiring quality certifications while only 42.1% from Alternate Medicine has got some quality accreditations.

Problems Faced by Medical Tourism

The general feeling is that the issue of Medical Visas are reasonably fast and without problems. The low level of problems mentioned is perhaps due to the very small number of medical tourists visiting these hospitals presently and most of them coming through references from friends (word of mouth) and hence are fully aware of the limitations and risks as also the advantages associated with treatment in India. But as the scale of operations increase in future more problems relating to insurance, risk of legal actions etc., are likely to arise. Chi-Squire test was conducted for the above data and found that at 95% confidence level;

- For Alternate Medicine all values are statistically significant excepting 'Getting the incentives relating to foreign exchange earnings.
- For Modern Medicine the values of 'Getting the incentives relating to foreign exchange earnings' and 'Visa permission restriction/delay' are statistically significant.

Discussion

Relevance of Health Tourism in Kerala

Kerala is an established tourist destination. Ayurveda is already popular and Kerala is recognised as the number one source for Wellness solution. The Alternative medicine sector led by Ayurveda has been showing vibrant growth in recent years. There is also tremendous scope for Modern medicine including Dentistry in the state.

The Advantages of Kerala in Medical Tourism

- Nobody can beat India Kerala cost-wise.
- Our doctors and nurses are accepted all over the world.
- We are known as compassionate people (even Thailand lack this)
- Kerala Hospitals give many consultancies under one roof
- Offer eco friendly environment
- NRIs all over the world function as ambassadors for Kerala
- Some US NRIs function as Entrepreneurs facilitating Medical Tourism to India & Kerala: (18 NRI Travel Agents operate in Medical tourism arranging to and fro travel, treatments and sight seeing).

Some Reasons for Travel of Foreign Patients to India/Kerala:

1. UK NHS—National Health Service for poor citizens is heavily burdened and the system almost collapsed. Indian costs being only 1/6 of UK attracts the lower and middle income groups to India.
2. In the U.S. the cost of medical treatment is so high that only 10% can afford the costs in US, while Indian costs are only 1/10.
3. The Middle East: Huge infrastructure facilities are available. But the expertise is insufficient.

After 9/11, they have reduced trips to U.S.

Role of CII

India and Kerala have only private institutions participating in Medical Tourism. CII has been attempting to bring several medical institutions under one umbrella. They have already succeeded in bringing 40 hospitals under the umbrella of medical tourism. CII started medical tourism promotion in Kerala with 12 hospitals. Some of them are Lakeshore, Amrita, Medical Trust, MIMS, Baby Memorial, KIMS, Ananthapuri, Uthradom Thirunal, EMS Coop.

Hospital etc. CII recently completed a study on the Scope of Medical Tourism in India. The study says that the medical tourists in modern medicine at present is hardly 12,000 to 16,000. (This is exclusive of Ayurveda which is already about 3.5 lakhs.) By 2012 it will hit 1 million visitors to India. Out of this Kerala's target is 20%, i.e.2 lakhs. It is expected that in 5 to 10 years

Medical Tourism will Overtake other Forms of Tourism

Reluctance of Hospitals Towards Tourism

Most of the Hospitals who participate in Medical Tourism do not give much significance to Tourism. As seen earlier only 28% felt that the desire of patients who come to Kerala because of opportunity for tourism is high. 25% thought that it is medium. The remaining 47% thought patients were not concerned about it at all.

Only less than half of the hospitals were found to take some initiative to help patients to club their medical travel with tourism. It was also revealed that only 33% of the hospitals were making some initiatives on their own to market their services and only 31% of them were participating in any collective effort for marketing medical tourism. This attitude will not help Medical Tourism. At the same time 64% of them claimed that they were taking initiatives for marketing their services in foreign countries even though in actual practice they were not doing anything more than relying on word of mouth publicity.

Need for Collective Promotion

Almost all the respondents had pointed out the need and relevance for Collective Promotion. The need to organise road shows, Medical Tourism Fares, and other efforts to convert Kerala as Destination for Medical/Dental Tourism were also suggested by some of them.

Accreditation of Hospitals

The attitude of Hospitals towards quality certification is very cold. For the successful participation in Medical Tourism, this should change because the foreign tourists value quality recognitions.

Government Involvement for the Growth and Promotion of Medical Tourism

The survey among hospitals engaged in Medical Tourism very clearly brought out the low key played by the Government in promoting Medical Tourism. Only 8.33% felt that the Government was successful. As high as 64% were of the opinion that Government efforts have failed. In our discussions with the officers of the Tourism Department they also admitted that not much was being done in this direction. So far the activity of the Tourism Department of the Government of Kerala is limited to accreditation of the Ayurvedic Hospitals as Green Leaf/Olive Leaf Classes. About 50 units have been given Green Leaf Accreditation and around 40 units given Olive Leaf Accreditation. In the area of Medical Tourism in the Modern Medicine area, other than identifying the scope for Medical Tourism and constituting an informal committee including personalities of prominent hospitals involved in Medical Tourism, nothing more has been done. The respondents of our survey strongly felt that the Government should involve more actively in the promotion of Medical Tourism.

Problems Faced by Medical Tourism

It is thankful to know that the level of perceived problems in Medical Tourism is low. However as pointed out earlier, when the scale of operation increases more problems are bound to occur.

Suggestions for Improvement of Medical Tourism in Kerala

Ayurveda in Medical Tourism

Ayurveda is a synonym for Medical Tourism in Kerala. There has been a spontaneous growth in Kerala for Ayurveda, which has no competition in the whole world. By unorganized but collective effort the name

Ayurveda got branded all over the world. The present problem in the market is the overcrowding of unqualified people conducting massage parlours in the name of Ayurveda. If immediate measures are not taken to control such fake set ups, the tourists who come in search of genuine Ayurveda treatment will get cheated and carry back a wrong message about Ayurveda. This is especially so because Ayurveda is not very strong in standardization and scientific data. Another problem facing Ayurveda is the scarcity of certain essential herbs and medicines, which will affect the quality of the treatment.

Environment and Infrastructure

The various suggestions from the respondents and the discussions we had with the resource persons have emphasised the point that we need improvement in physical and social environment. The physical environment includes the improvement in basic infrastructure, standard of cleanliness etc. Basic amenities should be good—toilets should be user friendly and well maintained. Good standards at lesser cost will make the state a more attractive, value for money destination. For this we have to improve the physical

infrastructure and connectivity. The social environment includes the improvement in human culture and behaviour. People have to be friendly to the visitors and guests. Our old manthra, 'Athidhi devo bhava' or 'guest is equal to god' is very relevant in this context. We should have a responsible political culture. The overcrowded schedules of Harthals and strikes will spoil the image of Kerala as a tourist friendly state.

Promote Dental Tourism

With over 3000 dentists and 1200 dental clinics Kerala has a distinct advantage in dental tourism. The fact that the treatment requires multiple sittings with liberal gaps in between sittings and hence requiring around 30-40 days stay makes the dental patient an ideal candidate for medical tourism. Hence, more efforts should be made to market the dental tourism product.

Government Involvement for the Growth and Promotion of Medical Tourism

The government should take more active role for the growth of tourism. It should function as a facilitator and catalyst. There has been a suggestion that Hospitals should be given industry status for power, import of machinery, equipments etc. It would be advisable to follow a Private-Pubic-Partnership Model (PPP) in promoting Medical Tourism as suggested in the study conducted by CII. The Central

Government could also help popularise Medical Tourism through Embassies and through Health Ministries in various foreign countries. More financial and fiscal concessions need also be offered to this sector which has tremendous employment and foreign exchange earning potential. Only then they can be encouraged to make the necessary investments needed for upgradation, standardisation and accreditation of the medical facilities/institutions. Other areas which will require government/ statutory support is in the field of insurance facilities, visa on arrival with special facilities for medical visas, quality control and certification/accreditation.

Dental Tourism India

India is emerging as one of the preferred destinations for dental tourism in the world. Thousands of people from USA, Europe and other parts of the world fly to India every year seeking dental treatment. Though tourists attach a variety of reasons for their travel, the major indicator is the cost for dental implants and dental surgery, which is generally cheap in India.

Dental Tourism India

Irrespective of recession and slump downs in the market, many people still travel to India for various dental treatments. Among many reasons, the major one could be the cost and dental insurance. In U.S, only 50% of the total population has dental insurance. Even those with comprehensive medical packages do not a have dental coverage.

Dental procedure	*Cost in USA ($)*		*Cost in India ($)*
	General Dentist	*Top End Dentist*	*Top End Dentist*
Smile designing	-	8,000	1,000*
Metal Free Bridge	-	5,500	500*
Dental Implants	-	3,500	800*
Porcelain Metal Bridge	1,800	3,000	300*
Porcelain Metal Crown	600	1,000	80*
Tooth impactions	500	2,000	100*
Root canal Treatment	600	1,000	100*
Tooth whitening	350	800	110*
Tooth coloured composite fillings	200	500	25*
Tooth cleaning	100	300	75*

Source: health-tourism-india.com

Apart from the low dental insurance coverage, cost of the dental treatments is also extremely high in these western countries. For instance, a patient requiring root canal treatment might cost up to $600 and a tooth crowning may cost around $40000. However, same procedures cost around $35-125 in India.

Listed below is the cost comparison of dental treatment between USA and India. The figures are indicative and might vary as you approach your dental tourism provider.

The Indian dental tourist provider offer a combination pack that enables the visiting patients to correct their teeth as well enjoy the attractions of the country, rich in culture and heritage.

Dental Surgery Offered in India

India is well equipped with quality hospitals and experienced dentists that assure reliable treatment. Many dental tourism providers in India offer you worthwhile dental packages. Most of them include the following dental surgery/treatment options:

- Intra mouth dental scanning
- Extraction of normal/fractured teeth under local anesthesia
- Extraction of impacted wisdom teeth
- Ceramic caps without gold under microscopic control
- Maxillary Surgery
- Dental Bridges, Porcelain/Ceramic crowns
- Bleaching
- Prosthesis on the implant/ Dental Implants
- Vertical and horizontal bone grafting
- Gum Grafting/ Gums treatment
- Palatal orthodontics
- Fluoride treatments for children
- Cosmetic dentistry
- Smile designing.
- Root Canal
- Teeth whitening
- Tooth contouring and reshaping
- Dental Fillings.

Dental Implants

India is popular for successful dental surgery treatments like dental implants and implantology. Dental implants are titanium fixtures or artificial teeth that are surgically placed in the jawbone. Over a period the titanium fixtures merges with the teeth bone through a process called osseo-integration. Once this foundation becomes strong, a crown or bridge is placed on the respective teeth. There are different types of surgical dental implants procedure. If you are coming for dental implants to India, check with your dentist for the dental implant procedure you might require. The types of dental implant procedures include:

Root form Implant: This implant looks like the root of a tooth. If your jawbone is wide and deep enough then the implant is placed on your bone surgically with local anesthesia. However, in conditions where there is not enough width or depth in the jawbone, grafting is done to place the same. Once the implant is placed, the gums are stitched and take three to six months to heal.

Plate form Implant: If your jawbone is too narrow for bone grafting, then a plate form implant is suggested. After local anesthesia, a cosmetic dentist will place the implant on your bone and stitch the gums. While few implants are healed quickly, some might take three to six months for restoration.

Subperiosteal Implants: This is suggested in cases where the jawbone does not have enough height/width to accommodate either the root form or the plate form implant. This is a custom-made solution for your teeth and is usually placed via any of the two special methods. The first method involves making an impression of your jawbone by a cosmetic dentist. After which, he/she comes up with a custom-fit implant to suit your bone. The second methodology involves CAT scan of your jawbone. The CAT scans your jawbone and provides the dentist with a model of the same. With this model, the dental labs create an implant suitable for your jawbone.

Dental implants are usually costlier abroad. A dental implant by a senior dentist in US might cost around $3500. While dental implants in India by an experienced dentist may just cost around $800. Listed below are the indicative figures of dental implants in India

Dental Implant Procedures	*Cost in INR*
Alpha Bio Dental Implant with straight abutment	25,000
Nobel Biocare-Groovy Dental Implants	40,000
Computer Guided Implant Surgery	50,000
Procelain based Metal Crown	4, 500
Procera-Crown & Veneer	15,000

Cosmetic Dentistry in India

Many dental tourism providers in India also offer cosmetic dentistry package to enhance your smile and appearance. The cosmetic dentistry packages to India may include one or all of the following depending on your dental tourism provider.

Tooth whitening-If you have stained or dull teeth then this is the best option for you.

Dental Bonding-If you have a minor repair on your gaps or repair of the placed chips, then dental bonding might suit you. Dental bonding in India is relatively cheaper and solves all aesthetic problems arising from colour and shape.

Dental Veneers-These custom-made moldings made of porcelain/ceramic are perfect for spaces, chips, fractures, rotated or maligned teeth, distorted, or discolored teeth.

Tooth Reshaping/Cosmetic Contouring-This is done to straighten the contour teeth.

Gum Reshaping/Gum Contouring-The procedure is done to correct excessive or uneven gums through cosmetic dental procedures/gigivoplasty that makes your smile more appealing.

Gum Depigmentation-This is done to re-colour the pigments of the gum that are black or brown at times.

Inlays/Onlays-This procedure involves placing porcelain, resin, or gold filling bonds to restore a decayed or broken tooth.

Sports Tourism

Sports tourism refers to international trips specifically taken to watch sporting events. Common examples include international events such as world cups (soccer, rugby, cricket, etc.), the Olympics and Formula 1 Grand Prix, regional events (such as the soccer European Champions League), and individual (non-team) participant sports such as tennis, golf and horse racing.

Estimate of Global Market Size

The most popular global sporting events are the soccer FIFA World Cup and the Olympics, followed by the European Football Championships. However other popular sporting events also attract a large number of international visitors. These include the Rugby Union World Cup and Formula 1 Grand Prix.

- The FIFA Football World Cup held in France in 1998 attracted 900,000 international football fans and generated $12.3 billion.
- It is estimated that the 2000 Olympics in Sydney generated 111,000 additional international arrivals to Australia specifically travelling for sports tourism.
- Euro 2004 (the European Football Championships) attracted 500,000 sports tourists to Portugal, generating $320 million for the Portuguese economy.
- The Monaco Grand Prix (which alongside the Indy 500 and Le Mans is one of the most famous motor racing fixtures of the year) attracts 200,000 visitors over its four-day duration.
- The 2007 Cricket World Cup staged in the Caribbean was thought to have generated an additional 100,000 visitors who travelled specifically for the tournament.

Whilst the number of sports tourists fluctuates on an annual basis depending on the events taking place (it is greatest during FIFA World Cup and Olympics years), on average an estimated 12 million international trips are made for the main purpose of watching a sporting event.

Potential for Growth

Increased media exposure of sporting events over the last decade has raised the profile of many sports, and although TV coverage is better than at any time in the past, an increasing number of sports fans want to experience live events. The media also has the ability to make national and international icons of sporting stars, thereby generating greater demand, as fans want to see their sporting idols "in the flesh".

Sporting events themselves are being made increasingly appealing to attend, with greater levels of comfort, and other events – such as festivals-being created around them (such as horse racing weekends, boating regattas, etc.). Low-cost regional airlines (and more affordable long haul flights), are also driving demand for sporting events as flights become more convenient, more regular, and of course more affordable. Overall, the sports tourism niche market is expected to grow annually at around 6% for the next five years.

Brief Profile of Consumers

Sports tourists are more easily profiled according to the sports they follow. However, in general terms the bulk of the market tends to be young-between 18 and 34 years, and in the C1 and C2 (middle) socio-economic groups. This would also be the typical profile of a sports tourist following soccer matches. Rugby and cricket followers tend to be slightly older and with greater disposable income. Horse racing has a broad range of followers with no clear demographic structure. Followers of athletics tend to be young, low spenders, whilst those following the Formula 1 Grand Prix circuit tend to be skewed towards males in their 40s with above average disposable income.

Main Source Markets

The main source markets for sports tourism are those that are most interested in the main international sports. These include:

- United Kingdom
- United States
- Germany
- Italy
- Spain
- Scandinavia
- Australia
- South Africa.

Main Competing Destinations

The main competing destinations tend to vary depending on where the large events, such as the FIFA World Cup and Olympics are held. However, those holding key annual tournaments of global sporting interest include:

- United States
- United Kingdom
- France
- Australia
- Spain.

For specific sports, such as golf, motor racing, or yachting, this list of competing destinations would vary considerably.

Index

N

O

P

R

S

□□□